Tourism and

ONE WEEK

Tourism and the Lodging Sector

Dallen J. Timothy
Professor, School of Community Resources and Development, Arizona State University, Phoenix, Arizona

Victor B. Teye
Associate Professor, School of Community Resources and Development, Arizona State University, Phoenix, Arizona

AMSTERDAM · BOSTON · HEIDELBERG · LONDON · NEW YORK · OXFORD
PARIS · SAN DIEGO · SAN FRANCISCO · SINGAPORE ·SYDNEY · TOKYO
Butterworth-Heinemann is an imprint of Elsevier

Butterworth-Heinemann is an Imprint of Elsevier
Linacre House, Jordan Hill, Oxford OX2 8DP, UK
30 Corporate Drive, Suite 400, Burlington, MA 01803, USA

First edition 2009

Library of Congress Cataloging-in-Publication Data

Timothy, Dallen J.
  Tourism and the lodging sector / Dallen J. Timothy and Victor B. Teye. – 1st ed.
    p. cm.
  ISBN 978-0-7506-8659-4
  1. Hotels. 2. Tourist camps, hostels, etc. 3. Tourism. 4. Hospitality industry. I. Teye, Victor B.
  II. Title.
  TX911.T56 2009
  910.46–dc22

                                    2009008310

A catalog record for this book is available from the Library of Congress

British Library Cataloguing in Publication Data

A catalogue record for this book is available from the British Library

For information on all Butterworth-Heinemann
publications visit our web site at books.elsevier.com

Printed and bound in United States of America

09 10 10 9 8 7 6 5 4 3 2 1

ISBN: 978-0-7506-8659-4

Table of Contents

LIST OF FIGURE AND TABLES vii

CHAPTER 1: Tourism and Tourist Accommodations.............................. 1

SECTION I: CONTEMPORARY ISSUES IN THE LODGING SECTOR **11**

CHAPTER 2: Demand for Lodging and Tourism 13

CHAPTER 3: Current Issues in Human Resources, Structural Change, and e-Commerce in the Global Lodging Sector............... 29

CHAPTER 4: The Socio-Economic Implications in the Destination 47

CHAPTER 5: Globalization and Inclusiveness in the Lodging Sector..... 63

CHAPTER 6: Accommodations and the Green Movement 81

CHAPTER 7: Safety and Security Issues in a Globalizing World 101

CHAPTER 8: Food and Beverage Services, Gaming and Conferences.. 117

SECTION II: TOURIST LODGING TYPES AND FORMS **131**

CHAPTER 9: Hotels, Motels and Resorts 133

CHAPTER 10: Second Homes and Timeshares................................... 155

CHAPTER 11: Small-Scale Boutique Accommodations: Inns, Bed & Breakfasts, Lodges, Farm Stays and Pensions 177

CHAPTER 12: Mobile Lodging... 197

CHAPTER 13: Youth Hostels and Backpacker Accommodation........... 213

CHAPTER 14: Camping 227

CHAPTER 15: Novelty and Alternative Lodging 239

CHAPTER 16: Critical Issues and the Future of Lodging 259

Index **263**

List of Figure and Tables

Figure 2.1 Monthly tourist arrivals in Sri Lanka, 2007–2008 23

Table 1.1 Existing Canadian Pacific Railway hotels from the early years...3

Table 2.1 Growth of international tourist arrivals since the Second World War 14

Table 2.2 Countries expected to grow their tourism economies fastest in 2008.. 15

Table 2.3 International arrivals by sub-region, 2007 17

Table 2.4 Top ten personal traveler origin countries by expenditures, 2008..18

Table 2.5 Top ten business traveler origin countries by expenditures, 2008..18

Table 3.1 Employment in hotels and other accommodations by occupation, USA, 2006...31

Table 4.1 Top ten tourism employment-generating countries, 2008.....48

Table 4.2 Top ten tourism-dependent countries in relative terms, 2008..52

Table 4.3 The top ten tourism-dependent countries in terms of employment, 2008..53

Table 5.1 Top ten hotel groups in the world, 2007 67

Table 5.2 Top 20 international hotel brands/chains, 2007 68

Table 5.3 Recommendations and strategic actions of the Bali Declaration on Barrier-Free Tourism 73

Table 5.4 General requirements for adapting public spaces for people with disabilities, according to the ADA.................74

Table 5.5   Number of rooms required to be fully accessible 75

Table 6.1   Accommodation providers' views of renewable
energy sources, Queensland, Australia 86

Table 6.2   A selection of ECOTEL-certified lodging facilities in Latin
America and Asia 91

Table 6.3   Business travellers' green expectations of lodging
establishments, $n = 1155$ 93

Table 6.4   Business travellers' own green behaviour in lodging
establishments, $n = 1155$ 93

Table 8.1   Restaurant facts in the United States, 2008–2009 119

Table 8.2   Indian Gaming Revenues in the United States, 2000–2007
($ billions) 123

Table 8.3   Recent facts and figures associated with MICE tourism
in the United States 125

Table 8.4   Top 15 countries for conferences and meetings in 2007 125

Table 9.1   Examples of famous historic hotels 138

Table 9.2   Hotel and Resort Classification 145

Table 9.3   Top Ten Hotel Chains in 2006 146

Table 10.1 Second homes and populations in the Nordic countries 157

Table 10.2 Seasonal housing in the United States by year
(in thousands) 157

Table 10.3 Timeshare Characteristics in the United States,
as of January 1, 2008 166

Table 10.4 Economics of Timeshares in the United States, 2008 167

Table 10.5 Problems/Issues facing the US timeshare industry 168

Table 12.1 Passengers and passenger kilometers in the world's
most train-dependent countries, 2006 201

Table 12.2 Cruises departing from the 15 most popular US
cruise ports, 2003–2004 205

Table 12.3 Geography of Cruise Destinations by Bed Days,
2008 (000's) 206

Table 12.4 Growth of North American Cruise Capacity
(Lower Berths) 1981–2007 208

Table 13.1 Backpacker and hostel accommodation in Australia,
2005–2007 216

Table 13.2 Characteristics of backpacker travel in Australia, 2007 216

Table 13.3 A selection of international hostel chains 221

Table 14.1 Top ten activities undertaken by KOA campers in 2007 231

Table 15.1 Examples of Tree House Accommodations and their
Characteristics 244

Table 15.2 Examples of Cave and Underground Tourist
Accommodations 248

Table 15.3 Examples of Lighthouse Accommodations 249

CHAPTER 1

Tourism and Tourist Accommodations

Tourism is an economic powerhouse that has become the service industry of the new millennium. It has experienced a steady and rapid growth since the middle of the twentieth century, but even centuries and millennia ago, it was a force to be reckoned with. Many historians argue that the modern-day concept of travel and tourism originated with medieval Christian pilgrimages to Rome and the Holy Land. Others, however, maintain that Hinduism and Buddhism are the forerunners to modern mass tourism. Hinduism, commonly referred to as the world's oldest religion, may have originated as long ago as 4000 years BC, although claims range from 4000 to 1500 BC depending on how its origins are defined. What we do know is that already more than 2000 years ago Hindu pilgrims were traveling through South Asia to bathe in holy rivers and participate in sacred rituals associated with temples built to worship diverse deity.

Buddhist pilgrims were said to have traveled in great numbers more than 2000 years ago to be enlightened by visits to the locations in Nepal and India where Lord Buddha was born (between 600 and 400 BC), received enlightenment, preached, and died. Today these locations are connected via a pilgrimage circuit and still function as important destinations for pilgrims and cultural tourists. Following the death of Jesus Christ, Christian pilgrimage to Jerusalem, and later to Rome, was the basis of an important circulation between Europe and the Roman lands of today's Middle East. Long distance travel waned with the fall of the Eastern

CONTENTS

Tourism, Hospitality and this Book

Summary and Conclusion

Reference

Further Reading

Jerusalem was the center of ancient and medieval Christian pilgrimage

Roman (Byzantine) Empire in the thirteenth century but intra-regional travel flourished in the medieval period with the Grand Tour in Southern Europe. Global explorations characterized the Middle Ages, resulting in the colonization of most of the world's territory by European superpowers. The Industrial Revolution of the early nineteenth century and the subsequent invention and widespread adoption of steam trains and steam ships, automobiles, and airplanes characterized the early modern era from the 1820s until the Second World War. The end of World War II unleashed the speediest phase of global and extraterrestrial exploration and travel of any period of time before in human history.

Where does the lodging sector fit in with this long history of travel? Each of these historical periods had its own lodging needs. The early rest houses of Hindu and Buddhist pilgrims (*dharamshalas*—charitable rest houses) are still used today to provide shelter and sustenance to pilgrims in various places in India. The ruins of ancient roadside inns can be found throughout India and Israel/Palestine, and many others that are already several centuries old are still functioning as pilgrim rest houses. During medieval times, inns and roadside watering holes (for horses and their drivers) were developed to refresh weary travelers and meet their sleeping needs. These early pilgrim rest houses and roadside inns are often cited as the original concept behind today's hospitality sector.

The development of trains and railway networks during the early and mid-1800s saw a rapid spread of travel in Europe, the UK, North America, Australia, and parts of Asia. In fact, railway lines were critical to the settlement of the American west and in the development of popular resorts on the US east coast (e.g. Ocean City, Atlantic City, Cape May), as well as on the coast of Great Britain (e.g. Brighton, Blackpool, Llandudno). Resort communities like Atlantic City and Cape May developed rapidly during the mid-1800s with the train-induced mobilization of crowds from the growing population centers of the northeast (e.g. New York City, Boston, Baltimore, Philadelphia). Resorts and hotels were built

Ruins of an ancient way station, or roadside inn in Palestine

rapidly to accommodate this newfound socio-economic force known as seaside tourism. Many of the original hotels still function as hotels and have been listed on America's Register of Historic Places.

Trans-continental railway development in Canada created a string of large luxury hotels from the east coast to the west coast. Several have since been demolished or no longer function as hotels, but the remaining properties are still considered luxury lodging options and provide some of the most exclusive accommodations in Nova Scotia, New Brunswick, Quebec, Ontario, Saskatchewan, Alberta, and British Columbia. Several are now operated by Fairmont Hotels and Resorts (Table 1.1).

At the end of the nineteenth century with the invention of the combustible engine, automobiles became popular. During the 1920s and 1930s, personal cars became more widespread as more and more families were able to afford them. This fueled the development of coastal resort towns and other inland destinations throughout the world, including the colonial highland resorts in Indonesia and India, to which European colonizers flocked to escape the tropical heat of the lowlands. Cars also enabled people to explore. While few highways existed in the early twentieth century, travelers began to penetrate areas that had before been accessible only by foot or carriage, or through which trains passed without stopping. The popularity of the automobile also fueled the growth of mountain, forest, and coastal destinations and increased demand for

Table 1.1	Existing Canadian Pacific Railway Hotels from the Early Years	
Year Opened	**Hotel**	**Location**
1888	Banff Springs Hotel	Banff, Alberta
1889	The Algonquin	St Andrews, New Brunswick
1890	Chateau Lake Louise	Lake Louise, Alberta
1893	Château Frontenac	Quebec City, Quebec
1908	Empress Hotel	Victoria, British Columbia
1914	Palliser Hotel	Calgary, Alberta
1917	Digby Pines Resort	Digby, Nova Scotia
1927	Lord Nelson Hotel	Halifax, Nova Scotia
1927	Hotel Saskatchewan	Regina, Saskatchewan
1929	Cornwallis Inn	Kentville, Nova Scotia
1929	Royal York Hotel	Toronto, Ontario
1930	Château Montebello	Montebello, Quebec
1930	Lakeside Inn	Yarmouth, Nova Scotia
1939	Hotel Vancouver	Vancouver, British Columbia

lodging and dining services. It was during this period that the notion of motels, or motor hotels, developed.

Air travel took off in the early twentieth century with the first commercial flight in 1914 in Florida, where Tony Jannus flew 21 miles (34 km) from St Petersburg to Tampa in a two-seater machine at an altitude of only 50 feet (15 m). The first trans-Atlantic flight occurred in 1919. Advances in airplane technology came about via the two world wars. The mid-1900s saw the growth of larger and more efficient aircrafts that enabled larger cohorts of society to travel overseas and domestically. This fueled demand for tourism and the need for accommodations even further.

Today in the late modern era we face such rapid technological transformations that it is unsettling to many people. The Internet has become a mechanism that allows people to arrange their own travel, including hotel reservations, bypassing industry intermediaries, which has expanded hotel and resort profit margins and given direct access and control to the customer. The Internet is constantly being refined and applied in ever more diverse contexts and for more uses. Transportation innovations continue to develop, with one of the most recent developments being the largest passenger aircraft ever made—the Airbus A380, which can accommodate 853 people and fly at a maximum cruising speed of 945 kmp/587 mph. Likewise, super cruise ships have developed to carry more than 3000 passengers at one time, and new apartment cruises have become vogue among the world's wealthy elites. Higher capacity transportation modes have the potential to increase global travel, if there is adequate demand. If history is any predictor of the future, it is very likely that such demand will meet the challenge. As such there is an obvious need for lodging providers to keep pace and to meet the needs of a growing global marketplace, particularly as new destinations open up, demand characteristics change, international relations improve, and cross-border travel and trade are liberalized.

The importance and magnitude of global tourism cannot be overstressed. Nearly a billion international overnight trips were taken in 2007, with expenditures measuring in the trillions of dollars. In the United States, domestic and international travelers spend an average of $2 billion a day, $84.5 million an hour, $1.4 million a minute, and $23 500 per second (American Hotel and Lodging Association, 2008). Because in most instances between 25 and 35% of all tourist spending, varying from case to case, goes to accommodations, the importance of lodging in tourism also cannot be overstressed. This is a substantial portion of travel expenditures and amounts to hundreds of billions of dollars every year. In the United States alone, there were 48 062 lodging properties in 2007 with 4.5 million guest rooms. Direct spending by travelers on overnight stays was just under $140 billion, and the year's average occupancy rate was 63.1% (American Hotel and Lodging Association, 2008).

Given these magnanimous figures associated with tourism, it is little wonder that tourists and their hotels contribute a great deal to the economic well-being of tourist destinations, especially in terms of regional income, employment, taxes, and the stimulation of entrepreneurialism. By the same token, such masses of people have contributed to the degradation of destination environments and resulted in disillusioned communities whose residents often loathe outsiders, even if their very livelihoods depend on them. In response to these conditions, destination planners and hotel managers realize the need to develop facilities and destinations that are more socially and environmentally sustainable. The green movement and various forms of community-based, or pro-poor, tourism have emerged in the lodging domain to minimize the ecological impacts of hotels, lodges, and resorts on the environment and involve destination residents in tourism decision making and in providing more sustainable and scale-appropriate forms of accommodation.

With the globalization of the lodging sector has come exposure to a bigger world, where cultures meet and often clash, supranationalist bodies now control tourism with more authority and power than individual states, and where firms and corporations are exposed to more volatile socio-economic environments. Part of this broader process of globalization is a deepening concern over safety and security, which affects all components of the tourism system; hotels, motels, and resorts are not immune. All tourist lodging businesses have had to adapt to changing security landscapes to ensure the safety of their guests and to contribute to a collective sense of security in the destination.

If there is one thing in life that remains the same, it is change. This old cliché holds true for tourism and accommodations as well. As mentioned above, technological development has facilitated a more rapid growth in supply and demand for accommodations. While technological change is difficult to keep pace with, it has enabled many companies to become more efficient in managing human resources, budgets, and service departments through advanced management information systems. It has also saved considerable sums of money through online advertising and by eliminating many fee-based travel intermediaries. Another aspect of change that has affected most lodging businesses is the need to expand the bottom line to meet the profit requirements of shareholders and business partners by expanding the product to include conference sales, special events, food and beverage services, and gaming. All of these issues and many others are examined in the chapters that follow.

TOURISM, HOSPITALITY AND THIS BOOK

Tourism entails people traveling away from home and comprises a global network of services, suppliers and systems in the traveler's home base, in transit, and in the destination that facilitate travel away from home. This includes travel agents and airport shuttles at the place of origin, gas stations, and restaurants along the way, and attractions, accommodations, eating establishments, souvenir shops, motor coach companies, and tour guides in the destination. It also includes services and suppliers that are often not considered part of tourism, yet they are. Banks, post offices, department stores, and laundries are important services in the point of origin that assist in preparing for a trip. In the destination, farmers, fishermen, and public utilities providers are equally important in the broad framework of tourism supply. In addition, tourism entails intangible elements such as motives, experiences, beliefs and values, expectations, and personal relationships. Thus, tourism is an extremely complex and multidimensional phenomenon that touches the lives of nearly everyone on earth, whether or not they have ever traveled away from home.

Students of tourism from a business perspective tend to have an interest in the everyday functioning of the industry and its agencies. Marketing and promotional effectiveness, human resource management to recruit and retain the best talent, budgeting and financial resource management, agency development and understanding visitor characteristics, expectations, and satisfaction with the destination or product are often the focus of business studies in tourism. The less business-oriented side of tourism studies tends to focus more on theoretical questions and examines the broader social and ecological implications of tourism development, including the historical, geographical, social, cultural, ecological, and political repercussions of the industry. These two broad perspectives are not mutually exclusive but are equally important. Business researchers, for instance, need to understand the psychology of travel to be able to segment the market for promotional purposes. Those who study the political theories related to tourism need to understand the practical functioning side of the industry (e.g. labor laws and marketing approaches) to be able to formulate sound research questions. Some observers have suggested that the business approach to studying tourism is more interested in the demand side, while the science of tourism is more inclined to focus on supply. We submit, however, that this is a false dichotomy, because tourism is a single system that cannot be disconnected from any of its parts; tourism is a business and network of businesses, but it is also a socio-cultural, ecological, political, geographical, and historical phenomenon that is big enough for all perspectives.

Having said this, in the domain of accommodation services, academic work has focused overwhelmingly on the business management side of lodging with a concentration on marketing, human resources, facilities, guest satisfaction, reservation systems, budgeting, and housekeeping. Textbooks that deal specifically with the lodging sector have been written from a hospitality management perspective, to prepare students to work in hotels and resorts as desk clerks, accountants, supervisors, food and beverage managers, groundskeeping and housekeeping supervisors, or human resource managers. While this approach and these jobs are extremely important, textbooks have in general ignored the broader role of lodging as part of the global tourism system. With this realization, the idea for this book was born. The purpose of this book, therefore, is not to provide a hospitality management perspective about hotels and resorts. This has been done many times already. Instead it aims to place the accommodation sector firmly within tourism and situate its viewpoints and discussions within the broader sets of concepts and issues of concern to tourism scholars today, which include both business and social science perspectives, as well as elements of supply and demand. These include such issues as environmental sustainability, social and cultural accountability, safety and security in times of political turmoil, and globalization and geopolitical restructuring. While this book is not about hotel management, it most certainly elucidates issues that have profound management implications.

This textbook is divided into two sections. Besides this introduction, the first eight chapters examine many of the broad tourism-related issues noted above and how they affect the lodging sector of tourism. The second half of the book, comprising chapters 9 through 15, examines these issues and many others within the specific context of individual types of lodging facilities, including hotels, motels, resorts, second homes, boutique accommodations (e.g. B&Bs, inns), mobile forms of lodging, hostels, campgrounds, and post-modern novelty types of accommodations, including lighthouses, ice hotels, and tree house lodges. All of these forms of lodging have unique management challenges. These are examined along with larger social movements that affect their successes or failures.

There are in fact dozens of different sorts of lodging facilities. Sometimes these are regional or country-specific. This book only touches on the most common ones and a few innovative novelty forms, but a lack of coverage does not reflect a lack of importance in the regions where other facilities dominate. For instance, a *ryokan* is a traditional place to stay in Japan, which originated during the seventeenth century along well-demarcated travel routes. Today *ryokan*s (a type of inn) are located in scenic areas of high amenity and cater to a wide market base. They are an important part of traditional Japanese culture and represent a romanticized version of Japan's heritage. There is even a Japan Ryokan Association to help member facilities market themselves and promote the *ryokan* experience. *Ryokan*s are important in Japanese society but are not highlighted in this text.

SUMMARY AND CONCLUSION

Tourism comprises a huge global network of product suppliers, many of which are often not conceived of as being part of tourism. One of the most easily recognized elements of tourism supply is accommodation businesses. Aside from transportation to the destination, lodging is usually the largest investment made by people traveling for business or pleasure. In tourism studies, the role of lodging has been almost entirely ignored, although business and hospitality specialists have made pioneering achievements in understanding various aspects of hotel management. This book aims to place the lodging sector more squarely in the midst of tourism studies, and it is our hope that its readers will appreciate the hospitality management side of lodging but look beyond it to see the broader implications it holds for tourism studies.

REFERENCE

American Hotel and Lodging Association, 2008. 2008 lodging industry profile. Online <http://www.ahla.com/content.aspx?id=23744> Accessed January 29, 2009.

FURTHER READING

Bhardwaj, S.M., 1973. Hindu places of pilgrimage in India: a study in cultural geography. University of California Press, Berkeley.

Black, J., 2003. Italy and the grand tour. Yale University Press, New Haven.

Clarke, J., 1995. The effective marketing of small-scale tourism enterprises through national structures: lessons from a two-way comparative study of farm tourism accommodation in the United Kingdom and New Zealand. Journal of Vacation Marketing 1 (2), 137–153.

Clegg, A., Essex, S., 2000. Restructuring in tourism: the accommodation sector in a major British coastal resort. International Journal of Tourism Research 2 (2), 77–95.

Dillon, M., 1997. Pilgrims and pilgrimage in Ancient Greece. Routledge, London.

Hobson, K., Essex, S., 2001. Sustainable tourism: a view from accommodation businesses. Service Industries Journal 21 (4), 133–146.

Kendall, A., 1970. Medieval pilgrims. Wayland, London.

Lee-Ross, D., 1998. Comment: Australia and the small to medium sized hotel sector. International Journal of Contemporary Hospitality Management 10 (5), 177–179.

Pearce, D.G., Grimmeau, J.P., 1984. The spatial structure of tourist accommodation and hotel demand in Spain. Geoforum 15 (4), 37–50.

Pratt, J.B., 1996. The pilgrimage of Buddhism and a Buddhist pilgrimage. Asian Educational Services, New Delhi.

Timothy, D.J., Wall, G., 1995. Tourist accommodation in an Asian historic city. Journal of Tourism Studies 6 (2), 63–73.

Towner, J., 1985. The Grand Tour: a key phase in the history of tourism. Annals of Tourism Research 12, 297–333.

Walford, N., 2001. Patterns of development in tourist accommodation enterprises on farms in England and Wales. Applied Geography 21 (4), 331–345.

Wall, G., Long, V., 1996. Balinese homestays: an indigenous response to tourism opportunities. In: Butler, R., Hinch, T. (Eds.), Tourism and Indigenous People. Thomson International Business Press, London, pp. 27–48.

Contemporary Issues in the Lodging Sector

CHAPTER 2

Demand for Lodging and Tourism

INTRODUCTION

As noted in the first chapter, tourism is a huge global phenomenon, which with only a few notable exceptions, continues to grow each year. At any given moment there are millions of people undertaking leisure or business trips in all corners of the world. With these millions of travelers, there are likewise millions of purposes and thousands of motives for undertaking their journeys. Years of scholarly research have shown that different people travel for different reasons—to fulfill a variety of psychological, emotional, physical, or economic needs. Because everyone is different and might be motivated differently, and they come from different places, the tourism product sought varies from person to person and place to place. Thus, motives and interests, coupled with what the destination has to offer potential visitors, create an array of tourism types and market types that can be divided and subdivided for the purposes of marketing planning and research.

In addition, demand, or the consumption of the tourism product, is not uniform through time and space. Thus, certain places have different patterns of demand at different times of the year. Likewise, global forces that cannot always be predicted, and some that can, are at play in causing people to avoid or flock to certain destinations. Understanding tourism demand is very important for marketing, regional tourism planning, and managing attractions and other services (e.g. transportation and accommodations). This chapter examines tourism demand, what it is, how it is changed via 'demand shifters', and how understanding patterns of demand is crucial for tourism planning and development.

CONTENTS

Introduction

Demand for Tourism and Lodging Services

Travel Motives and Accommodation Selection

Demand Shifters

Market Segmentation

Summary and Conclusion

References

Further Reading

Useful Internet Resources

DEMAND FOR TOURISM AND LODGING SERVICES

Demand for tourism refers to the consumption of tourism products. The supply side of tourism and lodging is not the focus of this chapter but is the focus of the majority of the next 14 chapters that follow. Demand entails the travelers themselves, intermediaries (e.g. travel agents and tour operators), and service suppliers consuming or purchasing products and services that make the travel experience possible. Tourists buying food, train tickets, souvenirs, and hotel nights is an example of demand; travelers in this sense are consuming the supply of tourism directly. Tour operators also form part of the demand for tourism as they too purchase products from suppliers such as airlines, motor coaches, hotels, and dining establishments. Likewise, airlines, hotels, and other direct suppliers are equally important consumers because they purchase petroleum, bathroom supplies, food and drinks, laundry services, and so on. Thus, the tourism demand system is as complex as the supply system; it involves many levels of consumption and entails more than just tourists staying in hotels or dining in cafés. Nonetheless, this chapter focuses primarily on the tourist and his/her role in the demand side of tourism.

Worldwide, there has been significant growth in demand for international travel since the mid-1900s. With the close of the Second World War and the technological advancements in long-distance air transportation that developed during and after the war (e.g. larger and more efficient airplanes), air ticket costs became more within reach of the average traveler. As a result, the world opened up to greater flows of people. During the 1990s and early 2000s, international travel has seen an annual growth rate of between 4 and 7%, depending on the year and economic and political forces at play. Since 2000, international travel has grown by nearly 30% (Table 2.1). Between 1950 and 2007, in only 57 years, international arrivals have

Table 2.1	Growth of International Tourist Arrivals Since the Second World War
1950	25 million
1960	69 million
1970	166 million
1980	288 million
1990	457 million
2000	698 million
2007	903 million

Source: UNWTO (2008).

multiplied more than 35 times. Few other industries have realized such rapid and widespread growth.

Although nearly a billion international tourist trips is remarkable and noteworthy, domestic travel, which is much harder to measure and estimate, increases global tourism totals by several times. Mid-2000s industry estimates in the United States, where domestic travel is a very important part of tourism demand, place the number of domestic trips at around two billion. Approximately 44% of lodging nights in the US were spent by business travelers, while 56% were spent by leisure tourists. Most leisure hotel guests travel by car, are aged 35–54, make reservations ahead of time and pay an average of $109 per room per night. From a business traveler perspective, 41% spend three or more nights at a hotel. In contrast, only 28% of leisure travelers spend three or more nights (American Hotel and Lodging Association, 2008).

There are also some interesting geographical patterns associated with growing global demand for tourism. For instance, in 1950, the top 15 destination countries in the world accounted for approximately 98% of all international tourist arrivals. In 1970, this had fallen to 75%, while in 2007 the top 15 destinations absorbed only 57% of all arrivals (UNWTO, 2008). These changes reflect the materialization of new destinations in the developing world and in peripheral regions. As more places open up to tourism, demand is spread to other destinations, breaking the monopoly traditionally held by only a handful of countries. This is particularly important in the past 20 years as tourists have expressed a lack of interest in the 'same old places' and a surge of interest in discovering places that have been heretofore relatively unexplored, including destinations such as Antarctica, and many countries in Asia, Africa, and Latin America. Countries such as Vietnam and Cambodia, which were

Table 2.2   Countries Expected to Grow their Tourism Economies Fastest in 2008

Rank	Country	Real Tourism GDP Growth %
1	Macau	23.8
2	Montenegro	17.0
3	Seychelles	14.1
4	Angola	13.7
5	Reunion	13.7
6	United Arab Emirates	13.5
7	Libya	13.2
8	Azerbaijan	11.4
9	China	11.3
10	Romania	9.3

Source: WTTC (2008).

until recently relatively unexplored by tourists and under strict communist control, have become popular destinations. Table 2.2 lists the countries that were expected to experience the most relative tourism-based economic growth in their GDPs in 2008, which is reflective of the point that new countries are becoming tourist destinations as the world continues to open up to tourism. As denoted in Table 2.2, Angola, Libya, and Azerbaijan are good examples of this change in global demand for new and different destinations. The World Travel and Tourism Council projects that between 2008 and 2018, other countries that traditionally have not been chief destinations will be listed as among the fastest growing and largest tourism-based economies, based on arrivals, employment, and relative growth in tourism GDP. These include Namibia, Vietnam, Vanuatu, Sao Tome and Principe, Cape Verde, Brunei, Qatar, Montenegro, Rwanda, Chile, and Romania.

As of 2007, the fastest growing tourism regions in the world are the Middle East, Southeast Asia, Northeast Asia, and Central America, as measured by international arrivals (Table 2.3). The Middle East experienced a remarkable growth of 16.4%, with most of this being shored up by increased arrivals to Egypt, Saudi Arabia, and the United Arab Emirates. Southeast Asia's tourist arrivals grew by 12.2%, reflecting in part the increasing popularity of Vietnam, Cambodia, and Malaysia as tourist destinations. Arrivals in 2007 in Northeast Asia exceeded 2006 numbers by nearly 11%, with Macau demonstrating the highest growth—an astonishing 21%. Japan experienced a 13% growth in one year, and a 10% growth was recorded for China. Central America's extraordinary 10% growth reflected notable enlargement in demand for Costa Rica, Honduras, and Panama.

It is also interesting and useful to examine where the demand comes from, not just where it goes. Table 2.4 shows the origins of people who travel for personal/leisure reasons in the order of how much is spent on travel. American tourists together spend more than any other individual nation, exceeding the second ranked country, Japan, by more than three times. China's position in the top ten demonstrates its burgeoning middle class, which can now afford to travel and which has benefited from the Chinese government's Approved Destination Status—a list of countries the Chinese are permitted to visit on holiday vacations, which continues to expand each year. Mexico's inclusion on the top-ten list also testifies to the growing affluence in that country and the high priority Mexicans place on international travel. Table 2.5 similarly shows expenditures on business-related travel. Not surprisingly, most states on the personal top-ten list also have a place on the business travel top-ten list. There has always been a positive relationship between pleasure- and business-oriented travel, as one tends to support the other.

Table 2.3 International Arrivals by Sub-region, 2007

Sub-region	International Arrivals 1990 (millions)	International Arrivals 1995 (millions)	International Arrivals 2000 (millions)	International Arrivals 2005 (millions)	International Arrivals 2007 (millions)	Growth between 2006 and 2007 (%)
EUROPE						
Northern Europe	28.6	35.8	43.7	52.8	57.6	2.2
Western Europe	108.6	112.2	139.7	142.4	154.9	3.6
Central/Eastern Europe	31.5	60.6	69.4	87.8	95.6	4.5
Southern Europe	93.9	102.7	140.8	157.3	176.2	7.0
ASIA AND THE PACIFIC						
Northeast Asia	26.4	41.3	58.3	87.5	104.2	10.6
Southeast Asia	21.1	28.2	35.6	48.5	59.6	12.2
Oceania	5.2	8.1	9.2	10.5	10.7	1.7
South Asia	3.2	4.2	6.1	8.1	9.8	8.2
AMERICAS						
North America	71.7	80.7	91.5	89.9	95.3	5.2
Caribbean	11.4	14.0	17.1	18.8	19.5	0.1
Central America	1.9	2.6	4.3	6.4	7.7	9.6
South America	7.7	11.7	15.3	18.2	19.9	6.4
AFRICA						
North Africa	8.4	7.3	10.2	13.9	16.3	7.9
Subsaharan Africa	6.8	12.8	17.7	23.3	28.2	7.1
MIDDLE EAST						
Middle East	9.6	13.7	24.4	37.8	47.6	16.4

Source: UNWTO (2008).

These global patterns are important to understand when considering the lodging needs of travelers. Most of the data presented above are based on overnight trips. The World Tourism Organization defines a tourist as someone who travels away from home and spends at least one night in the destination. While international and domestic day trips are an important part of tourism, they are not typically counted in international arrivals data. As a result, tourists undertaking these millions (or billions in a domestic context) of overnight trips require places to stay, so the relevance of lodging in this context is clear. For this reason, there has also been a concomitant increase of lodging facilities of various sorts throughout the world. These are discussed in greater detail in the second half of the book.

Table 2.4 Top Ten Personal Traveler Origin Countries by Expenditures, 2008

Rank	Country	Billions of $ US on Personal Travel
1	United States	889.5
2	Japan	274.4
3	United Kingdom	208.1
4	Germany	201.8
5	France	170.9
6	China	167.5
7	Italy	127.1
8	Spain	123.9
9	Canada	95.8
10	Mexico	77.1

Source: WTTC (2008).

Table 2.5 Top Ten Business Traveler Origin Countries by Expenditures, 2008

Rank	Country	Billions of $ US on Business Travel
1	United States	190.1
2	Japan	70.2
3	China	65.8
4	Germany	62.1
5	United Kingdom	51.1
6	France	43.3
7	Italy	40.3
8	Spain	21.7
9	Canada	20.2
10	Brazil	15.5

Source: WTTC (2008).

To illustrate the lodging impact of international travelers, their demand for lodging in the USA, one of the world's top destinations, can be examined briefly. Almost 19 million overseas travelers and nine million Canadians spent at least one night in the United States in 2007, accounting for some 22% of all room nights in the country. The average length of stay for overseas visitors was 7.9 nights with the main motives being leisure/holiday (53%) and business (35%). Most foreigners visited more than one state (average 1.6) and traveled by taxis (49%), rental cars (33%), and air (27%) (American Hotel and Lodging Association, 2008).

TRAVEL MOTIVES AND ACCOMMODATION SELECTION

To understand tourism demand, one must understand people's motives for traveling. There are nearly as many motives as there are travelers, but the primary underlying stimuli include the need to belong, seeking self fulfillment, spiritual growth, getting away from mundane environments at home, escaping inclement weather, psychological renewal, and altruism, to name just a few. These motives (push factors), when viewed together with what the destination has to offer (pull factors), result in various types of tourism and types of tourists. For example, people who travel to seek spiritual renewal or fulfill a religious obligation participate in 'religious tourism' and are known as religious tourists or pilgrims. People who want to enjoy nature but exact minimal impacts on the environment are referred to as ecotourists. There are many such types of tourism and tourist, too many to elaborate on here, but several will be described briefly and how they relate to demand for accommodation.

The largest tourist gatherings in the world are religious in nature—the hajj in Mecca, Saudi Arabia, the Kumbh Mela in India, and several others. Tens of millions of people attend the Kumbh Mela events every few years, and every year more than two million people undertake the hajj pilgrimage. While the poor who attend these religious events tend to stay in tents or pilgrim rest houses, there is a growing demand for hotels and guesthouses. International hotels, such as InterContinental and Ramada, have found favor in Mecca among wealthy Muslims undertaking the pilgrimage.

Ecotourists, or those who travel for enjoyment but also with an educational, altruistic, or environmental solidarity purpose, often select ecolodges or ecohotels that practice environmentally sensitive energy, waste management, and supply chain procedures. People whose primary desire is to get away from home to avoid bad weather, to relax, or simply to do nothing at all, typically elect to stay at a beach resort or take a cruise.

Outdoors enthusiasts usually choose camping, cabins, or ski lodges as their lodging medium because this allows them to be closer to nature and the outdoors. Tourists with an

Modern-day pilgrims at the Ganges River, Varanasi, India

Beach resort area on the Caribbean island of Anguilla

interest in rural areas and agricultural heritage often select farm stays or dude ranches as their preferred accommodations. Likewise, business travelers typically prefer high-class, brand-name hotels located either in urban centers or near airports. Road-based travelers have a tendency to stay in hotels or motels located near major thoroughfares, while youth and educational tourists usually stay in hostels, dormitories, or camp-grounds. People who travel to gamble usually end up staying in casino resorts or casino hotels, and of course VFR (visiting friends and relatives) travelers are more inclined to stay in private residences. Clearly there are direct relationships between travel motives or type of tourism, and the most common lodging choice.

DEMAND SHIFTERS

So far this chapter has illustrated the immensity of tourism and lodging demand. However, it should also be made clear that demand for accommodation services is not uniform, balanced or in any way absolute. Tourism demand is fickle, fluctuating quickly, and inconsistent with economic, social, political, and environmental changes. Forces that alter demand, both up or down, are known as demand shifters and can take on any number of forms such as terrorism, increased unemployment, or demographic changes.

One of the most common shifters is special events and holidays. These can include festivals, public holidays, school breaks, sporting events, or other periodic occurrences that increase demand for places and products. Mega sporting events, such as the World Cup, the Olympics, the World Series (baseball), and the Super Bowl (American football), are extremely popular events that draw tens of thousands of people physically to a place and deliver considerable media exposure to others. Communities throughout the world compete to host such large-scale events because of the numbers of tourists they produce. Accommodation properties are perhaps the most affected by big events and festivals, and sometimes new properties are erected specifi-cally to facilitate an expected influx of visitors.

Changing demographics is another demand shifter that is especially pertinent today with the retirement of baby boomers, who are living longer and are more affluent than their parents. These two variables alone (longevity and affluence) are part of the reason for the rapid growth in tourism, especially special niche forms of tourism such as adventure tours, ecotours, educational travel, genealogy-based journeys, and other forms of heritage tourism. Market research has shown that since the 1990s, retirees today are demanding higher levels of physical activity and adventure in their expectations and behaviors. Other demographic changes, such as immigration and ethnic composition, are having a significant impact on tourism demand as well. For instance, with escalating numbers of Hispanic Americans in the United States, there is a higher tendency for the populations of the southwestern states (e.g. California, Arizona, Nevada, New Mexico, and Texas) to travel back to Latin America on vacation to visit family and friends. Likewise, smaller family sizes since the 1950s have allowed more families to go on longer distance holidays more frequently.

In terms of economic trends, it is fairly obvious that when unemployment rates rise, travel declines. Travel is considered a dispensable luxury good during times of economic hardship. The current global economic crisis (2007–2009) is illustrative of this, as many people have cut travel completely out of their budgets until the economy begins to stabilize. Millions of people have recently lost their jobs and their homes; in these dire circumstances, travel is one of the first items to be trimmed from the family budget. As well, there is a direct correlation between currency exchange rates and international travel. When rates are favorable people will travel abroad. When exchange rates become unfavorable, travel slows down. Personal holiday travel is the most elastic in relation to exchange rates; business travel on the other hand tends to remain fairly constant during periods of currency devaluation.

Political circumstances also have a profound influence on demand for tourism. As already noted, an extreme example is terrorism and war. These have obvious downturn effects not only in the countries where the conflicts occur but also in their broader regions and throughout the entire world. One of the most momentous political shifters during the past two decades was the collapse of state socialism (communism) in Eastern and Central Europe. With the fall of communism in countries like Poland, Czech Republic, Bulgaria, Romania, Serbia, Albania, and the successor states of the former Soviet Union, there has been a huge influx of tourists to these countries. This fact elevated several of them to the World Tourism Organization's list of top 20 destinations because of the newfound freedom to visit there. People of Polish or Romanian decent living abroad could now visit their homelands freely without fear of detainment or government harassment. Many emigrants from the region who left following World War II were not permitted to return or they might face imprisonment in some cases. The disintegration of the communist system has created a huge global demand for the countries of Eastern Europe. Mongolia, China, Vietnam, and Cambodia have faced similar changes in Asia. Even though China, Cambodia, and Vietnam remain communist states, they have adopted economic systems that resemble capitalism; they welcome foreign visitors and are encouraging tourism growth, something the European communist states did not do.

Other political issues relate to travel restrictions, passports, and visas. In 2003, the Department of Homeland Security began requiring a transit visa for all passengers transferring between flights in US airports, even if they do not leave the airport building. This is only one of several new regulations initiated to fight the threat of terrorism. This has been a point of contention between the US and many of its allies. Citizens of most Latin American, Caribbean, Asian, African, and Pacific Island countries must now obtain a US transit visa to change airplanes in a US airport, even if their layover is an hour or less.

As part of its national security measures, the US government recently ratified a law that will require passports for all travel into and out of the United States, including by foot and car to Mexico and Canada. Canadians have always been permitted to enter the US on only proof of citizenship (e.g. birth certificate) and vice versa. Americans have long been able to visit Mexico without a passport. However, now passports will be required to re-enter the United States for everyone. At the time of writing, Americans could still enter the US by land or sea from Bermuda, the Caribbean, Mexico or Canada, using only a photo ID and birth certificate. After June 2009, however, all entrances into the country will require a valid passport. The governments of Canada, Mexico, and the Caribbean islands have protested the US government's decision, suggesting that such a passport requirement (only about one quarter of Americans possesses a valid passport) will create a huge drop in demand for regional tourism. For many Americans, travel to Canada, Mexico, and the Caribbean before 2008 was feasible because passports were unnecessary.

Seasonality

Seasonal changes in demand for tourism and accommodations are known as seasonality. There are two primary types of seasonality, namely natural and institutional. Natural seasonality is caused by naturally occurring demand shifters, such as weather and climatic patterns. Institutional seasonality happens as a result of human-induced variables, such as school breaks and summer vacations, public holidays, and special events. Low season occurs when demand for destinations and products is down. From a socio-economic perspective this is seen as one of the negative sides of tourism because it usually results in layoffs and other staff reductions, and it also means less tax and regional income. Lodging properties can do several things, including special events and offer special discounts to try to counter the effects of low season (this is discussed in greater detail in Chapter 4). Seasonal changes can be seen easily in the form of bar or line graphs. Figure 2.1 shows seasonal variations in demand among tourist arrivals in Sri Lanka. It is clear that Sri Lanka is in high demand between

A hotel in New Hampshire, USA, experiencing low season

November and February, with the peak months being December and January. Of course this is a result of the country's tropical warm weather, which appeals to tourists from Europe and other cold climes during the northern winter. During the summer months and monsoon periods there is considerably lower demand for the island's tourism product.

Colder climates, such as parts of Canada and Norway, typically have their high season in summer, when the weather is pleasant and warm. Winters are low seasons because of the cold and darkness associated with their northern locations. However, even in cold-weather climates there tends to be a bump in demand during the winter season, which reflects the popularity of winter sports (e.g. skiing) in many cold-climate destinations.

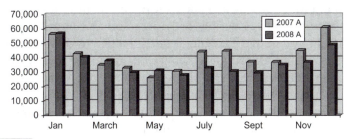

FIGURE 2.1 *Monthly tourist arrivals in Sri Lanka, 2007–2008.*
Source: Sri Lanka Tourism Board (2009).

MARKET SEGMENTATION

Demand for tourism and lodging can be studied from three or four main perspectives, including geographically as noted earlier, psychographically, demographically, and according to visitor behavior. Breaking the market into these categories is known as market segmentation. Segmentation is an important and very useful tool in understanding what consumers desire, how they behave, what they consume, and where they are from. All of these have salient implications for marketing and research.

The goal of geographic market segmentation is to understand visitor/guest origins. The most common question asked in this regard is where they are from. This allows destinations and accommodation facilities to decide their largest 'catchment area', or the region from which most of their visitors derive. This has long been an important approach to understand demand and catering to the needs of prominent markets. This is often broken down in aggregate into international and domestic markets. Likewise, individual businesses, such as attractions, restaurants, and ski resorts often divide their geographic market into local and non-local consumers.

Some observers suggest that geographic segmentation is losing some of its relevance with the rapid development of e-commerce and Internet-based advertising, because catchment areas can now be viewed as the entire world. Traditional political boundaries have therefore been breached and are slightly less relevant in today's e-commerce-oriented marketplace. Nonetheless, most destinations still desire to understand this important aspect of their markets. This is particularly true as new countries open up to global travel by way of increased affluence and greater political freedom to travel. China and India, demographically the two largest countries in the world, fall into these categories and are becoming key markets for global tourism. According to estimates by various international organizations, both countries will continue generating international tourists at high rates of growth far into the future.

Psychographic and behavioral segmentation assists planners and marketers in understanding demand as it manifests in visitor expectations, lifestyles, attitudes, values, desires, activities, motives, and behaviors. This is particularly important in the lodging sector, for different guests have different expectations regarding cleanliness, service quality, brand loyalty, and a wide range of other variables that can influence their experiences at a property and the way the property needs to be managed.

Demographic classifications are important in understanding the age, gender, marital status, sexual orientation, income, family size, occupation, level of education, race and ethnicity, religion, and social class of guests and potential guests. Many of these have a bearing on the types of lodging facilities they will choose. It seems obvious that people with low incomes will elect to stay at generally inexpensive properties, such as motels or campgrounds. Large families might be required to purchase two rooms for the night. Gay and lesbian travelers will probably select a hotel, resort, or cruise that is gay-friendly. Honeymooners or older couples might decide on a quiet location devoid of a mass party atmosphere. Certain religious adherents might choose one hotel over another if a prayer room is provided or if the kitchen can cater to their unique dietary needs. Once the demographic characteristics of a lodging facility's primary market(s) are know and understood, these issues can be highlighted in their promotional materials and on their websites. 'Kid-friendly', 'relaxing atmosphere', 'vibrant night-life', and 'good value for money' are examples of phrases that might be utilized to match supply with demand by understanding market demographics and psychographics.

To meet an increasingly sophisticated and segmented demand for resort products, some resort companies have paid close attention to demographic, psychographic and behavioral demand and have broadened their appeal to a wider market. Club Med, traditionally known for its active, singles lifestyle-oriented resorts, has now broadened its appeal and advertises family resorts, couples resorts, singles resorts, spa resorts, ski resorts, golf resorts, diving resorts, and tennis resorts. Other resort companies have narrowed their markets by specializing in a single niche, including the Sandals, which caters to 'couples in love' at its locations in St Lucia, the Bahamas, Jamaica, and Antigua.

SUMMARY AND CONCLUSION

This chapter has highlighted several aspects of the demand for tourism and lodging. It did not focus on the supply side, for this is the purpose of the rest of the book. It is clear that worldwide demand for tourism is tremendous. Lodging is perhaps the biggest beneficiary of the worldwide growth in arrivals, as the hundreds of millions (and billions in domestic terms) of overnight travelers require a place to stay. There are many things accommodation companies can do to understand various aspects of demand, including their market segments. This will help them target the correct population cohorts based on their demographic, psychographic, and behavioral characteristics. Geographic segmentation is also critical, as home location will often determine seasonal demand for hot- or cold-weather destinations.

There are many variables at play to determine the level of demand for destinations and accommodation services. These are primarily of an economic, natural, demographic, and political nature. In today's complex world, these demand shifters are becoming even more important in determining the success of resorts, hotels, and other lodging businesses.

REFERENCES

American Hotel and Lodging Association, 2008. 2008 Lodging industry profile. AHLA, Washington, DC.

Sri Lanka Tourism Board, 2009. Monthly statistical bulletin. Online < http://www.sltbstatistics.org/msb.html> Accessed January 29.

UNWTO, 2008. Tourism highlights, 2008 Edition. World Tourism Organization, Madrid.

WTTC, 2008. Tourism satellite accounting: the 2008 travel and tourism economic research executive summary. World Travel and Tourism Council, London.

FURTHER READING

Albaladejo Pina, I.P., Díaz Delfa, M.T., 2005. Rural tourism demand by type of accommodation. Tourism Management 26, 951–959.

Bai, B., Ghiselli, R., Pearson, T., 2000. Market characteristics in economy/budget lodging. FIU Hospitality Review 18 (2), 37–50.

Bender, B., Partlow, C., Roth, M., 2008. An examination of strategic drivers impacting U.S. multinational lodging corporations. International Journal of Hospitality and Tourism Administration 9 (3), 219–243.

Cai, L.A., 1999. Relationship of household characteristics and lodging expenditure on leisure trips. Journal of Hospitality and Leisure Marketing 6 (2), 5–18.

Capó-Parrilla, J., Riera-Font, A., Rosselló-Nadal, J., 2007. Accommodation determinants of seasonal patterns. Annals of Tourism Research 34, 422–436.

Chadee, D., Mieczkowski, Z., 1987. An empirical analysis of the effects of the exchange rate on Canadian tourism. Journal of Travel Research 26 (1), 13–17.

Chen, J.S., 2000. Norwegians' preferences for U.S. lodging facilities: market segmentation approach. Journal of Travel and Tourism Marketing 9 (4), 69–82.

Chhabra, D., 2005. Understanding the VFR market and their economic impacts. e-Review of Tourism Research 3 (4), 97–102.

Chung, K.Y., Oh, S.Y., Kim, S.S., Han, S.Y., 2004. Three representative market segmentation methodologies for hotel guest room customers. Tourism Management 25, 429–441.

Cope, R., 2001. USA outbound. Travel and Tourism Analyst 6, 29–58.

de Roos, J.A., 1999. Natural occupancy rates and development gaps—a look at the U.S. lodging industry. Cornell Hotel and Restaurant Administration Quarterly 40 (2), 14–19.

Fernández-Morales, A., Mayorga-Toledano, M.C., 2008. Seasonal concentration of the hotel demand in Costa del Sol: a decomposition by nationalities. Tourism Management 29, 940–949.

Gu, Z., 2003. The Chinese lodging industry: problems and solutions. International Journal of Contemporary Hospitality Management 15 (7), 386–392.

Hong, G.S., Kim, S.Y., Lee, J., 1999. Travel expenditure patterns of elderly households in the US. Tourism Recreation Research 24 (1), 43–52.

Jeffrey, D., Barden, R.R.D., 1999. An analysis of the nature, causes and marketing implications of seasonality in the occupancy performance of English hotels. Tourism Economics 5 (1), 69–91.

Jeffrey, D., Barden, R.R.D., Buckley, P.J., Hubbard, N.J., 2002. What makes for a successful hotel? Insights on hotel management following 15 years of hotel occupancy analysis in England. Service Industries Journal 22 (2), 73–88.

Jolliffe, L., Farnsworth, R., 2003. Seasonality in tourism employment: human resource challenges. International Journal of Contemporary Hospitality Management 15 (6), 312–316.

Koenig, N., Bischoff, E.E., 2004. Tourism demand patterns in turbulent times: analysing Welsh accommodation occupancy data for 1998–2001. International Journal of Tourism Research 6 (4), 205–220.

Krakover, S., 2000. Seasonal adjustment of employment to demand and revenues in tourist hotels during expansion and stagnation. International Journal of Hospitality and Tourism Administration 1 (2), 27–49.

Laesser, C., Crouch, G.I., 2006. Segmenting markets by travel expenditure patterns: the case of international visitors to Australia. Journal of Travel Research 44 (4), 397–406.

Laesser, C., Crouch, G.I., Beritelli, P., 2006. Market segmentation by reasons and influences to visit a destination: the case of international visitors to Australia. Tourism Analysis 11 (4), 241–249.

Lee, M.J., Jang, S.C., 2007. Market diversification and financial performance and stability: a study of hotel companies. International Journal of Hospitality Management 26 (2), 362–375.

Lieux, E.M., Weaver, P.A., McCleary, K.W., 1994. Lodging preferences of the senior tourism market. Annals of Tourism Research 21, 712–728.

Lim, C., 1997. Review of international tourism demand models. Annals of Tourism Research 24, 835–849.

Lundtorp, S., Rassing, C.R., Wanhill, S., 1999. The off-season is 'no season': the case of the Danish island of Bornholm. Tourism Economics 5 (1), 49–68.

Lynn, M., 2007. Brand segmentation in the hotel and cruise industries: fact or fiction? Cornell Hospitality Report 7 (4), 4–18.

Morrison, A.M., Braunlich, C.G., Cai, L.A., O'Leary, J.T., 1996. A profile of the casino resort vacationer. Journal of Travel Research 35 (2), 55–61.

Moschis, G.P., Ünal, B., 2008. Travel and leisure services preferences and patronage motives of older consumers. Journal of Travel and Tourism Marketing 24 (4), 259–269.

Oh, H.M., Jeong, M.Y., 2004. Moderating effects of travel purpose and past experience on the relationship between product performance and lodging repurchase. Journal of Hospitality and Leisure Marketing 11 (2/3), 139–158.

Palakurthi, R.R., Parks, S.J., 2000. The effect of selected socio-demographic factors on lodging demand in the USA. International Journal of Contemporary Hospitality Management 12 (2/3), 135–142.

Pan, C.M., 2007. Market demand variations, room capacity, and optimal hotel room rates. International Journal of Hospitality Management 26 (3), 748–753.

Patrick, J.M., Renforth, W., 1996. The effects of the peso devaluation on cross-border retailing. Journal of Borderlands Studies 11 (1), 25–41.

Perdue, R.R., 2004. Skiers, ski bums, trust fund babies, migrants, techies, and entrepreneurs: the changing face of the Colorado ski industry. In: Weiermair, K., Mathies, C. (Eds.), The Tourism and Leisure Industry: Shaping the Future. Haworth, New York, pp. 209–225.

Perucic, D., 2007. The impact of globalization on supply and demand in the cruise industry. Tourism and Hospitality Management 13 (3), 665–680.

Prodanic, I.J., Timothy, D.J., 2007. Effects of the Yugoslavian wars on tourism in the Republic of Montenegro. Journal of Hospitality and Tourism 5 (1), 67–82.

Scarinci, J., Richins, H., 2008. Specialist lodging in the USA: motivations of bed and breakfast accommodation guests. Tourism 56 (3), 271–282.

Smith, R.A., Lesure, J.D., 1999. The U.S. lodging industry today. Cornell Hotel and Restaurant Administration Quarterly 40 (1), 18–25.

Smith, S., Timothy, D.J., 2006. Demand for tourism in North America. In: Fennell, D. (Ed.), North America: A Tourism Handbook. Channel View Publications, Clevedon, UK, pp. 32–52.

Timothy, D.J., Teye, V.B., 2005. Informal sector business travelers in the developing world: a borderlands perspective. Journal of Tourism Studies 16 (1), 82–92.

Verma, R., 2007. Unlocking the secrets of customers' choices. Cornell Hospitality Report 7 (2), 4–20.

Walker, B.H., 1993. What's ahead: a strategic look at lodging trends. Cornell Hotel and Restaurant Administration Quarterly 34 (5), 28–34.

Walsh, K., Enz, C.A., Canina, L., 2004. The impact of gasoline price fluctuations on lodging demand for US brand hotels. International Journal of Hospitality Management 23 (5), 505–521.

Webber, A.G., 2001. Exchange rate volatility and cointegration in tourism demand. Journal of Travel Research 39 (4), 398–405.

USEFUL INTERNET RESOURCES

World Tourism Organization: www.world-tourism.org.

World Travel and Tourism Council: http://www.wttc.org/.

Current Issues in Human Resources, Structural Change, and e-Commerce in the Global Lodging Sector

INTRODUCTION

Tourism is a labor-intensive industry. It requires great effort and many key players to achieve success. Hotels, resorts, bed and breakfasts, and other places to stay comprise one of the most labor-demanding sectors in tourism. In an increasingly global marketplace in terms of both demand and supply, and in a world of rapid technological growth, there are many pressing concerns for lodging managers and company officials. This chapter examines several of these, including certain human resource issues, corporate ownership (e.g. mergers, franchises, and acquisitions), and e-commerce and Internet-based technology.

Managers of lodging properties face a multitude of issues in a variety of departments that could be discussed in this chapter, including budgeting, human resources, staff training, program certification, event management, laundry services, housekeeping, maintenance and custodial work, and others. However, as the first chapter mentioned, this book is not designed to be a hotel management text, even though the material presented in the chapters clearly has important management implications. Dozens of hospitality and hotel management textbooks already exist, so this chapter aims to highlight only a selected few of the most pressing and noteworthy issues that managers and marketers are facing in this sector today. In particular, the chapter examines several contemporary human resource issues, patterns of mergers and acquisitions, and e-commerce and technology as they relate to the lodging sector.

CONTENTS

Introduction

Human Resource Issues

Franchises, Mergers and Acquisition

E-Commerce and Information Technology

Summary and Conclusion

References

Further Reading

Useful Internet Resources

HUMAN RESOURCE ISSUES

Staff and personnel are one of the most important assets an accommodation facility possesses. Because tourism is volatile and potential guests have a wide array of lodging options, it is important that the right staff members are hired, trained, and retained to provide the best experiences possible for guests. Human resource management (HRM) is a broad sub-field within hospitality management, and there already is a multitude of books and articles that describe and teach about the nuances and best practices associated with HRM. This section, therefore, underscores some of the critical issues and themes that are currently facing human resource (HR) managers, as they are required to work in the broader field of tourism, which is on an upward trajectory of globalization, inclusiveness, and increased competition.

There is a huge assortment of jobs involved in the accommodation sector. These range from groundskeepers to chambermaids, to wait staff, and to general managers. All of these positions are important in the smooth functioning of a property, although each one has a certain set of skills that have to be developed. Table 3.1 lists the lodging-affiliated jobs that are officially recognized in the United States for statistical purposes by the US Department of Labor. In 2006, there were approximately 1.833 million jobs in the accommodation sector in the United States.

More than 80% of workers in the lodging sector are employed as service, office, and administrative support personnel. In most cases, people in these positions learn the necessary skills on the job, with relatively few having pursued a post-secondary education. For this category of workers, personality, people skills, and communications skills are often more important than a formal education. Service workers are a very important and large part of the success of accommodation properties. Housekeeping, maintenance, food preparations, and food services' staffers are all included in this category. In addition to people who work directly in room and facilities maintenance, there are also important roles for workers in the amenities area, including recreation and fitness workers, casino dealers, chauffeurs, and camp counselors.

Upper-level management is hired to coordinate personnel, finances, food services, security, transportation, marketing and sales, and other high-profile tasks. Many of these people have post-secondary university or college degrees in areas of management, marketing, accounting, law enforcement, culinary arts, or tourism.

Most contemporary concerns associated with human resources in the hotel and lodging sector rotate around recruitment and retention, service quality, and training and development. Each of these is multidimensional and not mutually exclusive of one another.

Recruitment and retention

There is a vast and growing hospitality-based literature about the nuances of job skills and qualifications, recruitment methods, employee benefits and

Table 3.1	Employment in Hotels and Other Accommodations by Occupation, USA, 2006	
Occupation	**Number of Jobs (in thousands)**	**Percent of Total**
ALL OCCUPATIONS IN LODGING	1,833	100
MANAGEMENT, BUSINESS, AND ACCOUTING	94	5.1
General and operations managers	12	0.7
Lodging managers	29	1.6
Meeting and convention planners	8	0.5
Accountants and auditors	8	0.4
SERVICE OCCUPATIONS	1,184	64.6
Security guards	30	1.7
Chefs and head cooks	13	0.1
First-line supervisors/managers of food preparation and serving workers	23	1.3
Cooks, restaurant	57	3.1
Food preparation workers	21	1.1
Bartenders	36	2.0
Fast food and counter workers	28	1.5
Waiters and waitresses (wait staff)	133	7.2
Food servers, non-restaurant	41	2.3
Dining room and cafeteria attendants and bartender helpers	46	2.5
Dishwashers	33	1.8
Hosts/hostesses, restaurant, lounge and coffee shop	19	1.0
First-line supervisors/managers of housekeeping and janitorial workers	32	1.7
Janitors and cleaners, except maids and housekeeping cleaners	52	2.9
Maids and housekeeping cleaners	424	23.1
Landscaping and groundskeeping workers	22	1.2
Gaming supervisors	11	0.6
Gaming dealers	34	1.9
Amusement and recreation attendants	12	0.6
Baggage porters and bellhops	25	1.4
Concierges	8	0.4
Recreation workers	10	0.5
SALES AND RELATED OCCUPATIONS	52	2.9
Cashiers, except gaming	15	0.8
Gaming change persons and booth cashiers	7	0.4
Sales representatives, services	12	0.7

(continued)

Table 3.1	Employment in Hotels and Other Accommodations by Occupation, USA, 2006—*Cont'd*	
Occupation	Number of Jobs (in thousands)	Percent of Total
OFFICE AND ADMINISTRATIVE SUPPORT OCCUPATIONS	345	18.8
First-line supervisors/managers of office and administrative support workers	25	1.3
Switchboard operators, including answering service	9	0.5
Bookkeeping, accounting, and auditing clerks	23	1.3
Hotel, motel, and resort desk clerks	207	11.3
Reservation and transportation ticket agents and travel clerks	13	0.7
Secretaries and administrative assistants	16	0.9
INSTALLATION, MAINTENANCE, AND REPAIR OCCUPATIONS	82	4.5
Maintenance and repair workers, general	70	3.8
PRODUCTION OCCUPATIONS	38	2.1
Laundry and dry-cleaning workers	31	1.7
TRANSPORTATION AND MATERIAL MOVING OCCUPATIONS	24	1.3
Taxi drivers and chauffeurs	8	0.4
Parking lot attendants	8	0.5

* *Note: Columns do not necessarily add to totals, as some occupations with small numbers have been omitted.*
Source: Bureau of Labor Statistics (2008).

Resort employees in Fiji preparing to meet arriving guests

incentives, hiring and firing, talent management, employee relations, and performance assessments. These are not the purpose of this section. Instead, we aim here to examine some of the other pertinent issues facing the lodging sector as they relate to human resources.

After hiring and training high-quality staff members, one of the most critical tasks HR managers face is retaining good talent. Common sense and research to support it suggest that retaining employees hinges on creating environments that are conducive to high levels of job satisfaction. Many things contribute to job satisfaction or dissatisfaction in the hospitality industry. Like many service industries, hospitality has a fairly high employee turnover rate in the developed world, which is a common concern and challenge for lodging managers. This is less the case in less-developed countries, where jobs in tourism are more coveted and appreciated. Most turnover takes place in food services and other direct service jobs, while managerial positions see the least turnover. One of the goals of managers and human resource experts is to understand what variables influence job satisfaction most. Giving voice to personnel rather than simply dictating what they must do, outweighing negative feedback with positive feedback, accommodating employees' personal needs in terms of schedules and salaries, providing clear job expectations, and providing rewarding incentives are key to job satisfaction and retaining high-quality workers. Research studies have shown that there is a positive relationship between employee voice and ownership of issues and a company's ability to retain talent. Aside from competitive salaries, bonuses, recognitions, and awards, there are other social factors that contribute to satisfied staff and increased morale. One factor found to develop a sense of solidarity in the workplace and greater workplace satis-faction is having an empathetic and cooperative supervisor, who is person-able and accommodating when it comes to personal needs in the workplace.

One interesting perspective on this that a few researchers have begun examining is in some destinations, particularly in the Caribbean and Pacific Islands, job satisfaction is directly linked to religious adherence among workers. Faith and religion play an important role in many people's lives. In fact, while religiosity is declining in some places, in Europe for example, it is continuing to intensify in other places with important implications for overall wellbeing and harmony in everyday life. By extension then, research has found that if employees are allowed to observe the Sabbath by not being scheduled to work or having places to worship on the job, there is generally a higher level of job satisfaction. In Fiji and other Pacific destinations, island resorts often provide chapels for workers, who meet together in evenings for Bible study and music, as well as church services on Sundays. Essentially at the core of this trend is a flexible and adaptive work environment that empowers employees and allows them to meld personal and work relation-ships and accommodate special needs. A management approach that shares responsibility with the workers is a relatively new concept that appears to be working in recruiting and maintaining high-quality talent.

Employee recruitment is a common concern throughout the hospitality sector. One of the most notable recruitment and retaining issues and trends since the 1990s is inclusiveness, or lack of discrimination, in the workforce. This refers to several foci of discrimination that have long existed, albeit often covertly, in the sub-sectors associated with tourism. Marital status, age, sexual orientation, gender, race, ethnic heritage, and physical disabilities are the most common human characteristics that are referred to in recent discussions of anti-discrimination and inclusiveness. While all of these touch tourism and hospitality in some form, the issue at the forefront of discussions today is the role of people with disabilities in the workforce. The United States is one of relatively few countries in the world that have good legislation to assure equality for people with disabilities, largely put into place with the passing of the Americans with Disabilities Act in 1990 and other subsequent laws. In many countries, including Canada, there is still a lack of definition of what constitutes a physical, visual, hearing, developmental, or psychological disability or disorder, which makes legislation and enforcement to protect special needs populations more difficult.

Unfortunately there are still prejudices in the workforce related to physical attractiveness, aesthetics, and skills, which often preclude people with special needs and visible disabilities. However, conditions are improving and it is becoming more commonplace to see people in wheelchairs or hearing- or visually-impaired persons working in tourism and hospitality.

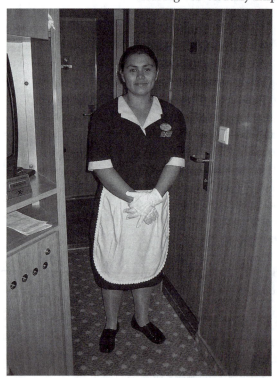

Some hotel companies are actively seeking employees with disabilities. Not only does this build bridges with the broader community and demonstrate goodwill, it makes good business sense; the disabilities community is large with considerable spending power. Research shows that employing people with visible disabilities can attract clients and guests who also have physical impairments, who might feel a common connection and see the respectability demonstrated by the company toward people with special needs.

A well-trained cruise stateroom attendant

Training and service quality

Service quality is the standard by which a lodging facility is judged. Tarnished service reputations are difficult to overcome. Training is seen as a way of improving service quality and can encompass formal education, short training courses, and worksite orientation courses that train people in skills directly pertinent to their jobs and the establishment where they work. There is some concern in the field today that there is a gap between what is taught in universities and colleges and the realities of working in the industry. This is a critical problem that must be addressed by inviting industry representatives to participate in curriculum development and outcomes articulation.

Training to meet the needs of a more globalized market is imperative if hotels and other lodging facilities desire to expand their market base and find success with a growing international clientele. Cross-cultural knowledge is important in today's tourism industry. Without appropriate training, cross-cultural encounters can result in miscommunications and frustration on the part of guests and hotel workers. Cross-cultural training and skills development need to focus on several areas. First, lodging property managers should understand their international markets well and do all they can to hire people with appropriate language skills. In most US states, for example, foreign-language visitors originate primarily in Germany, Italy, Mexico, Japan, Korea, the Netherlands, and increasingly, China. While many overseas guests are able to communicate in English, many are not. It would be prudent for managers to have at least one German-speaking, Japanese-speaking, or Spanish-speaking service, management, or administrative support employee on duty at all times. The lodging sector in Australia, New Zealand, and most of Europe is better at staffing bilingual or multilingual administrative support staff, particularly front-line employees who work directly with guests. This is especially the case in Australia in gift shops and front desk positions. With the United States being placed on China's Approved Destination List in 2007, it would be judicious to seek Mandarin-speaking employees for the near future.

Second, it is good business to ensure that employees understand cultural sensitivities and cultural differences between their own backgrounds and those of the guests. Proper ways to address guests or refer to their nationality or religion should be learned. In some cultures, titles and the way people are addressed are very important. For someone with a doctorate degree to be referred to as Mr or Mrs instead of Dr might be highly offensive. Likewise, to assume that all Arab guests are Muslims or all Indians are Hindus is an avoidable mistake. Bowing, shaking hands, or kissing on the cheek might be considered appropriate or inappropriate greeting gestures, depending on where the guests are from and how formal or informal the relationship is.

Third, there are national and cultural differences regarding expectations from service providers. Japanese guests, for example, expect very high levels of customer service and prefer to be pampered. They are also extremely sensitive to gift-giving, small extras, and outward presentation. Satisfied Japanese clients can be won by providing special gifts, special prices, or otherwise going the extra mile to make them feel welcome.

There are several other cross-cultural areas that are directly pertinent to hospitality. Managing all of them breaks down barriers, builds trust and confidence, and develops interpersonal skills. Considerable research has shown that employees with high levels of cross-cultural sensitivity score much higher than those with low intercultural sensitivity in areas of job satisfaction, social satisfaction, service attentiveness, interpersonal skills, and contribution to revenue (Sizoo, 2008).

FRANCHISES, MERGERS AND ACQUISITION

The past few decades have been a period of unprecedented tourism growth. Along with that growth has come unprecedented change in the management and ownership structures of large hotel and resort companies. The traditional model of hotel administration is independent ownership or title holdings. In most areas of the world, this is still the primary model, which simply refers to individuals, companies, or large corporations owning lodging properties independently. In this instance, the building or property is usually owned by the company in question and the business is operated and managed directly by the owners. Some of the services, such as landscaping and laundry might be subcontracted out, but the hotel itself is owned and operated by the proprietor or proprietary corporation. This model which is also very common in many developing countries tends to appeal to operations in small lodging facilities.

Another very common but very different managerial/ownership structure is franchising. During the mid-1900s, there were only a few large hotel companies (e.g. Hilton and Sheraton). As tourism began to grow and develop quite rapidly after the Second World War and into the 1950s and 1960s, other companies came onto the scene, including Ramada, Howard Johnson, and Holiday Inn. What these companies all had in common was a desire to increase growth and market penetration. This normally would require a great deal of upfront capital for building new properties, but with the goal of increased profits, several hotel companies decided to partner with airlines and other non-hotel companies to lease various properties from other sources. This effectively expanded their property holdings without having to build or purchase real estate, even though there were more facilities with the Sheraton or Westin brand attached to them. This saved the companies hundreds of millions of dollars. The idea soon caught on, and the idea of hotel franchising began.

Today, franchising is one of the most popular ownership models in the accommodation sector. It allows individuals or investment companies to construct or purchase a hotel and then buy or lease a brand name that will give their property the distinction of being part of a larger hotel trademark with all that this entails, including customer brand loyalty, standardized business practices, standard facilities, staff training, a huge promotional and marketing network, a companywide reservation system, established partnerships with other sectors, and many other benefits. A franchise agreement with a hotel company means that for a fee the franchisee (owner/developer) can use the franchisor's name and agrees to adhere to the company's management framework and maintain companywide structural, business, cleanliness, and personnel standards. The franchisee typically is required to pay several different fees, including an upfront franchise fee, a marketing fee, a reservation fee, and a royalty fee. Some fees are lump sum amounts, with others are based on a percentage of sales (Lattin, 2002).

There are several risks and benefits associated with franchises. Perhaps the biggest risk is not having as much total control over each property as independent hotel owners have. A property owner that does not live up to a company's standard of cleanliness or friendly customer service, for example, can be a significant liability for the franchisor. There probably are, however, more benefits than costs. A franchising system allows a hotel company to expand its holdings and grow in terms of properties and revenue without the costs, hassles, and risks associated with constructing hotels themselves. In fact, many hotel companies today have sold off all their real estate properties and operate almost solely in name only as a leasable brand.

Relatively few franchise agreements in the lodging sector have gone global. Franchise agreements are more prevalent in the United States, Canada, and the United Kingdom, although they are spreading in Europe and several areas of Asia and the Middle East. In locations outside of North America, independent ownership is still the most common management model.

The third common ownership/management approach is the management contract—a service offered by certain companies to manage a hotel or resort for its owners. Management contracts allow hotel companies to have more control over the quality and standards of a facility than simple franchise arrangements do, and they have now become the most common method that hotel companies use to penetrate the market (Kim, 2008). Management companies receive a fee, usually a percentage of revenues, for their services and essentially have full authority to make all business decisions on behalf of the owner. In fact, according to some contracts, the actual lodging owners have little voice and authority to make any kind of management decision. This relationship is clearly spelled out in the contract, which can be in effect for as little as a few years or as long as two or three decades. It appears that time periods for management contracts are getting shorter as time goes on, which could be indicative of hotel owners desiring the option of changing brands sooner if they feel it is necessary. Most of the large hotel companies today (e.g. Hyatt, Marriott, Accor, Sheraton, Hilton, and others) are deeply involved in selling management contracts. Some of them still also sell franchises, while others are phasing out their franchise operations in favor of the management contract model.

These unique American- and western-based management models have faced some critical challenges as they have expanded into the international arena. This is especially the case in China, where the communist system is loathe to accept decentralization of hotel ownership from the central government to companies that give the government little voice in management decision making (management contracts).

Since the 1980s, there has been a dizzying climate of rapid consolidation, mergers, and expanding partnerships. Confusing networks of brands owning other brands, buying and selling names, and merging and selling off, dominate the accommodation business landscape today. While there are still plenty of independent hotels and hotel chains, the standard of today is consolidations and mergers. Part of this has been the expansion of international companies going into countries and buying up several independent chains, as France-based Accor group did with the US budget company Motel 6.

Critics of the consolidation movement argue that the industry will eventually be owned by only a few international brands, reducing competition and selection. Critics also question whether or not mergers are good for the sector or only for executives' increased remunerations and benefits. It is also suggested that brands might lose their identity under mega-companies, since bigger is not necessarily always better, and consolidation could result in loss of employment (Lattin, 2002).

E-COMMERCE AND INFORMATION TECHNOLOGY

Information technology (IT) is one of the fastest growing areas of study in tourism and among the most important specializations of industry workers. Many large companies today have their own IT departments that oversee Internet use, website design, marketing, equipment maintenance, and telecommunications. IT applications in lodging operations include front office applications, back office operations, banquet and restaurant management, and guest service interfaces. The most salient aspect of IT today is the Internet and its multitudinous uses.

In the not-so-distant past, most travel arrangements were made through a travel agent. Travel agents in turn worked with other intermediaries that include wholesalers, tour operators, airlines, hotel companies, and car rental agencies to meet the travel needs of their clients. Agents' primary source of income was commissions from the suppliers of travel products and services, mainly the airlines, hotels, and car rental companies. With the development of the Internet, however, travel agents have, overall, been skipped over in the tourism system because consumers now have access to airline and hotel booking sites, even to discount travel consolidators who buy tickets and bed nights in bulk to resell for a profit. The main exception here is cruise line products, which are still predominantly purchased from travel agents. This ability to purchase directly from the service providers has caused airlines (mostly in the United States) to cancel travel agent commissions. In response, many agencies have declared bankruptcy since the 1990s; others that remain successful stay in business by specializing in particular destinations, travel products, or consumer markets and by levying customer fees for booking tickets. The Internet has made hotel selection, reservations, payment and stays, as well as airline tickets and rental cars more accessible to the masses at the cost of a traditionally important travel intermediary. Several research studies have pointed to user friendliness and information completeness of the main hotel websites that determine people's satisfaction.

There has also been a rapid growth in online auctions for vacation rentals, hotel nights, selling timeshares, vacation packages, and cruises. Many such products can be found on ebay or other online auctions. In terms of the regular marketplace, there are hotel-owned reservation websites and third-party reservations websites. There is some evidence that the third-party systems are favored among travel shoppers, owing to the wider accommodation options available on one system, as well as the fact that some of them function as, or have direct links with, consolidators, which are able to get discounted rates not available on company-specific distribution channels. Most business observers believe it is good for lodging establishments to have a variety of booking systems, including direct phone lines, central reservation systems that work with many different properties, and a hotel's own website. Having a variety of booking options is seen to increase profitability and survivability in the modern competitive market.

It also provides a good research tool for hotels as they are able to track their market segments, seasonal variations, advance bookings, and overall yield management. The information technology provides opportunities to collect personal data that are useful in marketing and management. Almost all hotels collect identifying data by encouraging guest to join loyalty programs. Frequent stay programs, designed much the same way as frequent flyer programs, are now being utilized by hotel companies to build brand loyalty, promote special offers, and assist guests in their travel planning endeavors.

Marketing and other promotional efforts are perhaps one of the best uses of the Internet, and nearly all lodging operations from the largest resort companies to the smallest family-owned bed and breakfast are taking advantage of its widespread market penetration and the low cost of designing and maintaining a website. Although most accommodation companies still work with intermediaries like travel agents, or communicate with the public via magazine ads and brochures, websites are now considered one of the most effective ways of reaching a wide global market. This effect is compounded even further with the prolific diffusion of online travel agents (e.g. Travelocity, Orbitz, and Expedia) that make individual trip planning easy and convenient. While traditional advertising forms are still widely used by the lodging sector, and tourism more broadly, Internet-based marketing is much less expensive, is easier to control, extends the traditional market catchment area, and allows for easy data collection on web users and potential customers.

Hundreds of millions of people each year make purchases on the Internet. This is known as e-commerce and has become nearly as commonplace as shopping at a supermarket, department store, or mall, at least in the developed world. E-commerce is growing even bigger as high-speed Internet and comprehensive search engines allow consumers to find almost any product or service available on the market. As well, vendors and merchants the world over are beginning to realize the benefits of selling online. Rather than struggling to survive in strictly a local market, the Internet now broadens the customer base to all corners of the globe, so that even the smallest souvenir producer or T-shirt shop can expand its reach across the world, accepting orders to customize souvenirs to fit demand for different destinations. The emergence of online auctions and supermarkets, such as ebay and Amazon. com, has played a crucial role in the development of e-commerce; other online markets and service providers have followed suit. Without doubt, e-commerce and information technology are one of the most salient notions in tourism studies today, and one of the most crucial considerations in the area of accommodation marketing and management.

There is also a trend toward consumer-generated media (CGM) in online technology, referring to consumers posting comments about facilities and services. Online ratings of hotels, guesthouses, motels, cruise ships, resorts, and other lodging facilities have become a staple source of knowledge for people seeking information about lodging, food services, and tourist destinations. Tripadvisor.com and Lonely Planet's Thorn Tree Travel Forum are two of the more popular venues for posting reviews and experiences, although hundreds more can be found on the Internet. As an extension to this, geographic information systems (GIS) mechanisms, such as Google Earth, have become popularized and accessible to the masses in recent years.

Google Earth and other satellite imagery conveyed to hand-held devices and global positioning systems have begun to play an important role in user-generated information about quality, prices, and accessibility in relation to places to stay. While these media provide highly subjective information—what is a luxurious resort to some might be unacceptable to others—their use is widespread in people's travel decision making. Thus, CGM can be an important and economical (free) promotion tool, but a few negative comments might also deter would-be guests from booking a stay.

Information seeking has long been of research interest to tourism scholars in relation to people's travel decision making. Information sources, frequency of use, depth of use, and types of information are some of the primary interests of those who research this concept. Consumer information searches have always existed, evolved from word of mouth, newspapers, books, and magazines, to the Internet, which has become the primary information source since the mid-1990s. Most Internet users feel secure while using the Internet in their information searches, and the perceived benefits of using online searches and the satisfaction associated with it often determine people's future usage. The Internet has become the most widespread information source for destination information and tourism service providers, including hotels, resorts, and other lodging establishments.

SUMMARY AND CONCLUSION

This chapter examined some currents issues that are critical to the operations and management of the lodging sector. Hotels and resorts have several attributes similar to many other tourism and hospitality service providers. However, there are others unique only to the lodging industry. For example, the vast majority of hotels and resorts operate 24 hours throughout the year, and are homes away from home for guests. The line of service can be quite considerable extending from accommodations, food and beverage, entertainment, recreational facilities, health and spa, sports (golf), gaming, meetings and conferences, and even local events such as catering for weddings and anniversaries. Delivery of that quality service in this age of intense competition and demanding local, domestic and diverse international guests requires a pool of trained quality personnel. The relevant issues include recruitment, training, retention, compensation and benefits, turnovers, and continuing education. The hospitality sector has a long history of education and training with the establishment of hotel schools, first in Europe and now in many parts of the world. While standards vary, these institutions continue to provide the human capacity building to meet the demands of the industry.

Structural changes in the areas on ownership, management, chain affil-iations, and franchising are also part of the broader evolution of corporate structure in the global marketplace in the last 25 years. The economic challenges in the late 2000s will also affect the lodging sector with respect to availability of credit and investment capital for new developments as well as upgrades and renovations. Already, destinations from Las Vegas to Macau and Dubai are either putting new projects on hold, while many of the large chain hotels are going ahead with restructuring. One recent development in this regard is the emergence of the sub-field of hospitality law that aims at managing legal issues in the hospitality industry.

The applications of information technology are broad and quite signifi-cant but still in the inception stage. Many hold the view that the future potential as a tool for e-tourism (as part or the broad e-commerce industry) is quite revolutionary and will affect all aspects of the travel and hospitality industry. This could be similar to the Computer Reservations Systems (CRS) developed initially for and by the airlines (Sabre, Apollo, Worldspan, Amadeus, etc.). The benefits could be geographically far reaching, as the tourism and lodging industries in even remote areas of the developing world find applications to their operations. Already, satellite systems and Google Earth have made mobile phones and other hand-held devices the main instruments of communication in many remote areas on the earth.

REFERENCES

Bureau of Labor Statistics, 2008. Hotels and Other Accommodations. Online < http://www.bls.gov/oco/cg/cgs036.htm#emply> Accessed January 20, 2009.

Lattin, G., 2002. The Lodging and Food Service Industry. Educational Institute of the American Hotel and Lodging Association, Lansing, MI.

Sizoo, S., 2008. Analysis of employee performance during cross-cultural service encounters at luxury hotels in Hawaii, London and Florida. Asia Pacific Journal of Tourism Research 13 (2), 113–128.

FURTHER READING

Baum, T., 2006. Human resource management for tourism, hospitality and leisure: an international perspective. Thomson Learning, London.

Buhalis, D., 2003. eTourism: information technology for strategic tourism management. Financial Times Prentice Hall, Harlow.

Buhalis, D., Kaldis, K., 2008. e-Enabled Internet distribution for small and medium sized hotels: the case of Athens. Tourism Recreation Research 33 (1), 67–81.

Butler, M., Pidd, I., 2006. As franchising becomes a priority tool for global hotel growth, PricewaterhouseCoopers asks, can you trust your franchisee? Hospitality Directions—Europe Edition 13, 1–4.

Buttle, F., 1986. Hotel and food service marketing: a managerial approach. Cassell, London.

Cabañas, B., 1992. A marketing strategy for resort conference centers. Cornell Hotel and Restaurant Administration Quarterly 33 (3), 45–49.

Cahill, D., 1997. How consumers pick a hotel: strategic segmentation and target marketing. Haworth, New York.

Chow, C.W., Haddad, K., Singh, G., 2007. Human resource management, job satisfaction, morale, optimism, and turnover. International Journal of Hospitality and Tourism Administration 8 (2), 73–88.

Eraqi, M.I., Abd-Alla, G., 2008. Information systems and tourism marketing: new challenges for tourism business sector in Egypt. Information Technology in Hospitality 5 (1), 35–47.

Eyster, J.J., 1997. Hotel management contracts in the U.S. Cornell Hotel and Restaurant Administration Quarterly 38 (3), 14–20.

Gröschl, S., 2004. Current human resources practices affecting the employment of persons with disabilities in selected Toronto hotels: a case study. International Journal of Hospitality and Tourism Administration 5 (3), 15–30.

Gröschl, S., 2007. An exploration of HR policies and practices affecting the integration of persons with disabilities in the hotel industry in major Canadian tourism destinations. International Journal of Hospitality Management 26 (3), 666–686.

Hanai, T., Oguchi, T., 2008. Features of lodging information in promotion of reservation through the internet: what kind of lodgings are popular in Shinjuku? Asia Pacific Journal of Tourism Research 13 (1), 33–40.

Hart, C.W.L., Troy, D.A., 1986. Strategic hotel/motel marketing. Educational Institute of the American Hotel & Lodging Assocation, Lansing, MI.

Hayes, D.K., Ninemeier, J.D., 2009. Human resources management in the hospitality industry. Wiley, Hoboken, NJ.

Heung, V.C.S., Zhang, H.Q., Jian, C., 2008. International franchising: opportunities for China's state-owned hotels? International Journal of Hospitality Management 27 (3), 368–380.

Hinds, M., Browne, Y., Henry, B., Jayawardena, C., Butcher, W., 2004. Current human resource challenges in the Caribbean hospitality industry. International Journal of Contemporary Hospitality Management 16 (7), 415–418.

Ho, J.K., 2008. Online auction markets in tourism. Information Technology and Tourism 10 (1), 19–29.

Hoque, K., 2000. Human resource management in the hotel industry: strategy, innovation and performance. Routledge, London.

Hsu, C.H.C., Powers, T., 2002. Marketing Hospitality. Wiley, New York.

Hughes, J.C., Rog, E., 2008. Talent management: a strategy for improving employee recruitment, retention and engagement within hospitality organizations. International Journal of Contemporary Hospitality Management 20 (7), 734–757.

Huntley, E., Barnes-Reid, C., 2003. The feasibility of Sabbath-keeping in the Caribbean hospitality industry. International Journal of Contemporary Hospitality Management 15 (3), 172–175.

Huyan, C., Heung, V.C.S., 2005. Impacts of internet and e-commerce on travelers' behaviors: implications for hotel management in China. China Tourism Research 1 (2/3), 259–286.

Jeong, M.Y., Jeon, M.H.M., 2008. Customer reviews of hotel experiences through consumer generated media (CGM). Journal of Hospitality and Leisure Marketing 17 (1/2), 121–138.

Jeong, M.Y., Oh, H.M., Gregoire, M., 2005. The role of website quality in online hotel reservations. Information Technology in Hospitality 4 (1), 3–13.

Kang, B., Brewer, K.P., Baloglu, S., 2007. Profitability and survivability of hotel distribution channels: an industry perspective. Journal of Travel and Tourism Marketing 22 (1), 37–50.

Karen, J., 1999. Hotel management contract terms: still in flux. Cornell Hotel and Restaurant Administration Quarterly 40 (2), 34–39.

Kim, S.Y., 2008. Hotel management contract: impact on performance in the Korean hotel sector. Service Industries Journal 28 (5/6), 701–718.

Kothari, T., Hu, C., Roehl, W.S., 2007. Adopting e-procurement technology in a china hotel: an exploratory case study. International Journal of Hospitality Management 26 (4), 886–898.

Law, R., Hsu, C.H.C., 2005. Customers' perceptions on the importance of hotel web site dimensions and attributes. International Journal of Contemporary Hospitality Management 17 (6), 493–503.

Law, R., Jogaratnam, G., 2005. A study of hotel information technology applications. International Journal of Contemporary Hospitality Management 17 (2), 170–180.

Liu, A., Liu, H.J., 2008. Tourism employment issues in Malaysia. Journal of Human Resources in Hospitality and Tourism 7 (2), 163–179.

Marvel, M., 2005. Hotel technology—international. Travel and Tourism Analyst 11, 1–42.

Medlik, S., Ingram, H., 2000. The business of hotels. Butterworth-Heinemann, Oxford.

Mikula, J.R., Chon, K.S., 1997. International hotel marketing in the age of globalization. International Journal of Contemporary Hospitality Management 9 (1), 31–34.

Mill, R.C., 2007. Resorts: management and operation. Wiley, New York.

Miller, B., 2004. Building e-loyalty of lodging brands: avoiding brand erosion. Journal of Travel and Tourism Marketing 17 (2/3), 133–142.

Mohsin, A., 2007. Human resource concerns: an assessment of motels in Hamilton, New Zealand. Journal of Human Resources in Hospitality and Tourism 6 (2), 27–41.

Morosan, C., Jeong, M.Y., 2008. The role of the internet in the process of travel information search. Information Technology in Hospitality 5 (1), 13–23.

Ng, C.W., Pine, R., 2003. Women and men in hotel management in Hong Kong: perceptions of gender and career development issues. International Journal of Hospitality Management 22 (1), 85–102.

Nickson, D., 2007. Human resource management for the hospitality and tourism industries. Butterworth-Heinemann, Oxford.

O'Connor, P., 2005. Who's watching you? Data collection by hotel chain websites. Information Technology in Hospitality 4 (2/3), 63–70.

Orfila-Sintes, F., Crespí-Cladera, R., Martínez-Ros, E., 2005. Innovation activity in the hotel industry: evidence from Balearic Islands. Tourism Management 26 (6), 851–865.

Pfeffer, E.E., 2000. Hotel franchising: perspectives and prospects. FIU Hospitality Review 18 (1), 81–86.

Piccoli, G., 2008. Information technology in hotel management: a framework for evaluating the sustainability of IT-dependent competitive advantage. Cornell Hospitality Quarterly 49 (3), 282–296.

Renard, J.S., Motley, K., 2003. The agency challenge: how Woolley, Woodley, and other cases rearranged the hotel-management landscape. Cornell Hotel and Restaurant Administration Quarterly 44 (3), 58–76.

Sims, W.J., 2007. Antecedents of labor turnover in Australian alpine resorts. Journal of Human Resources in Hospitality and Tourism 6 (2), 1–26.

Sizoo, S., Iskat, W., Plank, R., Serrie, H., 2003. Cross-cultural service encounters in the hospitality industry and the effect of intercultural sensitivity on employee performance. International Journal of Hospitality and Tourism Administration 4 (2), 61–77.

Vallen, G., Cothran, C.C., Combrink, T.E., 1998. Indian gaming—are tribal employees being promoted to management positions in Arizona casinos? Cornell Hotel and Restaurant Administration Quarterly 39 (4), 56–63.

Waddoups, C.J., 2001. Unionism and poverty-level wages in the service sector: the case of Nevada's hotel-casino industry. Applied Economics Letters 8 (3), 163–167.

Wei, S., Ruys, H.F., van Hoof, H.B., Combrink, T.E., 2001. Uses of the Internet in the global hotel industry. Journal of Business Research 54 (3), 235–241.

Xiao, Q., O'Neill, J.W., Wang, H.Y., 2008. International hotel development: a study of potential franchisees in China. International Journal of Hospitality Management 27 (3), 325–336.

Yang, H.O., Cherry, N., 2008. Human resource management challenges in the hotel industry in Taiwan. Asia Pacific Journal of Tourism Research 13 (4), 399–410.

Zhang, H.Q., Wu, E., 2004. Human resources issues facing the hotel and travel industry in China. International Journal of Contemporary Hospitality Management 16 (7), 424–428.

Zhou, Z., 2004. E-commerce and information technology in hospitality and tourism. Thomson, London.

USEFUL INTERNET RESOURCES

Americans with Disabilities Act: www.ada.gov.

Choice Hotels Franchises: http://www.choicehotelsfranchise.com/.

e-commerce for hotels blog: http://ecommerceforhotels.blogspot.com/.

e-tourism Newsletter: http://www.etourismnewsletter.com/ecommerce.htm.

Expedia: http://www.expedia.com.

Hotel Resources: http://www.hotelresource.com.

Orbitz: http://www.orbitz.com.

Travelocity: http://www.travelocity.com.

Wyndham Franchises: http://www.hotelfranchise.wyndhamworldwide.com/.

CHAPTER 4

The Socio-Economic Implications in the Destination

INTRODUCTION

Tourism is frequently viewed as an economic liberator because it creates jobs directly, generates tax revenues for government agencies, brings in additional business, and its ripple effects stimulate additional employment and revenues. Unfortunately, to achieve these desired goals, there has been a history of blind promotion and unmitigated growth in most areas of the world, which have resulted in many negative consequences as well. When tourism grows, economies grow. In addition, however, decades of research have shown that as tourism grows, so do its socio-cultural and ecological consequences. Chapter 6 will probe more deeply into the physical environmental impacts of tourism; this chapter focuses on the social and economic changes that take place in destinations when tourism arrives and grows.

ECONOMIC IMPACTS OF TOURISM AND LODGING

As already noted, nearly all places throughout the world have an interest in growing tourism for its potential to stimulate economic growth. One of the most beneficial outcomes of tourism is increased regional income and positive balance of payments, which means that more money is brought into an economy than that leaving the economy. Such regional income can be measured using a tourism satellite account—an accounting system that measures the total direct impact of tourism and its sub-sectors on a regional or national economy. It measures employment creation, balance of payments, and makes industry comparisons easier and more systematic. With increased regional income come additional jobs, higher tax revenues, and entrepreneurial growth. Each of these will be examined below.

CONTENTS

Introduction

Economic Impacts of Tourism and Lodging

Socio-Cultural Impacts of Tourism and Lodging

Summary and Conclusion

References

Further Reading

Useful Internet Resources

Perhaps the most influential factor is job creation. The World Travel and Tourism Council (WTTC) estimates that global tourism employs 80.75 million people directly in the industry and approximately 240 million people indirectly, constituting more than 8% of the world's total employment. The WTTC predicts that indirect employment will grow to nearly 300 million jobs by the year 2018 (WTTC, 2008). These figures for indirect employment are probably a bit too conservative, given that tourism induces hundreds of millions of additional jobs in agriculture, fishing, education, mining, manufacturing, and many other industries that are difficult to measure. This concept is usually referred to as the multiplier effect, meaning how many additional dollars or jobs are created by tourists' expenditures and direct tourism jobs in a given economy. Regardless of a lack of exactness in measuring tourism employment, it is clear that tourism is a major player in the world economy in terms of job creation. Table 4.1 highlights the top ten tourism job-generating countries in 2008.

Tourism employs people in all services that facilitate travel away from home, in the place of origin, in transit, and in the destination. Transportation, food services, tour agencies and guiding, tourist attractions, shops, and shopping centers are the most visible, but it is important to remember that tourism also supports employment in customs and immigration offices, banks, post offices, handicraft centers, supermarkets, department stores, churches, theaters, sports arenas, and schools. Of considerable interest today is tourism's ability to stimulate jobs in small and medium-sized enterprises for skilled and unskilled workers, in cities and rural areas, for the poor, the wealthy, for men and women, and for indigenous communities.

Table 4.1 Top Ten Tourism Employment-Generating Countries, 2008

Rank	Country	Number of Jobs ('000)
1	China	74 498
2	India	30 491
3	United States	14 933
4	Japan	6 833
5	Mexico	6 633
6	Indonesia	5 936
7	Brazil	5 500
8	Vietnam	4 891
9	Russia	4 126
10	Thailand	3 911

Source: WTTC (2008).

The lodging sector is one of the most labor-intensive segments of tourism, in company with transportation and food services. Accommodations are an extremely important part of the tourism economy and absorb much of the labor force in popular tourist destinations. From most countries' statistical data on employment it is difficult to distinguish jobs in the accommodation sector from other service-based employment. Often, tourism is reported as a whole industry, without a sectoral itemization, making an understanding of the lodging sector difficult; worse yet, sometimes tourism is reported in an undifferentiated way in conjunction with other services, such as education and banking. In the United States, however, the Bureau of Labor Statistics, under the US Department of Labor, keeps detailed statistics about work in the hospitality and tourism arena.

In 2006, lodging of all kinds, including hotels, motels, resorts, campgrounds, youth hostels, inns, bed and breakfasts, and all others, provided direct employment for 1.8 million people in the USA. In addition, some 40 000 people were self-employed or volunteered in small-scale, family-operated accommodations, such as camps or bed and breakfasts. Tourism and hospitality employment tends to be concentrated in urban areas and resort towns, and the relative staff size of hotels and other lodging facilities tends to be smaller than in other industries. For instance, in the US, three quarters of lodging providers employ fewer than 20 people, while 55% employ less than 10. Although most lodging businesses are small, most jobs are located in larger hotels with staff in excess of 100 (Bureau of Labor Statistics, 2008).

Hotels and other lodging providers play an important role in the employment environment—that of providing many first-time jobs for new entrants into the labor force. In 2006, in the US, some 17% of all accommodation workers were younger than 25, compared to 13–14% in other industries (Bureau of Labor Statistics, 2008).

Another important economic benefit of tourism is the generation of taxes for destination governments. There are several tourism-specific taxes. These include hotel and other bed taxes, car rental taxes, airport taxes, food and beverage taxes, and port taxes. In addition, destinations earn a great deal of revenue from the same taxes local residents also pay, including sales tax, liquor and tobacco taxes, property tax, and income tax. Destination governments at all levels, municipal, state/provincial, regional, and national, realize the value of tourism in generating tax revenues. In addition to jobs, this is one of the most favored reasons for targeting tourism as a development tool. In Europe and many other parts of the world, a generic value added tax (VAT) is charged for goods and services, including accommodations. In the United States and Canada, taxes are levied at all levels of administration: national, state, county, and municipality. The United States' top three destination states for international and domestic arrivals are California, Florida, and New York. In California, $2.2 billion were raised for local governments via tourism in 2007. The same year, tourism-based state tax revenues amounted to $3.6 billion. Tourist expenditures in the state of New York in 2007 produced $6.8 billion in state and local taxes, as well as $7 billion in federal tax income. Florida's state tax earnings from tourism the same year were $3.9 billion. Occupancy taxes are extremely important for municipalities as well. In Anchorage, Alaska, lodging taxes earned $18 million for the city's coffers in 2006. New York City annually receives approximately $400 million in hotel tax revenue. In 2007, San Francisco, earned nearly $2 million from hotel taxes. In Canada, tourism generated $19.7 billion (CAD) in tax income for local, provincial/territorial, and federal governments in 2007.

It is common in many places for tourism-specific tax earnings to be put back into tourism via promotional efforts and infrastructure development. Bed taxes and other tourism taxes are especially important revenue streams for local governments, primarily because they are paid by outsiders rather than local people. Thus, community leaders can raise tourist taxes without directly upsetting the destination population, in theory at least. There is often a tourism industry backlash whenever taxes are raised or initiated, arguing that such taxes will reduce arrivals and cause valuable tourists to select alternative destinations.

Another important economic effect of tourism is the stimulation of entrepreneurial activity. Tourism gets people thinking about ways to earn a living and often brings out creative ideas. In addition, it employs destination residents and typically depends on local products. The establishments of souvenir shops, transportation services, and food services are common entrepreneurial responses to tourism. In most cases, when tourism shows signs of success in a destination, large-scale multinational lodging companies come to town. In addition, however, local residents are often inspired to open up shops of various sorts and provide lodging for visitors. These activities generally fall into one of two categories of officialdom: the formal economy and the informal economy. Formal economic activities are those that are recognized, enumerated, and registered by government agencies. Restaurants, hotels, taxi companies, tour operators, banks, shopping centers, and supermarkets generally fall within this category. Informal ventures are not recognized, taxes, registered, or enumerated by the government, and usually they are considered illegal. These include many street vendors, unofficial guides, transport providers (if they own their own car, motorcycle, or pedicab), food sellers, beach sellers, and prostitutes. They also sometimes include lodging providers.

In some places, particularly in the developing world, many official accommodation businesses began as informal-sector entities. In popular destinations like Bali and Yogyakarta, Indonesia, guesthouses and home-stays in tourism neighborhoods often began as unofficial businesses. When children grew up and left home, it was lucrative to rent out the extra room in the house. As money was saved, the house was expanded vertically with extra rooms that could be let out to visitors. In the process, these establishments grew into guesthouses with several guest rooms and were officially recognized and licensed by the local government. These provide low-budget lodging options for backpackers and other independent travelers, and several of them have been elevated to one- or two-star hotels.

Small-scale entrepreneurs selling handicrafts in Dominica

Negative economic implications

One of the most notable negative issues related to tourism is economic leakage, or the amount of money spent by tourists that does not remain in, or benefit, the destination economy. This predicament is especially austere in the less-developed parts of the world. It is not uncommon for less than 20% of the cost of a journey to remain in the destination, as the remaining 80% leaks out. This leakage is caused by a number of practices and trends. Resorts and hotels are among the biggest perpetrators of the problem, particularly international brand-name establishments. The quandary derives from the use of imported building materials, operational supplies, food and drink supplies, vehicles, furnishings, and human resources. Many of the top management staff are expatriates, who are paid higher salaries than local personnel, and much of their own salary ends up in their home country bank accounts in the United States, France, Canada, the UK, Australia, or wherever else they might call home. Often the only positive tourist expenditure in the developing destination for the destination is souvenir purchases and hotel employee salaries, which in most less-affluent countries hover around $30–50 per month. The importation of supplies and high-paid staff is compounded by the use of foreign air carriers and lodging brands, which reap profits without contributing much to the local economy.

Another salient problem facing many destinations is an economic over-dependence on tourism. There is always danger involved when a place is too dependent on one industry. The demise of many mining towns in the US, Canada, Australia, the UK and Europe because of changes in demand for certain raw materials attests to this situation. The same can happen in the context of tourism. There are many tourist destinations that are far too dependent on tourism as their only, or overwhelmingly prevalent, economic generator. These most typically are small island nations rich in tourism amenities (sun, sea, and sand) but which have limited natural resources that can be exploited for their economic worth. Table 4.2 shows the ten most tourism-dependent countries in the world in terms of total value of tourism to overall economy. Likewise, Table 4.3 illustrates tourism overdependence in another way: the ratio of total tourism employees to total national workforce.

The dangers associated with overdependence on tourism are clear; the economic future lies at the mercy of external forces that are beyond their control. Tourism-dependent countries risk economic failure when global demand changes, as unemployment rates rise in market regions, source regions are plagued with economic instability, or the world is tarnished by political conflict or security concerns. In addition, more and more places are facing increased levels of competition as new destinations emerge, and as the tastes and preferences of the traveling public transform. Scores of the most dependent destinations are also prone to natural disasters (e.g. hurricanes,

Table 4.2	Top Ten Tourism-Dependent Countries in Relative Terms, 2008	
Rank	Country	Percentage of Total GDP Comprised of Direct and Indirect Tourism Earnings
1	Macau	82.5
2	Antigua and Barbuda	76.5
3	Anguilla	69.6
4	Aruba	69.3
5	Maldives	67.0
6	Seychelles	56.3
7	Bahamas	50.8
8	Barbados	40.7
9	St Lucia	40.6
10	Vanuatu	38.8

Source: WTTC (2008).

Rank	Country	Percentage of Total Workforce Employed Directly or Indirectly in Tourism
	Table 4.3 The Top Ten Tourism-Dependent Countries in Terms of Employment, 2008	
1	Antigua and Barbuda	87.1
2	Aruba	81.4
3	Macau	74.6
4	Anguilla	73.7
5	Seychelles	71.1
6	Bahamas	63.5
7	Maldives	57.9
8	US Virgin Islands	46.1
9	Barbados	45.8
10	British Virgin Islands	45.2

Source: WTTC (2008).

floods, and earthquakes), which can not only deter would-be visitors, but also destroy entire infrastructures that will have to be rebuilt, thereby taxing already damaged economies even further. This is a common occurrence on several islands in the Caribbean that are repeatedly swept by hurricanes each year.

Seasonal changes in demand, as noted in Chapter 2, are an influential matter in the lodging sector as well. Low season is a vital concern for destination and property managers, because regional income and tax revenues decline, resulting in seasonal or permanent layoffs and an oversupply of services and facilities. Destinations that have a notable seasonal variation in demand are typically used to the idea of part-time and cyclical work patterns. A more balanced, yearlong demand for tourism would be ideal, but the vagaries of weather, climate, school breaks, and special events determine people's interest in visiting a place.

The Caribbean islands are known as a winter destination because of their subtropical or tropical weather, which Canadians, Americans, and Europeans flock to when their own home regions are cold. The Northeastern United States and Canada's Atlantic Provinces are popular destinations in autumn when the deciduous trees change colors. Alaska, Canada, Greenland, Sweden, Norway, and Finland are usually seen as summer holiday destinations, unless one has a special interest in snowshoeing, skiing, dog-sledding, or ice fishing. Seasonal differences do not affect all places in the same way. Some destinations, such as Las Vegas, Orlando, or southern California, in the USA, as well as a number of Mediterranean and Asian destinations have a fairly consistent, year-round stream of arrivals.

There are several options accommodation facilities can choose from to offset the effects of seasonality. First, during the off season, hotels, resorts, bed and breakfasts, and hostels can host special events, such as dog shows, art exhibits, concerts, family reunions, weddings, or outdoor theater. Second, a resort or other property can change its focus altogether. Ski resorts, for instance, often install seasonal 'Alpine slides' or bobsled tracks, using their motorized lifts to transport sliders and hikers to the mountain tops. A third option is to offer special prices and package deals. Off-season price reductions are the most common coping mechanism in the lodging sector, but beyond lowering prices, partnerships can also be formed with airlines, car rental companies, or attractions to provide specially package deals that are lower in price and interesting to consumers. Fourth, promotional campaigns can be modified to attract more local guests, or destination residents who might have an interest in spending time at a luxury hotel or resort. Enticing locals to spend a night, play a round of golf, visit the spa, swim, or shop is a common summertime practice among resorts in Phoenix and Scottsdale, Arizona, where summer temperatures sometimes reach 118–120 F (48–49 °C), causing a distinct low season.

Tourism is also often blamed for increased inflation and over-inflated land values. When tourists arrive in town, prices tend to go up, and this includes prices for local products as well. Thus, living in tourist destinations becomes unaffordable for many people, and the higher prices brought about by tourism often drive long-time residents out of the community to more affordable locations. In addition, the historical record shows that as resorts and hotels develop, property values and property taxes in general rise, making owning or buying a home a prohibitive or impossible alternative for newcomers, which also drives many native peoples from their traditional lands and precludes in-migration of potential new workers.

SOCIO-CULTURAL IMPACTS OF TOURISM AND LODGING

The economy is not the only element of the human environment to be affected by tourism. Social structures and social mores are also influenced, as are cultural traditions and rituals. Tourism can be seen as a positive force in socio-cultural terms when it enhances the quality of life of destination residents by building social capital, improving public services (e.g. health care, education, and infrastructure), and resurrecting lost traditions or helping to preserve culture that might otherwise be lost in the unavoidable process of modernization.

Unfortunately, though, most of the social and cultural ramifications of tourism are negative and contribute to the demise of culture or an upsurge in discontent among community residents. This is, once again, particularly evident in the less-developed parts of the world, although it is evident everywhere. Research in American and Canadian destinations such as Niagara Falls, Orlando, and New England, as well as in various European and Australian destinations reveals that first-world regions are not less prone to the social consequences of tourism.

This unfortunate situation derives primarily from the history of global mass tourism, which developed following the Second World War and continues to this day as one of the most prominent manifestations of tourism. It entails large masses of people traveling to destinations, having little positive economic effect because of leakage and inflation, yet producing devastating environmental and socio-cultural consequences. It has been spurred by rapid growth, blind promotion with the false understanding that tourism is all good so it should be promoted at all costs, and a lack of systematic planning. Traditional boosterism and unmitigated tourism growth also has precluded marginal peoples in society, such as the poor, women, and ethnic and racial minorities, from receiving benefits from tourism or participating in planning and decision making.

This has given rise to arguments that modern-day mass tourism resembles colonialism (neocolonialism) in that a subservient relationship is created and resources and destinations in the third world are exploited for the pleasure and utility of western elites, while the destination is left to bear the burden of the tourist onslaught. Beach resort-based tourism, cruises, and coach-based package tours are often looked upon as the epitome of mass tourism. Hotels and mega resorts are thus seen as salient culprits, while smaller lodging businesses (e.g. hostels, campgrounds, inns, pensions, and bed and breakfasts) are considered more destination-friendly, since they are locally owned and more of their income remains in the destination.

Mass tourism consumers are typically seen as arrogant and overly demanding of destination residents and industry workers; ignorant about the world around them, especially the places they visit; culturally unrefined; immoral hedonists whose activities clash with local values; and flaunters of wealth in places where most tourism workers earn less than $600 per year.

The demands associated with mass tourism are seen to hasten cultural deterioration as music and dance performances, handicrafts and artworks, and ceremonies and traditions are altered to meet the needs of visitors in terms of size, duration, content, performance venue, and mass production. The notion of authenticity comes into play here, as many cultural traditions lose authenticity when they are altered or performed under spotlights in hotel

Maori dancers in New Zealand staging a performance for tourists

lobbies. Likewise, handicrafts and art forms are said to become inauthentic as their value, meaning, spiritual connotations, or utilitarian function is lost by being mass produced by assembly line workers who have little or no personal connection to the culture being represented.

From a strictly social perspective, the growth of mass tourism has also been shown to increase prostitution, crime, drug use, and illegal gambling. Uncontrolled tourism growth also generates crowded conditions, sometimes to the point that local residents are unable to access their own schools, shops, public services, and even their homes. All of these conditions and tourism-induced problems combine to drive a wedge between the visitors and the visited. Rather than gracious hosts, community members frequently become antagonistic toward tourists and tourism, even many whose livelihood depends on the industry.

Armed with the knowledge of what mass tourism can do to a destination, many community residents fear the growth of tourism in their communities. Considerable scientific research in recent years has been undertaken to understand residents' perceptions of tourism and its potential growth. Most of the research suggests a fairly large cohort of the population voicing grave concerns over tourism and its potential harm to their communities, even in light of its potential economic contributions.

Regional planning specialists have, for several decades, realized the importance of participatory forms of development and planning where community members are empowered to make decisions and take responsibility for themselves, in addition to receiving an enhanced standard of living through improved development. It has taken a significantly long time for tourism development specialists to realize the same is true for tourism. In response to the negative legacy of traditional tourism, and with growing global pressure to promote the principles of sustainable development (e.g. ecological and social integrity, holistic growth, scale-appropriate development, social and economic equity, empowered citizens, and indigenous knowledge), observers of tourism, and the industry itself, began to rethink tourism's growing popularity in terms of social equity and intergenerational longevity, or sustainability. As a result, during the 1980s, 1990s, and 2000s, alternatives to mass tourism ('alternative tourism') have emerged, which claim to reduce the negative environmental and social consequences of tourism. These new forms, it is claimed, are sensitive to the needs and concerns of destination communities and ecosystems, have minimal impacts, involve a wider cohort of the local population in the benefits of tourism, and suppress economic leakage by buying local products and hiring local employees.

Ecotourism is perhaps the best known of these new movements. Volunteer tourism, wherein people donate their own time and travel on their own expense for altruistic reasons, is also on the rise. Cultural and heritage tourism, geotourism, and educational tourism are examples of alternatives to mass tourism that are said to empower communities, utilize local products and services, reduce environmental problems, and provide inclusive economic impacts. Unfortunately, so many people are becoming more conscientious in their travel choices that we are now beginning to see the likes of mass ecotourism, mass volunteer tourism, and other forms of mass alternative tourism. Fortunately, however, there are many modern examples of true community-based tourism development initiatives that have kept many of the negative impacts at bay. Some of them are directly linked to the lodging sector in tourism.

One of the best examples, for instance, is the Toledo Ecotourism Association, which was founded in 1990 by indigenous people in the rural periphery of Belize. Its aim was to enhance the standard of living of the indigenous Maya people of southern Belize by building guesthouses of indigenous building materials and in traditional fashion. Families in the villages shared in the profits equitably, decisions were made from the ground up, rather than being imposed from above, and efforts have been kept to a small scale to minimize crowdedness and the complications that arise from mass tourism. In general, these people had two things going against them: they were indigenous minorities who felt they were tangential to the interests of the central state and they were located on the country's physical periphery away from the economic center where policy decisions were usually made. Nonetheless, their efforts have been a considerable success and have spread to other villages in the region. Their example has also been used as a beacon in other less-developed countries for communities to take charge of their futures and develop forms of tourism that are less destructive and which retain a higher percentage of income in the local economy. Many examples exist of guesthouses and other indigenous housing being used to support a community's growth aspirations in an equitable and sustainable manner.

SUMMARY AND CONCLUSION

This chapter has highlighted the dark side of tourism and the lodging facilities that accompany it. While traditional mass tourism has had provable negative repercussions for socio-economic and natural environments in the past, new forms of tourism and more community-friendly accommodation options suggest that there are sustainable alternatives to older, more destructive kinds of tourism growth. Indigenous and small-scale lodging can play an important role in this change.

Not all of the impacts of tourism are negative. On the contrary, there are many positive outcomes of tourism, and increasingly more places are vying for tourists because community members and leaders see the employment, tax, regional income, and small business growth that tourism can contribute. Tourism is, worldwide, one of the most targeted economic growth engines. As long as communities, regions, and nations have people who need work and public services to provide, they will continue to target tourism as a growth mechanism. As this chapter highlights, hotels, resorts, motels, and other lodging businesses are one of the most pervasive components of tourism, as indicated in most tourism satellite account-based research. Inasmuch as lodging properties are able to minimize their carbon footprint and their role in socio-cultural deterioration, they have the most potential to satisfy the economic needs of tourist destinations.

REFERENCES

Bureau of Labor Statistics, 2008. Hotels and other accommodations. Online <http://www.bls.gov/oco/cg/cgs036.htm#emply> Accessed January 20, 2009.

WTTC, 2008. Tourism satellite accounting: the 2008 travel and tourism economic research executive summary. World Travel and Tourism Council, London.

FURTHER READING

Andriotis, K., 2008. Integrated resort development: the case of Cavo Sidero, Crete. Journal of Sustainable Tourism 16 (4), 428–444.

Ashley, C., Haysom, G., 2006. From philanthropy to a different way of doing business: strategies and challenges in integrating pro-poor approaches into tourism business. Development Southern Africa 23 (2), 265–280.

Baum, T., Lundtorp, S., 2001. Seasonality in tourism. Elsevier, Amsterdam.

Beeton, S., 2006. Community development through tourism. CSIRO Publishing, Collingwood, Australia.

Bista, R., 2006. A tourism plan to alleviate rural poverty in Nepal. e-Review of Tourism Research 4 (3), 50–55.

Bowden, J., 2005. Pro-poor tourism and the Chinese experience. Asia Pacific Journal of Tourism Research 10 (4), 379–398.

Braunlich, C.G., 1996. Lessons from the Atlantic City casino experience. Journal of Travel Research 34 (3), 46–56.

Burns, G.L., 2003. Indigenous responses to tourism in Fiji: what is happening? In: Harrison, D. (Ed.), Pacific Island Tourism. Cognizant, New York, pp. 82–93.

Cavus, S., Tanrisevdi, A., 2003. Residents' attitudes toward tourism development: a case study in Kusadasi, Turkey. Tourism Analysis 7 (3/4), 259–269.

Chheang, V., 2008. The political economy of tourism in Cambodia. Asia Pacific Journal of Tourism Research 13 (3), 281–297.

Cho, M.H., 2002. Tourism redevelopment strategy: the case of the Kangwon Land Resort. Anatolia 13 (2), 185–197.

Craig-Smith, S.J., French, C.N., 1994. Learning to live with tourism. Pitman, Boston.

D'Hauteserre, A.M., 2001. Representations of rurality: is Foxwoods Casino Resort threatening the quality of life in southeastern Connecticut? Tourism Geographies 3 (4), 405–429.

Diakomihalis, M.N., Lagos, D.G., 2008. Estimation of the economic impacts of yachting in Greece via the tourism satellite account. Tourism Economics 14 (4), 871–887.

Fayissa, B., Nsiah, C., Tadasse, B., 2008. Impact of tourism on economic growth and development in Africa. Tourism Economics 14 (4), 807–818.

Fisher, J.B., Nawaz, R., Fauzi, R., Nawaz, F., Eran Sadek, S.M.S., Zulkiflee, A.L., Blackett, M., 2008. Balancing water, religion and tourism on Redang Island, Malaysia. Environmental Research Letters 3 (2), 10–20.

Gooroochurn, N., Sinclair, M.T., 2005. Economics of tourism taxation: evidence from Mauritius. Annals of Tourism Research 32, 478–498.

Hall, C.M., 2007. Pro-poor tourism: who benefits? perspectives on tourism and poverty reduction. Channel View, Clevedon, UK.

Harrison, D., 1992. Tourism and the less developed countries. Wiley, Chichester.

Harrison, D., Schipani, S., 2007. Lao tourism and poverty alleviation: community-based tourism and the private sector. Current Issues in Tourism 10 (2/3), 194–230.

Higgins-Desbiolles, F., 2008. Justice tourism and alternative globalisation. Journal of Sustainable Tourism 16 (3), 345–364.

Huybers, T., 2007. Tourism in developing countries. Edward Elgar, Cheltenham.

Jarvis, J., Kallas, P., 2008. Estonian tourism and the accession effect: the impact of European Union membership on the contemporary development of the Estonian tourism industry. Tourism Geographies 10 (4), 474–494.

León, Y.M., 2007. The impact of tourism on rural livelihoods in the Dominican Republic's coastal areas. Journal of Development Studies 43 (2), 340–359.

Lindberg, K., Andersson, T.D., Dellaert, B.G.C., 2001. Tourism development: assessing social gains and losses. Annals of Tourism Research 28 (4), 1010–1030.

Macpherson, C., 2008. Golden goose or Trojan horse? Cruise ship tourism in Pacific development. Asia Pacific Viewpoint 49 (2), 185–197.

Manwa, H., 2008. Enhancing participation of women in tourism. In: Moscardo, G. (Ed.), Building community capacity for tourism development. CAB International, Wallingford, UK, pp. 116–122.

Meyer, D., 2007. Pro-poor tourism: from leakages to linkages. A conceptual framework for creating linkages between the accommodation sector and 'poor' neighbouring communities. Current Issues in Tourism 10 (6), 558–583.

Mitchell, J., Faal, J., 2007. Holiday package tourism and the poor in The Gambia. Development Southern Africa 24 (3), 445–464.

Pattullo, P., 1996. Last resorts: the cost of tourism in the Caribbean. Ian Randle Publishers, Kingston, Jamaica.

Porier, R.A., Wright, S., 1993. The political economy of tourism in Tunisia. Journal of Modern African Studies 31 (1), 149–162.

Pryce, A., 2001. Sustainability in the hotel industry. Travel and Tourism Analyst 6, 95–114.

Roessingh, C., Duijnhove, H., 2004. Small entrepreneurs and shifting identities: the case of tourism in Puerto Plata (northern Dominican Republic). Journal of Tourism and Cultural Change 2 (3), 185–201.

Rogerson, C.M., 2006. Pro-poor local economic development in South Africa: the role of pro-poor tourism. Local Environment 11 (1), 37–60.

Scheyvens, R., 2006. Sun, sand, and beach fales: benefiting from backpackers—the Samoan way. Tourism Recreation Research 31 (3), 75–86.

Scheyvens, R., 2007. Exploring the tourism-poverty nexus. Current Issues in Tourism 10 (2/3), 231–254.

Sirakaya, E., Teye, V.B., Sönmez, S.S., 2002. Understanding residents' support for tourism development in the central region of Ghana. Journal of Travel Research 41 (1), 57–67.

Smith, C., Jenner, P., 1989. Tourism and the environment. Travel and Tourism Analyst 5, 68–86.

Stuebner, S., 1991. Valbois: Idaho's fiercely debated mega-resort. Ski Area Management 30 (6), 36–37. 54–55.

Teye, V.B., Sirakaya, E., Sönmez, S.S., 2002. Residents' attitudes toward tourism development. Annals of Tourism Research 29, 668–688.

Thompson, W.N., Pinney, J.K., Schibrowsky, J.A., 1996. The family that gambles together: business and social concerns. Journal of Travel Research 34 (3), 70–74.

Timothy, D.J., 1999. Participatory planning: a view of tourism in Indonesia. Annals of Tourism Research 26, 371–391.

Timothy, D.J., Wall, G., 1995. Tourist accommodation in an Asian historic city. Journal of Tourism Studies 6 (2), 63–73.

Timothy, D.J., Wall, G., 1997. Selling to tourists: Indonesian street vendors. Annals of Tourism Research 24, 322–340.

Timothy, D.J., White, K., 1999. Community-based ecotourism development on the periphery of Belize. Current Issues in Tourism 2 (2/3), 226–242.

Tsuyuzaki, S., 1994. Environmental deterioration resulting from ski-resort construction in Japan. Environmental Conservation 21 (2), 121–125.

van der Dulma, V.R., Caaldersb, J., 2008. Tourism chains and pro-poor tourism development: an actor-network analysis of a pilot project in Costa Rica. Current Issues in Tourism 11 (2), 109–125.

Wall, G., Mathieson, A., 2006. Tourism: change, impacts and opportunities. Prentice Hall, Harlow.

Wang, Y., Wall, G., 2005. Resorts and residents: stress and conservatism in a displaced community. Tourism Analysis 10 (1), 37–53.

Yahya, F., Parameswaran, A., Ahmed, I., Sebastian, R., 2005. The economic cost of tourism in Maldives. Tourism 53 (1), 33–44.

USEFUL INTERNET RESOURCES

Caribbean Tourism Organization: http://www.onecaribbean.org/.

Office of Travel and Tourism Industries, Tourism Satellite Account Program: http://tinet.ita.doc.gov/research/programs/satellite/index.html.

Tourism Concern: http://www.tourismconcern.org.uk/.

Travel Industry Association of America: http://www.tia.org/index.html.

UN Statistical Commission Tourism Satellite Account: http://unstats.un.org/unsd/statcom/doc08/BG-TSA.pdf.

UN World Tourism Organization: http://www.unwto.org/index.php.

World Travel and Tourism Council: http://www.wttc.org/.

CHAPTER 5

Globalization and Inclusiveness in the Lodging Sector

INTRODUCTION

When modern-day tourism was relatively new following the Second World War, international travel was the domain of the world's most affluent people. Service providers catered to the selected few who were able to travel overseas, with little thought about a larger diversity of potential travelers. However, as tourism grew rapidly between the 1970s and 2000s, and as lodging and transport service providers, as well as attraction managers, began to prioritize profit-making and business expansion, they soon recognized a much larger diversity of latent travelers who could, because of increased wealth and leisure time, pursue their interest in travel. As a result, lodging establishments and other service providers now compete for special populations and cater to their unique demands, because satisfied guests means increased revenue.

Likewise as traditional barrier effects of political and social boundaries have been reduced during the past quarter century, more people than ever before are traveling to new destinations. Tourist destinations and service providers are becoming more concerned with meeting the needs of an increasingly diverse market to improve visitor satisfaction and win business. This chapter will focus on some of the key globalization and diversity issues and their relevance to the lodging and hospitality industry.

GLOBALIZATION AND TOURISM

Globalization is the process by which the world becomes a smaller place, and nowhere is this shrinking world more apparent than in the realm of tourism. Technological advancements, more widespread wealth, and more awareness of the world have all facilitated and encouraged more people to travel now

CONTENTS

Introduction

Globalization and Tourism

Internationalization of the Lodging Sector

Inclusiveness

Summary and Conclusion

References

Further Reading

Useful Internet Resources

than ever before in history. In this sense, then, the world is a smaller place, and there are very few locations on earth that have not been exposed to tourism.

One of the prime indicators of globalization is supranationalism, or the unification of nation states into large-scale trading blocs, customs unions, or economic alliances. There are a lot of supranationalist alliances in Europe, Asia, Latin America, the Caribbean, Africa, North America, and the Pacific Islands. Some of these trade blocs emphasize tourism as an important focus, primarily those in Europe, Asia, and the Caribbean, with important implications for the accommodation sector. Other types of international alliances also exist, such as the United Nations, the World Trade Organization, and the North Atlantic Treaty Organization. Membership in some of these multinational coalitions requires countries to standardize some hospitality-related regulations and eliminate trade barriers in the services sectors. For example, when China joined the World Trade Organization in 2001, it was required to change its regulations governing hotel investments, including the requirement for foreign companies to be involved in a joint venture with a Chinese company in developing a hotel, allowing more private ownership of businesses and real estate property, and permitting competition from international firms.

One of the most successful supranational alliances is the European Union (EU), which has evolved in varying stages since the Second World War and today includes 27 independent countries. The primary purposes of the EU are to enhance trade between countries, reduce import restrictions, improve and balance the standards of living among member states, and reduce the barriers to cross-border travel and trade. To facilitate easy intra-regional movement by its citizens, the EU countries issue a standardized passport. Member states that belong to the European Monetary Union utilize a common currency, which eliminates much of the accounting headache that existed in Europe before 2002 when 15 different currencies were in use in the EU's 15 member states at that time. And 25 member states (and three non-EU states—Switzerland, Norway, and Iceland) have signed the Schengen Agreement, which eliminates border controls, lifts restrictions on cross-border travel, and provides a single Schengen visa.

The EU and its affiliated Schengen Agreement have important connotations for hotels and other lodging facilities. For instance, properties are now free to import building materials and supplies from neighboring countries without having to declare their goods at borders or pay taxes on them. In human resource terms, it means that hospitality and tourism workers are able to work anywhere within the EU without having to obtain special work permits. The same is true for students wishing to pursue hospitality-related degrees in another EU member nation. The recent admission of several Eastern European countries into the Union (e.g. Romania, Bulgaria, and Slovakia) has seen a notable shift in human resources from east to west. However, this goes beyond the EU, as citizens of many Eastern European countries that are not members of the Union have also been able to secure work visas in increasing numbers for tourism-related employment in the EU and other parts of the world. It is also much more common now, for example, for Eastern Europeans to obtain work permits on cruise ships. Many traditional cruise service positions filled by Filipino and Central American workers have been filled by employees from Croatia, Serbia, Bosnia and Herzegovina, Romania and Ukraine, reflecting an increasingly globalized and mobilized workforce and providing a multinational atmosphere, which according to Perucic's (2007) study, can be effectively marketed as part of the cruise experience.

Clearly, then, tourism is a stimulus for employment migration in Europe, but similar patterns can be seen elsewhere. The United States is experiencing a similar situation to that in Europe, but the labor movement in the North American context is from south to north. Many immigrants, both legal and illegal, are employed in a variety of service occupations, including tourism and hospitality. Hotels, motels, resorts, restaurants, casinos, and other tourism suppliers in the US depend heavily on migrants from Mexico, Guatemala, El Salvador, and other Latin American and Caribbean countries. These émigrés provide inexpensive labor and are known as hard and dependable workers who appreciate the opportunity to work.

Other legislation has been passed in the EU that expands the rights of travelers and business owners, including hotels and inns. Environmental regulations and fair trade laws impact the accommodation sector in a variety of ways, including operational practices related to construction, recycling, pollution, and energy use. One goal of the EU is to assure that these policies are implemented uniformly throughout the alliance. Cruise ships are a special case. While they are expected to abide by international treaties related to environmental care and fair treatment of employees, they have some special dispensation because they ply international waters and a significant number are usually registered in countries other than those where they are docked. These 'flags of convenience' allow cruise companies to access a global workforce and reduce operating costs.

Another important trend in the process of globalization is the opening up of formerly closed regions of the world and the collapse of state socialism (communism) in Eastern Europe and parts of Asia. With the collapse of European communism in the early 1990s, new destinations opened up with an immediate growth in the two-way flow of travel between East and West.

Albania, one of the most tightly controlled and prohibitive destinations in the world, opened up to previously restricted markets. Countries such as Poland, Romania, Bulgaria, and the new countries of the former Soviet Union eliminated their visa requirements, and their citizens were free to visit the west after years of autocratic rule. Returning Poles, Romanians, Bulgarians, and others from the region, as well as westerners' curiosity about the area, shot several of these eastern-bloc countries into the top 20 destinations in the world. Even North Korea, the last remaining closed nation, is gradually opening to more tourists, including a limited number of US passport holders.

One of the most critical issues in the world today in relation to global tourism is the opening up of China for outbound travel. Until fairly recently, citizens of China were unable to travel outside their country for pleasure. Most travel was relegated to students studying abroad, business people traveling for meetings, and occasional permission to visit relatives in other parts of the world. Today, however, China operates under a dual politico-economic system; it is a communist country with a capitalistic economy. It is an unusual model but appears to be working well for China. Because of this model, middle and wealthy classes of Chinese are emerging. Increased disposable incomes, a newfound freedom to travel abroad, and a curiosity about the world around them have caused Chinese outbound travel to soar in the past few years, showing double-digit growth each consecutive year. In 2007, there were 41 million Chinese outbound trips, a growth of 18.6% over 2006 numbers.

Nonetheless, the Chinese government still controls the people's choice in holiday destinations with its Approved Destination Status (ADS) scheme. Each country that wishes to host Chinese tourists must petition the Chinese government and work out a bilateral agreement. Vacation travelers from China can only visit countries that have achieved this status. The current and future Chinese market is a lucrative one; estimates by the World Tourism Organization suggest that by the year 2020, China will be one of the top three tourist-generating countries in the world. To date more than 130 countries have received ADS. Others continue to work out agreements with the Chinese government to be included in the system. Countries in the Asia Pacific region especially have begun benefiting from increased inbound Chinese group tours, owing to their proximity to China and the lower cost for the Chinese associated with traveling shorter distances. Chinese tourism has become especially important for Australia, Thailand, South Korea, and Singapore. As noted already in Chapter 2, this new demand for travel to new destinations will have significant implications for the construction of hotels and management systems to deal with new and emerging market segments.

Other regions are being opened to increased tourism and new forms of accommodation. Cruises continue to be developed in new destinations, such as arctic and Antarctic regions, and more multinational cruise companies are plying the waters of the world far from their traditional ports of call. For example, Italian cruise lines that traditionally sailed in the Mediterranean and Scandinavia are now sailing more frequently in North America, the Caribbean, and South America than they did previously.

INTERNATIONALIZATION OF THE LODGING SECTOR

Chapter 3 discussed franchises and management contracts in the accommodation sector. This section takes this discussion forward to describe the emergence of multinational corporations and the spread of mergers and expansion throughout the world.

The most notable trends in the lodging sector associated with globalization are the current push for a broad and widespread geographic presence in critical overseas markets, the quest for global branding, expansion of brand loyalty, improving profitability, assuring durable shareholder value, international product positioning, and the pursuit of uniform service standards (Whitla et al., 2007). This has led, as already noted, to a widespread move toward mergers and consolidations on the international level. Several hotel companies have been extremely successful in their actions to spread throughout the globe, with InterContinental and Wyndham being the largest hotel groups in the world as measured by number of rooms (Table 5.1). The top 20 global hotel brands are listed in Table 5.2.

Table 5.1	Top Ten Hotel Groups in the World, 2007			
Rank	**Group**	**Home Base**	**Hotels**	**Rooms**
1	InterContinental Hotels Group	UK	3741	556246
2	Wyndham Worldwide	USA	6473	543237
3	Marriott International	USA	2775	502089
4	Hilton Corporation	USA	2901	497738
5	Accor	France	4121	486512
6	Choice	USA	5316	429401
7	Best Western	USA	4164	315401
8	Starwood Hotels and Resorts	USA	871	265598
9	Carlson Hospitality	USA	945	145933
10	Global Hyatt	USA	733	141011

Source: Adapted from Hotel Online (2007).

Table 5.2	Top 20 International Hotel Brands/Chains, 2007			
Rank	**Chain**	**Group**	**Properties**	**Rooms**
1	Best Western	Best Western	4 164	315 401
2	Holiday Inn	InterContinental	1 395	260 470
3	Marriott	Marriott International	537	190 431
4	Comfort	Choice	2 439	184 716
5	Hilton	Hilton Corporation	498	172 605
6	Days Inn of America	Wyndham World	1 859	151 438
7	Express by HI	InterContinental	1 686	143 582
8	Hampton Inn	Hilton Corporation	1 392	138 487
9	Sheraton	Starwood	396	135 859
10	Super 8 Motels	Wyndham World	2 054	126 175
11	Quality	Choice	1 128	112 173
12	Ramada Worldwide	Wyndham World	871	105 986
13	Courtyard	Marriott International	733	105 526
14	Motel 6	Accor	928	95 628
15	Hyatt Hotels	Global Hyatt	214	94 224
16	Mercure	Accor	732	89 624
17	Radisson Hotels	Carlson	400	89 365
18	Ibis	Accor	745	82 546
19	Crowne Plaza	InterContinental	275	75 632
20	Novotel	Accor	397	70 373

Source: Adapted from Hotel Online (2007).

Worldwide, there are approximately 5.5 million rooms in some 43 000 corporate operated hotels. As noted in an earlier chapter, the hotel and resort business are very complex, and there are always mergers, buyings, and sellings going on. In April 2007, for instance, Accor sold its American brand Red Roof for 1.3 billion dollars. Earlier in 2007, Hilton Hotels announced the purchase of Scandic Hotels for 833 million euros (Hotel Online, 2007).

North America is home to most corporate hotel chains. Some 60% of all the world's hotel rooms are located there. Most hotels outside of North America are still independently owned. This is especially the case in Europe, where independent hotels still persist; less than 25% of Europe's hotels belong to chain companies. European independents, however, are facing difficulties in staying competitive in a global marketplace and are slowly merging with larger international conglomerates, reflecting the common tendency toward consolidation and globalization. The economic advantage of going global, or joining a large chain, is being able to purchase supplies in bulk, adopting centralized reservation systems, brand-name visibility, improving pricing, and enhancing standardized service quality. For those

European properties that wish to remain independent, they are often advised to offer added value items and services that many of the international chains are unable to offer, such as bathroom products, special services (e.g. spa treatments), and one-on-one service. These, it is believed, will give them a competitive advantage and distinguish them from the brand-name establishments expanding throughout Europe.

According to some observers, consolidation and internationalization are inevitable for Europe, owing to the attractiveness of low brand penetration and high volumes of international arrivals. As well, Europe's economy, present conditions excep-

Globalized shops in Cairns, Australia, catering to their Japanese customers

ted, does quite well against other world economies with demonstrable growth on an annual basis. The European Monetary Union's single currency, the euro, is also an appealing advantage for most international chains, as is the growth in e-business. These advantages will likely increase the playing field among Europe's hotel properties and increase pressure from the outside to merge with international brands. In the recent past, however, since 2001, chain expansion in Europe has been slowed by threats of terrorism, economic recessions, and war.

During the past quarter century, large hotel chains, many of them based in the United States, have penetrated the global marketplace and formed alliances with other sectors of tourism, including the airlines. In most cases, international lodging companies see global expansion and inter-sectoral partnerships as a way of diversifying their geographical coverage and expanding their markets. This kind of diversification is believed to help assure profits when other markets and regions are down. Spreading to diverse destinations and regions is seen as a protective measure for hotel companies against the place-specific vagaries of bad economies, natural disasters, political unrest, tax increases, or otherwise shifting demand.

Entry into the global marketplace and international mergers is not without problems. On the contrary, there are many challenges and risks associated with internationalization of lodging businesses. These include, among others, different planning and legal systems, inefficient bureaucracies, unpredictable labor markets, corruption, political instability, and different organizational cultures. These challenges are extremely important to overcome as resort and hotel firms continue to expand into the international arena, particularly when management contracts or franchises are involved, as cultural miscommunication can result in image problems and failed business ventures.

A final perspective on the internationalization of lodging is the fact that because increasingly more companies are operating on the international stage, there are constant concerns associated with political instability, security crises, and economic downturns. Thus, there are high risks associated with going global and expanding ownership, franchises, or management into tenuous parts of the world. The Balkan and Middle East wars associated with the 1990s and 2000s, as well as recent economic downturns that have resulted in worldwide recessions between 2007 and 2009, have undermined the financial viability of many multinational hotel companies.

Publicly traded hotel corporations have suffered significant stock market losses, and foreclosures have become commonplace. Hotels in all parts of the world are laying off part of their workforce to remain viable. Most major accommodation companies have announced significant layoffs during 2008–2009, and this trend will likely continue into the foreseeable future. The economic crisis is exacerbated by terrorist threats against tourists and their accommodations providers, such as the November 2008 attacks on hotels in Mumbai, India.

INCLUSIVENESS

Also noted in Chapter 2, political change and tourism growth have brought about new demands in tourism and hospitality. The purpose of this section is not to repeat what was said in Chapter 2, but to bring it more directly into the discussion on globalization and modernization. As part of the 'shrinking of the world' mentioned earlier, service providers are required to acknowledge and meet the needs of an ever more disparate traveling public. One of the most important aspects of this change is recognition of the needs of foreign guests and cultural sensitivities that accompany doing business in a global marketplace.

Recent research shows that there are increasing numbers of people traveling for religious or spiritual purposes. In many parts of the world and among many groups of people there is a spiritual re-awakening, which affects travelers' destination choices and behaviors. In addition to this trend, there are more people traveling now who have special religious requirements. For example, orthodox Jews require special glatt kosher meals, certifiably prepared in kosher kitchens. Muslims are traveling now in greater numbers and have similar *halal* food requirements. Devout Muslims also are required to pray five times daily toward Mecca. It is incumbent on lodging facilities and other service providers who desire to cater to this affluent and booming market to provide prayer rooms, prayer rugs, and *halal* foods for their guests. This demonstrates cultural sensitivity and a desire to satisfy guests' needs, and goes a long way to make Muslim visitors feel welcome. There are many other religious groups that have certain dietary and behavioral requirements. Savvy accommodation managers will know their markets well and be able to satisfy people's unique necessities.

Knowledge of other cultural elements is also critical in delivering satisfying customer experiences. Much research in the area of hospitality and tourism demonstrates unique cultural differences between nationalities and cultures, including different levels of satisfaction with hotel services and quality and differences in customer complaints. There is also evidence to suggest that there are incongruent perceptions about service quality in some countries where clashes can occur between guests and hotel employees. Rubens (1995), for instance, argues that in North America the customer is king. The customer is always right, but in Russia the history of scarcity made the producer king. Even though conditions are changing much of this attitude remains.

Japanese, Korean, and Taiwanese tourists are among the most devout travelers in the world for whom special treatment is required. The Japanese expect high levels of service when they travel, and they almost always travel in groups. They love to shop, and packaging is very important. This goes not only for souvenirs and gifts, but for hotel rooms and their amenities as well. Shops that successfully serve Japanese visitors have learned to adapt by having Japanese-speaking staff, carrying clothing small enough for Asian women, stocking souvenirs and gifts that appeal to the market, providing special services (e.g. colorful gift wrapping) that make visitors feel valued, and posting prices in local currency as well as Japanese yen, Korean won, or Taiwanese dollars.

Politeness and being treated like royalty are expected by Asian visitors in all tourism service sectors, but especially in lodging and shopping contexts. Understanding the behaviors, likes, and dislikes of important and high-end markets like the Japanese and Koreans, is critical in today's global business environment. As noted earlier, the Chinese will continue to become a force to be reckoned with as affluence in China continues to increase and as more countries are enlisted with Approved Destination Status.

Inclusiveness also covers people with special needs or disabilities. Many hotels and other lodging businesses are making great strides to accommodate the needs of this important market segment. Small efforts go a long way in this regard as well. Some research evidence indicates that three primary changes can be made by lodging facilities to meet most of this group's special needs: structural changes, disseminating sufficient information while taking reservations and at check-in time, and sensitivity training for employees (Vladimir, 1998). Some hotels have located disabled-accessible rooms near elevators, so that wheelchair-bound customers or visually impaired guests will not have far to go to get to their rooms. Some rooms are equipped with special toilets and showers that are 'handicap accessible', and peepholes and locks have been installed much lower in the doors to be at eye level with someone in a wheelchair. Other measures that some properties have undertaken include contrasting color schemes to highlight the location of doors, raised beds, and fire alarms that include horns and strobe lights.

While supranational alliances have yet to address the notion of accessibility for people with physical disabilities, several international tourism organizations have begun to address this and encourage more open and inclusive policies and practices in the tourism industry. At the 2000 Bali Conference on Inclusive Tourism, the Bali Declaration on Barrier-Free Tourism for People with Disabilities was pronounced (Table 5.3). From a lodging perspective, its aims include adopting universal designs that create environments, products, and services that can be used by a wide spectrum of consumers, regardless of their knowledge, experience, skills, age, gender, or physical, sensory, cognitive, or communication abilities. This is especially true for hotels and restaurants. The declaration also suggested specific training exercises and competencies for educational institutions and inter-government organizations.

Hotel room door with wheelchair-accessible peep hole

While the Bali Declaration has yet to be adopted by many official public bodies, the conference was attended by government officials and tourism organizations, several of which agreed to begin implementing the recommendations of the accord. From a business perspective, the Declaration makes good business sense.

In the United States, anti-discrimination laws require the fair and equal treatment of people with disabilities. The 1990 Americans with Disabilities Act (ADA) requires accommodation properties to facilitate access for people with disabilities in common areas, kitchens, bedrooms, bathrooms, and conference rooms. The lodging sector is required to alter design or build new facilities that can assist people in getting around. They also are

Table 5.3	Recommendations and Strategic Actions of the Bali Declaration on Barrier-Free Tourism

For Government Authorities:

- train immigration officers about disability-friendly procedures
- develop uniform disabled people-friendly immigration procedures
- improve the accessibility of immigration offices
- exempt from customs tariffs all assistive devices required by people with disabilities that support their daily activities, including computers
- simplify customs clearance procedures for people with disabilities
- train customs and immigration officers about ways to communicate with hearing and visually impaired travelers

For Tourism Service Providers:

- develop in-house programs to build awareness, sensitivities, and skills to provide more appropriate services to people with disabilities
- communicate more with disabled people and their organizations to exchange accurate and reliable information to meet the clients' needs better
- make their websites accessible for the blind
- conduct regular accessibility surveys of the premises to improve tourism services
- introduce barrier-free tourism into their regular meeting agendas
- adopt accessibility as a criterion in the ranking of hotels and restaurants

required to provide auxiliary resources and devices. Table 5.4 lists the areas of hotels and other public buildings that are required to accommodate people with visual, mental, and physical disabilities. At first, there were negative reactions by tourism service providers, including hotels and motels, suggesting that they were being forced to accommodate what they saw as a small and non-lucrative market. Today, however, lodging properties are complying with the ADA and realizing the importance and value of meeting the needs of what has turned out to be an important market niche.

The ADA law defines areas of public accommodation as being inns, hotels, motels, or other places of lodging, except for an establishment located within a building that contains not more than five rooms for rent or hire and that is occupied by the owner of the establishment as the residence of the proprietor. Table 5.5 shows the minimum required number of disability-friendly rooms for a property to be considered in compliance as completely accessible.

Table 5.4	General Requirements for Adapting Public Spaces for People with Disabilities, According to the ADA

Areas and Amenities

- Parking
- Passenger loading zones
- Exterior accessible routes
- Curb ramps
- Drinking fountains
- Telephones
- Ramps
- Stairs
- Platform lifts
- Entrances and exits
- Doors and gates
- Lobbies and corridors
- Elevators
- Rooms and spaces
- Assembly areas (e.g. conference rooms)
- Toilet rooms and bathrooms
- Bathtubs and showers
- Dressing and fitting rooms
- Signage
- Alarms
- Detectable warnings
- Automated teller machines (ATMs)
- Sleeping quarters

In most parts of the world, tourist attractions and even tourist lodging are still inaccessible to people with disabilities, which severely limits some people's experiences and precludes an important market.

Unfortunately, one of the biggest deficiencies in the lodging sector today is accommodation for large families. While family sizes have decreased in relative terms since the 1960s, there are still large families who like to travel

Table 5.5	Number of Rooms Required to be Fully Accessible
Total Number of Rooms	**Accessible Rooms**
1–25	1
26–50	2
51–75	3
76–100	4
101–150	5
151–200	6
201–300	7
301–400	8
401–500	9
501–1000	2% of total rooms

together. Most hotels, resorts, bed and breakfasts, and other facilities do not accommodate large families well. Typically, two rooms have to be purchased to accommodate families with more than two children. Properties that have room and will allow several people to stay together will gain favor in large-family markets.

There has also been an increase in gay and lesbian travel in recent years as old prejudices have given way to higher levels of acceptability. With this change, homosexuals have experienced more freedom to express themselves, and resorts, hotels, and cruises have become more open-minded about catering to this specialized niche market. This market segment has unique interests and activities, so many resorts, especially in the Caribbean and the Mediterranean, have adapted their activities, programs, rooms, and physical facilities to accommodate the needs of this highly lucrative market.

SUMMARY AND CONCLUSION

Resorts, hotels, motels, and other lodging facilities may be considered the most visible assets of a destination's tourism sector. They are fixed assets that usually operate 24 hours a day, cater to both domestic and international guests, and can enhance the image of a destination's tourism trade. The arrival of an international hotel brand may signify a leap to the next level of a country's tourism development. While the hotel industry has become global, this chapter has shown that there are significant variations within regions. With increasing globalization in trade and commerce, the lodging sector will experience expansion and consolidation of its role in this arena. Some of the factors that have been discussed in this chapter will take center stage. First, more expansive supranationalism should lead to greater applications of codes for hotel standards. For example, although tourism is barely developed in West Africa, the Economic Community of West African States (ECOWAS) has already developed standards for hotel classification for all member states. Second, economic expansion in Asian countries, particularly China and India, and the rapid emergence of their middle class, will lead to greater domestic and international travel, as well as major investments in the hotel and resort sector. Third, to meet the demands for quality service delivery, capacity building of hotel personnel in the form of training institutions has also increased. Finally, at the core of the 'shrinking world' are transportation and information technology. For example, the development of the A380 aircraft by Airbus with the upper carrying capacity of over 800 passengers could also spur the expansion of hotel facilities at key international destinations. Similarly, Boeing's 787 'Dreamliner' aircraft, which will soon enter service, will save several hours on inter-continental flights, thereby indeed making the world a smaller place.

REFERENCES

Hotel Online, 2007. Worldwide hotel ranking 2007—final results. Online <www.hotel-online.com/News/PR2007_2nd/Jun07_HotelRaking.html> Accessed January 15, 2009.

Perucic, D., 2007. The impact of globalization on supply and demand in the cruise industry. Tourism and Hospitality Management 13 (3), 665–680.

Rubens, K., 1995. Changes in Russia: a challenge for HR. HR Magazine 40, 70–74.

Vladimir, A., 1998. Is there hospitality for disabled travelers? FIU Hospitality Review 16 (2), 13–21.

Whitla, P., Walters, P., Davies, H., 2007. Global strategies in the international hotel industry. International Journal of Hospitality Management 26 (4), 777–792.

FURTHER READING

Altinay, L., Altinay, M., 2003. How will growth be financed by the international hotel companies? International Journal of Contemporary Hospitality Management 15 (4/5), 274–282.

Baum, T., 2007. Skills and the hospitality sector in a transition economy: the case of front office employment in Kyrgyzstan. Asia Pacific Journal of Tourism Research 12 (2), 89–102.

Cho, M.H., 2001. Japanese, U.S. tourists: culture and hotel selections. FIU Hospitality Review 19 (1), 55–68.

Clifton, W.I., 2001. Circle the wagons, the Americans are coming!. Hospitality Review 3 (3), 7–15.

Connell, J., 1997. International hotel franchise relationships—UK franchisee perspectives. International Journal of Contemporary Hospitality Management 9 (4/6), 215–220.

Davies, T.D., Beasley, K.A., 1994. Accessible design for hospitality: ADA guidelines for planning accessible hotels, motels and other recreational facilities. McGraw-Hill, New York.

D'Annunzio-Green, N., 2002. An examination of the organizational and cross-cultural challenges facing international hotel managers in Russia. International Journal of Contemporary Hospitality Management 14 (6), 266–273.

DeFranco, A., Wortman, J., Lam, T., Countryman, C., 2005. A cross-cultural comparison of customer complaint behavior in restaurants in hotels. Asia Pacific Journal of Tourism Research 10 (2), 173–190.

Duncan, T., 2005. Current issues in the global hospitality industry. Tourism and Hospitality Research 5 (4), 359–366.

Frehse, J., 2005. Innovative product development in hotel operations. Journal of Quality Assurance in Hospitality and Tourism 6 (3/4), 129–146.

Gall, S., 1993. Staff training in disability etiquette: 43 million reasons to do business. Bottomline 7 (6), 22–23.

Garrigós-Simón, F.J., Palacios-Marqués, D., Narangajavana, Y., 2008. Improving the perceptions of hotel managers. Annals of Tourism Research 35 (2), 359–380.

Go, F.M., Pine, R., 1995. Globalization strategy in the hotel industry. Routledge, London.

Gröschl, S., 2005. Persons with disabilities: a source of nontraditional labor for Canada's hotel industry. Cornell Hotel and Restaurant Administration Quarterly 46 (2), 258–274.

Gröschl, S., 2007. An exploration of HR policies and practices affecting the integration of persons with disabilities in the hotel industry in major Canadian tourism destinations. International Journal of Hospitality Management 26 (3), 666–686.

Holjevac, I.A., 2003. A vision of tourism and the hotel industry in the 21st century. International Journal of Hospitality Management 22 (2), 129–134.

Huntley, E., Barnes-Reid, C., 2003. The feasibility of Sabbath-keeping in the Caribbean hospitality industry. International Journal of Contemporary Hospitality Management 15 (3), 172–175.

Johnson, C., Vanetti, M., 2005. Locational strategies of international hotel chains. Annals of Tourism Research 32 (4), 1077–1099.

Johnson, C., Vanetti, M., 2008. Internationalization and the hotel industry. In: Woodside, A.G., Martin, D. (Eds.), Tourism Management: Analysis, Behaviour and Strategy. CAB International, Wallingford, UK, pp. 285–301.

Kim, W.G., 2004. Implications of Chinese casino visitor characteristics in South Korea. Journal of Quality Assurance in Hospitality and Tourism 5 (1), 27–41.

Kivela, J., Leung, F.L.L., 2005. Doing business in the People's Republic of China. Cornell Hotel and Restaurant Administration Quarterly 46 (2), 125–152.

Kopnina, H., 2007. Migration and tourism: formation of new social classes. Cognizant, New York.

Lee, S.K., 2008. Internationalization of US multinational hotel companies: expansion to Asia versus Europe. International Journal of Hospitality Management 27 (4), 657–664.

Lindley-Highfield, M., 2008. 'Muslimization', mission, and modernity in Morelos: the problem of a combined hotel and prayer hall for the Muslims of Mexico. Tourism, Culture and Communication 8 (2), 85–96.

Littlejohn, D., 1997. Internationalization in hotels: current aspects and developments. International Journal of Contemporary Hospitality Management 9 (4/6), 187–192.

Marvel, M., 2004. European hotel chain expansion. Travel and Tourism Analyst 8, 1–48.

Mattila, A.S., 1999. An analysis of means-end hierarchies in cross-cultural context: what motivates Asian and Western business travellers to stay at luxury hotels? Journal of Hospitality and Leisure Marketing 6 (2), 19–28.

Mattila, A.S., Choi, S.M., 2006. A cross-cultural comparison of perceived fairness and satisfaction in the context of hotel room pricing. International Journal of Hospitality Management 25 (1), 146–153.

Mikula, J.R., Chon, K.S., 1997. International hotel marketing in the age of globalization. International Journal of Contemporary Hospitality Management 9 (1), 31–34.

Mok, C., Armstrong, R.W., 1998. Expectations for hotel service quality: do they differ from culture to culture? Journal of Vacation Marketing 4 (4), 381–391.

Ng, C.W., Pine, R., 2003. Women and men in hotel management in Hong Kong: perceptions of gender and career development issues. International Journal of Hospitality Management 22 (1), 85–102.

Nishiyama, K., 1996. Welcoming the Japanese visitor: insights, tips, tactics. University of Hawai'i Press, Honolulu.

Ohlin, J.B., 1993. Creative approaches to the Americans with Disabilities Act. Cornell Hotel and Restaurant Administration Quarterly 34 (5), 19–22.

O'Mahony, B., 2007. Uncontested space: case studies of the Irish involvement in the hospitality industry in colonial Victoria. International Journal of Culture, Tourism and Hospitality Research 1 (3), 203–213.

O'Neill, M., Knight, J.A., 2000. Disability tourism dollars in Western Australia hotels. FIU Hospitality Review 18 (2), 72–88.

Ozturk, Y., Yayli, A., Yesiltas, M., 2008. Is the Turkish tourism industry ready for a disabled customer's market? The views of hotel and travel agency managers. Tourism Management 29 (2), 382–389.

Peters, M., Frehse, J., 2005. The internationalization of the European hotel industry in the light of competition theories. Tourism 53 (1), 55–65.

Rob Tonge and Associates, 1995. How to do business with the Japanese visitor market: a guide for small tourist businesses, 5th Edition. Gull Publishing, Coolum Beach, Australia.

Salmen, J.P.S., 1992. The ADA and hotel technology. Bottomline 7 (3), 28–31.

Simons, T., Friedman, R., Liu, L.A., Parks, J.M., 2008. The importance of behavioral integrity in a multicultural workplace. Cornell Hospitality Report 8 (17), 4–20.

Sizoo, S., 2008. Analysis of employee performance during cross-cultural service encounters at luxury hotels in Hawaii, London and Florida. Asia Pacific Journal of Tourism Research 13 (2), 113–128.

Sizoo, S., Iskat, W., Plank, R., Serrie, H., 2003. Cross-cultural service encounters in the hospitality industry and the effect of intercultural sensitivity on employee performance. International Journal of Hospitality and Tourism Administration 4 (2), 61–77.

Tantawy, A., Kim, W.G., Pyo, S.S., 2004. Evaluation of hotels to accommodate disabled visitors. Journal of Quality Assurance in Hospitality and Tourism 5 (1), 91–101.

Weidenfeld, A., 2006. Religious needs in the hospitality industry. Tourism and Hospitality Research 6 (2), 143–159.

Williams, R., Rattray, R., Grimes, A., 2006. Meeting the on-line needs of disabled tourists: an assessment of UK-based hotel websites. International Journal of Tourism Research 8 (1), 59–73.

World Tourism Organization, 2002. Tourism in the age of alliances, mergers and acquisisions. UNWTO, Madrid.

Yu, L., Gu, H.M., 2005. Hotel reform in China: a SWOT analysis. Cornell Hotel and Restaurant Administration Quarterly 46 (2), 153–169.

Yuksel, A., Kilinc, U.K., Yuksel, F., 2006. Cross-national analysis of hotel customers' attitudes toward complaining and their complaining behaviours. Tourism Management 27 (1), 11–24.

USEFUL INTERNET RESOURCES

Accor: http://www.accorhotels.com/gb/home/index.shtml.

ADA Homepage: http://www.ada.gov/.

Best Western: http://www.bestwestern.com/.

Carlson Hospitality: http://www.carlson.com/.

Choice Hotels International: http://www.choicehotels.com/.

Gaytravel.com: http://www.gaytravel.com/.

Global Hyatt: http://www.hyatt.com/hyatt/index.jsp.

Hilton Corporation: http://hiltonworldwide1.hilton.com/en_US/ww/fob/index.do.
Hotels Online: http://www.hotel-online.com.
InterContinental Hotels Group: http://www.ichotelsgroup.com/.
Marriott International: http://www.marriott.com.
Starwood Hotels and Resorts: http://www.starwoodhotels.com/.
Wyndham Worldwide: http://www.wyndhamworldwide.com/.

CHAPTER 6

Accommodations and the Green Movement

INTRODUCTION

For many years, it has been clear, without fail, that unmitigated tourism growth results in environment degradation. The lodging sector has played an important role in ecological deterioration, although its impacts have not been as profound as those of automobiles, airliners, and cruise ships. Nonetheless, as part of the broader movement toward sustainable growth and development, resorts, hotels, motels, lodges, bed and breakfasts, and all other segments of the accommodation sector have begun to take action in doing their part to sustain the physical environment. It makes good business sense, and it is a characteristic of good ecological stewardship. This chapter examines the ecological impacts of tourism from an accommodation's perspective and highlights the ways in which the lodging sector is attempting to do its part in minimizing the negative effects of tourism in terms of recycling, waste management, and energy consumption.

CONTENTS

Introduction

Ecological Impacts of Tourism

Efforts to Mitigate Negative Impacts

Conclusion

References

Further Reading

Useful Internet Resources

ECOLOGICAL IMPACTS OF TOURISM

Tourism, in conjunction with most extractive economic activities such as mining, manufacturing, fishing, petroleum, as well as various manufacturing and service industries have played a salient role in environmental deterioration. The earliest research on the subject in the mid-1900s dealt with the overuse of the physical environment by outdoor recreationists and other nature enthusiasts. As tourism has grown to immense proportions since the Second World War, so too have its negative impacts in nearly every corner of the globe.

One of the most often-cited results of tourism is various forms of pollution, which affects air and water quality, as well as vegetation, bedrock and the entire ecosystem. The biggest culprit in this regard tends to be the

81

To control pollution and crowdedness, no gas-powered cars are allowed in Zermatt, Switzerland

transportation sector, but all parts of tourism, including accommodation and food services have a liable role as well. Water quality is typically affected in destinations by oil leakage, and garbage and sewage disposal, or lack thereof. In many parts of the world, accommodation-based sewage and trash are dumped directly into lakes, rivers, and seas without any kind of processing beforehand. This creates health hazards, is aesthetically unpleasant, affects coastlines and ocean floors, marine life and contributes directly to the destruction of coral reefs – an important ecosystem that protects shorelines, cleanses ocean waters, and provides a habitat for millions of species.

Wear and tear, vandalism, and collecting are also major problems associated with tourism. In areas that are heavily 'touristified', physical wear is ever-present on bedrock, historic sites, vegetation, and soils. At some of the world's most popular attractions, thousands of people per hour can visit during high season, creating irreversible impacts on the physical environment, including vandalism in the form of breaking, painting, scratching, and collecting. Excessive numbers of tourists viewing, chasing, photographing, and approaching can even affect the eating, mating, and migration patterns of wildlife species, and cause them to become more aggressive, which has been shown to be the case in several destinations in Africa, Asia, Australia, and North America.

While most physical impacts of tourism are negative, there is hope. For example, tourism is a major impetus for conserving and protecting natural and cultural areas. In essence, the world's national park movement, which began in the 1870s, was spurred in part at least by tourism and the recognized need to protect the environment. In addition, an increased awareness of humanity's negative environmental impacts has led to a culture of ecological awareness and 'cleaning and greening' in many tourist destinations. Individually owned lodging properties, as well as large multinational hotel corporations, have become involved in these efforts during the past 20 years, and more energy and resources are currently being put into achieving long- and short-term environmental objectives.

During the past century or so, it has become abundantly clear that the primary perpetrator of tourism's negative impacts (socio-cultural and ecological) is known as *mass tourism*. This is the traditional sun, sea and sand pleasure-based tourism in which place and environment were irrelevant and which was consequently allowed to grow spontaneously, without appropriate planning and oversight. The tourist destinations themselves are as much to blame as the tourists (perhaps more so), because of their 'boosterist' promotional tactics that encouraged unmitigated tourism growth and increased tourist arrivals and hotel/resort development at all costs. The results are very evident in a wide range of places in the United States, the Caribbean, Mexico, the Mediterranean region of Europe and North Africa, Great Britain, parts of Asia, and on some of the Pacific Islands.

This realization has led to new ways of thinking that tourism can no longer proceed to grow as it has for decades, rather there must be alternatives to the mass tourism of the past. Alternative forms of tourism ('alternative tourism') have thus developed as new ways of looking at the industry. Better planned, more sustainable and environmentally sensitive forms of travel have taken over significant segments of the marketplace since the late 1980s. Among the most important buzzwords and concepts in this regard today in planning, developing, promoting and researching tourism are ecotourism, community-based tourism, geotourism, responsible tourism, sustainable tourism and pro-poor tourism. These all refer to forms of travel that aim to minimize environmental and socio-cultural impacts, educate travellers and provide profound experiences, derive economic benefits for the destination community and its members, empower communities politically and psychologically, build mutual respect, and support the doctrines of sustainable development: equity, appropriate scale, cultural and ecological integrity, harmony, balance, and holistic development.

The accommodation sector, while not as perilous in environmental terms as the transport sector, does in fact bear much of the burden associated with the negative effects of tourism and has traditionally played a noteworthy role in the notions of mass tourism and boosterism. Today, however, changes are occurring as small-scale lodging and large hotel/resort companies are realizing that a sustainable future for tourism and hospitality is in their own best interest.

EFFORTS TO MITIGATE NEGATIVE IMPACTS

With the realization that they have contributed to environmental problems in tourist destinations and because the world in general is becoming more sustainability-minded, the accommodation and food service sectors have made significant and commendable strides toward 'greening up' their operations during the past quarter century. Several of their efforts are outlined below, although there are many more endeavours yet to be carried out. Some of the following initiatives are limited by geography and relative location, scale of lodging facility, accessibility, and market demand, although various adaptations can be made regardless of scale, location and market.

Buying green

One of the laudable efforts being made by lodging establishments is buying and selling green. Buying green can be as simple as using recyclable or glass drinking cups in guesthouse bathrooms, low-energy light bulbs in hotel corridors, or warm air hand dryers in public toilets instead of paper towels. Not only are such efforts good for the environment, but also they often reduce operating costs. Some establishments charge higher prices to offset the costs of recycling and buying green, but research shows that most environmentally aware guests are willing to pay a little extra for the assurance that the business they support is a green business.

Various recommendations have been made by many non-profit organizations and industry watchdogs as regards what constitutes green buying for lodging businesses. Biodegradable products such as eating utensils, cleaning solutions, soaps and shampoos, are an important part of any guest house or hotel environmental program. Similarly, for guest rooms, administrative offices, and kitchens, accommodation enterprises can purchase recycled content items such as take-out boxes and bags, stationary, toilet tissue, and other paper and plastic items made from previously recycled goods. Companies can also encourage consumers to utilize the Internet more so that fewer paper brochures and booklets will need to be produced. Likewise, some resorts and hotel companies are working with vendors to reduce the amount of packaging required for food and non-food items; the most influential companies are even attempting to work out ways in which transportation impacts might be reduced.

Being green (sustainable) is also more than just purchasing recycled and recyclable merchandize. It also entails using locally produced food items that are fresh, indigenous, and representative of the area, as well as supporting the local economy inasmuch as possible. This includes selling in hotel gift shops souvenirs and handicrafts that are produced with sustainable materials by local artisans. This not only helps the physical environment but also helps the community economically and builds bridges between the local population and the lodging sector.

Waste management

Part of being a sustainable tourism partner is not only reducing waste but also minimizing the amount of waste that goes into landfills or worse yet, rivers and oceans. Recycling is the most common waste-control measure being under-taken by the lodging sector in recent years. Recy-cling is particularly relevant and makes good business sense for ski resorts, which are among the world's leaders in recycling programs, in part because they realize that their sustainable future may be determined by the effects of global climate change. Ski resort recycling is done at the lodges and on the mountain slopes themselves. Tradi-tional recycled material comes from the hotels and lodges, but the on-mountain waste includes cardboard, water bottles, broken skis and snow-boards, boots, poles, and bindings. Broken ski equipment can be shredded and used in making furniture, flooring, and other home and yard products, and several resort companies have begun to participate in these important programs.

A self-contained waste treatment system at a resort in Fiji

Recycling programs are also done via green or blue deposit boxes in rooms and common areas for guests to use, but also important is employee recycling in kitchen and utility areas where plas-tics, paper, and metals are sorted. Some resort companies have even gone so far as to hire garbage separating companies that sort recyclable material from non-recyclable waste, saving landfills hundreds of millions of tons of trash every year. As

These recycling bins on a cruise ship help protect the environment

well, many establishments have decided to donate used furniture and elec-tronics to charities rather than sending them to landfills.

Composting is a novel idea that is beginning to catch on, particularly with small-scale lodging such as ecolodges, bed and breakfasts, inns, and guest houses. Usable kitchen waste can be placed in composting bins and turned into valuable, odourless, organic, and free fertilizer for flowerbeds and gardens. Lawn clippings, tree branches and leaves can be utilized as land-scaping mulch, which is normally very expensive to buy. While recycling and composting programs are probably more easily administered in small-scale lodging enterprises, there are numerous examples of large resorts and hotels also establishing successful green programs such as these. Vail Resorts in the United States, for example, initiated a kitchen food preparation composting pilot program at one of its properties, which the company estimates reduced landfill waste by 500 pounds (227 kg) per week and provided the property with plenty of organic fertilizer and mulch. Since that time, the program has expanded and keeps approximately three tons of vegetable and fruit discards per month from being dumped into local landfills (Vail Resorts, 2008).

Energy and water conservation

Research is currently being done to examine the feasibility of alternative energy sources for lodging establishments, and at present the general consensus is that stand-alone renewable energy supplies and alternative energy systems (e.g., wind and solar) can power all of a large-scale accommodation property's energy needs, including air conditioning and heating. The most cost-effective approach at present appears to be a combination of diesel and renewable energy configuration, which according to Dalton et al. (2008b), reduces costs by 50% and greenhouse gas emissions by 65%, and can pay for itself in less than five years. The study also concludes that wind energy is more cost-effective than solar energy in large-scale resorts and hotels. There is significant evidence that part of the green movement among accommodation providers includes seeking alternative fuels and reducing the carbon footprint not only of each individual establishment, but also the footprint of the tourists themselves. In Queensland, Australia, only a small portion of accommodation providers actually has renewable energy supplies, although nearly three quarters would consider installing them if it were cost-effective. More than half of the lodging businesses surveyed by Dalton et al. (2007) felt that renewable energy sources were a marketable commodity (Table 6.1).

Hotels, resorts, and small-scale lodging establishments can be built in ways that minimize energy use and waste and maximize natural energy and

Table 6.1 Accommodation Providers' Views of Renewable Energy Sources, Queensland, Australia		
Question	**Yes (%)**	**No (%)**
Do you have an installed renewable energy supply?	9.2	90.8
Would you consider installing a renewable energy Power supply?	71.0	29.0
For your operation, do you view the use of renewable energy as a tourism selling point?	54.0	46.0

Source: Dalton et al. (2007).

light. Designs that integrate skylights and face the direction of the sun during cooler seasons can lessen energy use and in the long-term be cost-effective. While such design implements cost money up front, they save capital in the long term. The U.S. Green Building Council, which certifies green construction, argues that the cost of construction according to LEED (Leadership in Energy and Environmental Design) standards is the same or only slightly more than traditional building, but the subsequent payoffs and savings are greater.

Water conservation is equally important, particularly in areas where water demands are high but supplies are low. This has gone to one extreme; however, in the US southwest, where in some cities (e.g., Las Vegas and Phoenix) residents' use of water for gardening and landscaping is restricted, or water-dependent landscaping in new home developments is curtailed because the area's hotels and resorts need the water for golf courses and swimming pools. Efficient sprinkler and dripper systems help keep water loss to a minimum, and compost and mulching help protect the moist soil from rapid evaporation and erosion. In addition, there is a strong movement going on to persuade resorts and hotels to use reclaimed or grey water for irrigating golf courses and landscaping. Many tourist lodging providers throughout the world have begun installing dual-flush toilets, which allow users to choose a light flush or heavy flush.

Concerns about the careless use of water resources led to the linen and towel reuse efforts adopted by most of the world's brand-name lodging during the past 15 years. This program promotes towel reuse in rooms where guests are staying more than one night by suggesting (via a placard or card in the bathroom) that if guests wish to reuse their towel again, they should hang it up, or leave it on the floor if they prefer to have a new one. In theory this program was supposed to reduce water and detergent use, and save on the cost of laundry. A few studies have been conducted on the effectiveness of this 'choose to reuse' campaign and have found that approximately three quarters of hotel guests choose to reuse their towels, and some would even be willing to pay more per night to reuse their towels as part of a hotel's sustainability program. Some observers, however, suggest that the linen reuse movement is facing two primary problems. The first problem is that guests are disregarding the cards or are now blind to them because of their ubiquity and simply leaving their towels on the floor. The second is that even when guests hang their towels up to be reused, cleaning staff replace them anyway.

Levying eco-taxes

Tourists are accustomed to paying taxes: departure taxes, bed taxes, fuel surcharges, duties and tariffs, sales/VAT taxes, security fees, and rental car taxes, just to name a few. One tax, however, has stirred considerable debate in the tourism realm: environmental use fees, which have been levied for many years on other industries, such as mining and manufacturing, to pay for the cleanup and monitoring of their ecological damage. Now, given the widespread recognition that tourism is damaging destination environments, the idea is trickling into the realm of tourism as well. Eco-taxes, as they are sometimes called, may be charged to tourists or service providers (e.g., tour operators) to help offset some of the environmental deterioration caused by tourism and to protect the environment from future damage. Common projects to utilize the money include beach and coastal rehabilitation, cleaning up the sea, collecting and disposing of waste, developing alternative energy sources, and protecting natural resources from further degradation.

While direct tourism eco-taxes are still rare, a few prominent examples exist, and several crowded tourist destinations in Europe and the Caribbean are considering implementing them. Most destinations that have implemented eco-taxes on tourism, and those that are considering it, typically collect the money through lodging facilities and base the rate on the type of accommodation being used and the length of stay in the destination. One exception to this, however, is the Caribbean nation of Dominica. Because most of the island's tourists come via cruise ship and therefore do not utilize land-based accommodation, the Dominican government levies a small environmental tax to all departing visitors. From Dominica's perspective, cruise passengers should pay the tax because they arrive on the island, produce considerable environmental impact (as do the cruise ships themselves), and contribute relatively little to the local economy. Most tourists are unaware that they are paying the tax since it is incorporated into the individual departure and port fees.

Probably the best known example of eco-taxes comes from the Balearic Islands of Spain. In popular Spanish destinations like Ibiza and Mallorca, where tourist arrivals outnumber residents by nearly 16 times, tourism became overdeveloped, and severe environmental damage had long occurred to the islands' infrastructure and environment. The most notable impacts are pressure on water resources, production of domestic waste at double the rate of the rest of Spain, and disproportionate consumption of energy. In response to the continued threat of ecological damage through tourism, the government of the Balearic Islands instituted an eco-tax (ecotasa), which everyone staying on the islands was required to pay and which would go toward protecting and restoring the destination environments in an effort known as the Tourist Area Restoration Fund. The program's primary goals were to restore and redesign tourist areas, reclaim open spaces and natural resources, revitalize rural economies and agriculture, and enhance heritage areas and attractions. The eco-tax was levied on every form of lodging, with each type having a different daily fee schedule. For example, five-star accommodation was taxed 2 euros per day. Three- and four-star lodging was taxed at 1 euro per day. Even campgrounds had to charge their customers, .75 euros per day, and guests in farm stay accommodations paid .25 euros per day.

The tourist eco-tax was collected between May 2002 and October 2003, at which time, under considerable pressure by the lodging and tour operators sectors, it was deemed illegal and discontinued by the conservative government of Spain. Even though similar user fees have been charged for years (e.g., entrance fees to national parks, which help pay for conservation and maintenance) in various parts of the world, there appears to have been a particular aversion to paying or requiring tourism eco-taxes. This is in spite of the successful diving tax in the Medes Islands (Spain), which generated nearly 70% of the Medes reserve's operating budget. While the idea of an environmental tourist user fee was popular among Balearic Islands' residents, and many tourists did not mind the low fees, enough pressure was exerted at the national level to lead to its demise.

Other countries also have enacted 'polluter-pays' taxes, including Sweden, which imposes environmental fees on a variety of industries. One of these is aviation; recognizing that airplanes are large contributors to greenhouse gas emissions, Sweden has imposed carbon-taxes on flights. Since much of the world's greenhouse gas problem derives from the transportation sector, other countries are considering taxes on bus/coach trips, air travel, ship transport, and automobile use. While accommodation establishments do not emit identical pollutants to those of the transport sector, they do have a deep carbon footprint in terms of energy consumption, waste production, and in some cases deforestation. Climate change observers argue that eco-taxes could help manage the impacts of tourism on the global environment. It is likely that tourism-based environmental taxes for transport and accommodations will become more commonplace in the future as countries begin to carry out the missions of supranational agreements on climate change and environmental conservation.

Eco-friendly certification

Stemming from the rush to adopt and embrace the notion of ecotourism and to dissociate themselves from the malevolence of mass tourism, many lodging proprietorships and large companies have become 'certified' eco-friendly establishments. There is a large number of fee-based ecologically sustainable certification programs throughout the world that endorse tour operators, transportation companies, food services, and lodging facilities, which adhere to basic minimum green standards. Owing to space constraints only a few of these will be mentioned in this section, although it should be borne in mind that they all base their eco-labelling on similar environmental and cultural obligations that uphold the principles of sustainability.

Established in 1990, the Green Restaurant Association is a non-profit organization based in Boston (USA) that aims to create an environmentally sustainable restaurant industry by certifying restaurants, cafes, bars, bakeries, museum snack bars, coffee and tea houses, caterers, and college/university cafeterias. Certification is based on adherence to criteria related to energy, water, waste, chemical and pollution reduction, sustainable food, and sustainable building materials and furnishings.

Ecotourism certification is also big business in Costa Rica and Australia and will be examined in more depth in Chapter 15. Costa Rica's Certification for Sustainable Tourism (CST), a creation of the Sustainability Programs Department of the Costa Rica Tourist Board and the Costa Rica National Accreditation Commission, endorses businesses that are managed according to principles of sustainable growth. Upon certification, lodging establishments can officially be called 'ecolodge' or 'ecohotel'. Ecotourism Australia is a comparable organization with the objective of approving tour operators, guides, and accommodations as ecologically responsible institutions. These two programs, and others such as Ecotourism, Kenya's eco-rating scheme, certify 'ecoresorts' if the establishment adheres to stringent policies associated with waste, water, energy and recycling management, and community-based development, including the enhancement of resident quality of life.

ECOTEL is another officially recognized program that approves hotels, resorts, inns and other properties inasmuch as they abide by eco-friendly practices. All certified properties are required to pass a detailed inspection and monitoring plan based on their commitment to the environment, waste management, energy efficiency, water conservation, community involvement and staff eco-training. More than 1000 hotels, inns and resorts have applied for ECOTEL certification, and it is becoming more widely recognized as a brand that image accommodation facilities should obtain. Table 6.2 provides a sample of some of the properties that have been certified by ECOTEL in Latin America and Asia.

Green Seal is not as closely connected to the accommodations industry as the other certifying organizations are. Instead it specializes in construction companies, cleaning products, food production and preparation services, transportation businesses, and utility services. However, since the late 1990s it has expanded into lodging and has so far certified 36 lodging facilities throughout the United States under its Greening the Lodging Industry

Table 6.2	A Selection of ECOTEL-certified Lodging Facilities in Latin America and Asia	
Property		**Location**
Costa de Cocos		Quintana Roo, Mexico
Villas Maya		Akumal, Mexico
Villa Castellanos		Peten, Guatemala
The Bayman Bay Club		Guanaja, Honduras
Maya Mountain Lodge		Cayo, Belize
Chaa Creek		San Ignacio, Belize
Arco Iris		Santa Elena, Costa Rica
El Sapo Dorado Mountain Suites		Santa Elena, Costa Rica
Selva Verde Lodge		Sarapiqui, Costa Rica
The Orchid ECOTEL		Mumbai, India
Hotel Rodas		Mumbai, India
Hilton Tokyo Bay		Tokyo, Japan
Eco Lodge Shimanto		Kochi-Ken, Japan

Program. It aims to promote environmentally responsible practices and products in hotels, resorts, and other lodging facilities and issues three levels of ecological achievement: bronze, silver and gold. Green Seal focuses on how sustainable management can benefit the environment while increasing net profits.

These various eco-certifications are not simply altruistic in nature; they create an environmental brand image that can be used in marketing and promotional campaigns. Official recognition by one or more of these 'authoritative' organizations demonstrates to tourists, tour operators, and travel agents that environmental accountability has been demonstrated by the property – a very appealing draw in today's eco-oriented western societies.

Tourism employee training

There are many examples of tourist destinations and lodging institutions requiring and providing training and education in the realm of environmental sustainability. Many observers suggest the only way to get tourism service providers to adhere to sustainability standards is to educate them about the importance and value of eco-sensitivity in tourism and to assure that there is an economic benefit as well. Several studies have demonstrated that hotel managers and other staff members do perceive the importance of conservation and renewable energy sources. Often as high as 80–90% of managerial staff recognize the importance of hotels and resorts becoming more aware and eco-friendly in their day-to-day operations, regardless of whether or not their motives are altruistic or financial.

The International Ecotourism Society has a Training and Education Program that endeavours to promote sustainable tourism education in official school and university curricula and promote the principles of ecotourism before various audiences, including tour operators, planning and development agencies, and government offices.

The Accor group is currently undertaking a scheme (Green Shield) that tries to educate staff members about the benefits of conservation and calculate the actual savings of reusing towels. Accor hopes to achieve a 5% reuse of towels, which will reportedly save some $4.8 million, but real savings are yet to be calculated. The core aim of Green Shield is to educate housekeeping staff, because as Accor Australia's vice president noted, "there is no point in asking guests to help out if the housekeeper just brings in new towels anyway" (Travel Weekly, 2008: n.p.). Marriott International claims to have saved an average of 11–17% in hot water and sewer costs in 2007 because of its linen reuse program (Weissenberg et al., 2008).

Educate the tourists

In general, the travelling public is becoming more environment conscious. Each time a tourist survey is conducted, it appears that more and more respondents are taking a personal interest in green travel. According to an October 2008 study, 48% of the American travelling public claimed to try to be green sensitive when they travel, a figure up from 41% the previous year (Deloitte, 2008). The environment in which each individual is best able to control his/her environmental impact is lodging, much more so than in transportation and food services. In an April 2008 study of 1155 business travellers, the consulting company (Deloitte) found some interesting results related to business travellers' ecological actions and expectations in the accommodation sector (Table 6.3). Some 95% of respondents in the study agreed that hotels and other lodging enterprises should be undertaking green initiatives, and more than a third (38%) make a point of searching for lodging that practices eco-friendly management principles.

The same survey found that business travellers themselves are overall environmentally savvy travellers (Table 6.4), with the majority responding that they do in fact practice specific energy-saving actions, such as turning off lights, conserving water, and adjusting heating and air conditioning when they are not in the room, and using toiletries sparingly. Interestingly, too, was

Table 6.3	Business Travellers' Green Expectations of Lodging Establishments, $n = 1155$

Environmental Actions Lodging Facilities Should be Undertaking	Percent
Recycling	77
Using energy-efficient lighting	74
Using energy-efficient windows	59
Using cards in bathrooms to remind guests to reuse their towels	52
Using environmentally safe cleaning products	49
Use water saving devices in rooms	46
Using green landscaping practices	45

Source: Adapted from Weissenberg et al., 2008.

Table 6.4	Business Travellers' Own Green Behaviour in Lodging Establishments, $n = 1155$

Traveller's Environmental Behaviour	Percent
Always or frequently turn off lights when leaving the room	92
Use toiletries conservatively or use their own	64
Always or frequently adjust the heat or air conditioning when leaving the room	61
Use water conservatively	60
Would be willing to pay more to stay in a green lodging establishment	40
Have taken initiatives to identify green lodging (e.g., internet searches, asked a travel agent)	38

Source: Adapted from Weissenberg et al., 2008.

that even though 97% of respondents claimed to be either extremely green or somewhat green during their hotel stays, only one-third regularly request that their bedding or towels not be changed, and 60% suggested they would not be willing to pay more for green lodging if they were paying for the room out of their own pockets. On the other hand, 4% said they would be willing to pay 50% more; 8% declared a willingness to pay 25% more; and 28% claimed to be willing to pay 10% more for green accommodations. A similar study in Australia found that 49% of holiday makers (including foreign visitors to Australia) would be willing to pay extra for hotels with renewable energy supplies (Dalton et al., 2008a).

Although business travellers and many other 'special interest' travellers do appear to be more ecologically informed than the general population, the majority of the world's tourists have a long way to go in understanding the implications of tourism and their own behaviour on the destinations they visit. This has resulted in many calls for codes of conduct for tourists, particularly in sensitive environments such as arctic tundra, Antarctica and tropical rain forests. In most cases, the responsibility lies with tour operators and travel agents to inform visitors about appropriate behaviour, and indeed travellers to Antarctica undergo rigorous 'educational' programs to learn about what is or is not acceptable behaviour and how best to protect that frail ecosystem. Several international organizations (e.g., the International Ecotourism Society) have as a mandate to educate and spread the public word about responsible travel.

It is also a common talking point that tourists should understand environmentally-friendly behaviour in lodging establishments and do their own part to help the hospitality sector become more sustainable. The linen reuse programs are a good example of these efforts and they are a good start. However, much more can be done. The Accor group's Green Shield project aims not only to educate staff but also to educate tourists about what they can do to save energy and reduce their carbon footprint.

CONCLUSION

As part of the broader movement of environmental ethics, or the ethical relationships between humans and the earth, there is a growing environmental consciousness on the part of tourists and lodging facilities, and more and more travellers are beginning to seek out accommodations that practice what is being preached about sustainability. Several of the world's largest hotel and resort companies have begun to realize the importance of being part of the global community and have started rallying around the sustainability movement. From their point of view it is a way to give back to the world and to create a lucrative competitive business advantage, since most guests would like to know that their money and stay are contributing to environmental protection.

The Accor hotel and resort group recently enacted its own Earth Guest Day, which corresponds with International Earth Day. On April 22, 2007, Accor mobilized thousands of its employees in 69 countries of Africa, Asia, Latin America and Europe to participate in simultaneous exercises of tree planting, orphanage and school rebuilding, blood donating, coastal and waterway rehabilitating, and many other environmentally and socially responsible initiatives. Accor carried out similar activities in even more countries in 2008 and plans to continue these efforts into the future under the theme of 'As Guests of the Earth, We Welcome the World'.

One point should be made quite clear that not all eco-friendly lodging practices are done out of pure altruism, even the Accor example above. In fact, it has now become common industry knowledge that green practices translate into increased earnings, because green practices amount to good marketing and better return on investment. With more leisure and business travellers expecting, and being willing to pay more for eco-friendly places to stay, green practices ought to be placed at the core if a company's marketing plan. A failure to do so will result in significant opportunities lost, not only for the physical environment but also for the competitive business environment of today.

REFERENCES

Dalton, G.J., Lockington, D.A., Baldock, T.E., 2007. A survey of tourist operator attitudes to renewable energy supply in Queensland, Australia. Renewable Energy 32 (4), 567–586.

Dalton, G.J., Lockington, D.A., Baldock, T.E. 2008a. A survey of tourist attitudes to renewable energy supply in Australian hotel accommodation. Renewable Energy, 33 (10), 2174–2185.

Dalton, G.J., Lockington, D.A., Baldock, T.E. 2008b. Feasibility analysis of stand-alone renewable energy supply options for a large hotel. Renewable Energy, 33 (7), 1475–1490.

Deloitte, 2008. 2009 Industry outlook: tourism, hospitality and leisure. Online <http://www.deloitte.com/dtt/article/0, 1002,sid%253D57196%2526cid%253 D238879,00.html> Accessed December 15.

Travel Weekly, 2008. Accor trials green scheme. Travel Weekly, 19 February. Online <http://www.travelweekly.com.au/articles/8f/0c05428f.asp>

Vail Resorts, 2008. Reducing, reusing and recycling. Online <http://www. vailresorts.com/Corp/info/reduce-reuse-recycle.aspx> Accessed November 30.

Weissenberg, A., Redington, N., Kutyla, D., 2008. The Staying Power of Sustainability: Balancing Opportunity and Risk in the Hospitality Industry. Deloitte & Touche, New York.

FURTHER READING

Agarwal, S., Shaw, G., 2007. Managing Coastal Tourism Resorts: A Global Perspective. Channel View, Clevedon, UK.

Ayala, H., 1996. Resort ecotourism: a master plan for experience management. Cornell Hotel and Restaurant Administration Quarterly 27 (5), 54–61.

Ayala, H., 2000. Surprising partners: hotel firms and scientists working together to enhance tourism. Cornell Hotel and Restaurant Administration Quarterly 41 (3), 42–57.

Azila, K., 2004. Environmental management in the hotel sector: searching for best practice in Penang, Malaysia. ASEAN Journal of Hospitality and Tourism 3 (2), 91–117.

Becken, S., Frampton, C., Simmons, D., 2001. Energy consumption patterns in the accommodation sector: the New Zealand case. Ecological Economics 39 (3), 371–386.

Bell, C.A., 1992. How to maintain a fragile resort. Cornell Hotel and Restaurant Administration Quarterly 33 (5), 28–31.

Bohdanowicz, P., 2006. Environmental awareness initiatives in the Swedish and Polish hotel industries: survey results. International Journal of Hospitality Management 25 (4), 662–682.

Bicknell, S., McManus, P., 2006. The canary in the coalmine: Australian ski resorts and their response to climate change. Geographical Research 44 (4), 386–400.

Butler, J., 2008. The compelling 'hard case' for 'green' hotel development. Cornell Hospitality Quarterly 49 (3), 234–244.

Chan, W.W., Lam, J.C., 2002. A study on pollutant emission through gas consumption in the Hong Kong hotel industry. Journal of Sustainable Tourism 10 (1), 70–81.

Chan, W.W., Mak, B.L., 2004. An estimation of the environmental impact of diesel oil usage in Hong Kong hotels. Journal of Sustainable Tourism 12 (4), 346–355.

Chan, W.W., 2005. Partial analysis of the environmental costs generated by hotels in Hong Kong. International Journal of Hospitality Management 24 (4), 517–531.

Chan, W.W., Wong, K.K.F., Lo, J.Y., 2008. Environmental quality index for the Hong Kong hotel sector. Tourism Economics 14 (4), 857–870.

Chan, W.W., Ho, K., 2006. Hotels' environmental management systems (ISO 14001): creative financing strategy. International Journal of Contemporary Hospitality Management 18 (4), 302–316.

Chatziathanassiou, A., Mavrogiorgos, D., Sioulas, K., 2004. Environmental initiatives in the hotel sector in Greece: case study of the 'Green Flags' project. In: Bramwell, B. (Ed.), Coastal Mass Tourism: Diversification and Sustainable Development in Southern Europe. Channel View, Clevedon, UK, pp. 249–268.

Clark, T., Gill, A., Hartmann, R., 2006. Mountain Resort Planning and Development in an Era of Globalization. Cognizant, New York.

Cummings, L.E., 1997. Waste management supporting urban tourism sustainability: a mega-resort case study. Journal of Sustainable Tourism 5 (2), 93–108.

Curtis, I.A., 2002. Environmentally sustainable tourism: a case for carbon trading at Northern Queensland hotels and resorts. Australian Journal of Environmental Management 9 (1), 27–36.

Dale, J.C., Kluga, T., 1992. Energy conservation more than a good idea. Cornell Hotel and Restaurant Administration Quarterly 33 (6), 30–35.

Dalton, G.J., Lockington, D.A., Baldock, T.E., 2008. A survey of tourist attitudes to renewable energy supply in Australian hotel accommodation. Renewable Energy 33 (10), 2174–2185.

Dalton, G.J., Lockington, D.A., Baldock, T.E., 2008. Feasibility analysis of stand-alone renewable energy supply options for a large hotel. Renewable Energy 33 (7), 1475–1490.

Enz, C.A., Siguaw, J.A., 1999. Best hotel environmental practices. Cornell Hotel and Restaurant Administration Quarterly 40 (5), 72–77.

Enz, C.A., Siguaw, J.A., 2003. Revisiting the best of the best: innovations in hotel practice. Cornell Hotel and Restaurant Administration Quarterly 44 (5/6), 115–123.

Erdogan, N., Baris, E., 2007. Environmental protection programs and conservation practices of hotels in Ankara, Turkey. Tourism Management 28 (2), 604–614.

Essex, S., Ken, M., Newnham, R., 2004. Tourism development in Mallorca: is water supply a constraint? Journal of Sustainable Tourism 12 (1), 4–28.

Fennell, D., 2007. Ecotourism, 3rd Edn. Routledge, London.

Goldstein, N.J., Griskevicius, V., Cialdini, R.B., 2007. Invoking social norms: a social psychology perspective on improving hotels' linen-reuse programs. Cornell Hotel and Restaurant Administration Quarterly 48 (2), 145–150.

Goldstein, N.J., Cialdini, R.B., Griskevicius, V., 2008. A room with a viewpoint: using social norms to motivate environmental conservation in hotels. Journal of Consumer Research 35 (3), 472–482.

González, M., León, C.J., 2001. The adoption of environmental innovations in the hotel industry of Gran Canaria. Tourism Economics 7 (2), 177–190.

Haden, L., 2007. Tourism and climate change. Travel and Tourism Analyst 1, 1–37.

Harrell, H., Chon, K.S., 1997. Hotel and resort industry trends in Asia-Pacific. In: Oppermann, M. (Ed.), Pacific Rim Tourism. CABI, Wallingford, UK, pp. 45–59.

Heung, V.C.S., Fei, C., Hu, C., 2006. Customer and employee perception of a green hotel—the case of five-star hotels in China. China Tourism Research 2 (3), 246–297.

Honey, M., 1999. Ecotourism and Sustainable Development. Who Owns Paradise? Island Press, Washington, DC.

International Hotels Environment Initiative, 1993. Environmental Management for Hotels: The Industry Guide to Best Practice. Butterworth, Oxford. Heinemann.

Iwanowski, K., Rushmore, S., 1994. Introducing the eco-friendly hotel. Cornell Hotel and Restaurant Administration Quarterly 35 (1), 34–38.

Johnson, C., 2002. Sustainable development in the hotel industry. Travel and Tourism Analyst 5, 3.1–3.24.

Lambert, J., 2001. Making tourism sustainable in the Maldives. Hospitality Review 3 (2), 22–29.

Manaktola, K., Jauhari, V., 2007. Exploring consumer attitude and behaviour towards green practices in the lodging industry in India. International Journal of Contemporary Hospitality Management 19 (5), 364–377.

Meade, B., Pringle, J., 2001. Environmental management systems for Caribbean hotels and resorts: a case study of five properties in Jamaica. Journal of Quality Assurance in Hospitality and Tourism 2 (3/4), 149–159.

Markandya, A., Harou, P., Bellu, L., Cistulli, V., 2002. Environmental Economics for Sustainable Growth: A Handbook for Practitioners. Edward Elgar, Cheltenham.

O'Malley, M., 2001. Energy management helps profits and the environment. Hotel and Catering Review 34 (5), 27–28.

Palmer, T., Riera, A., 2003. Tourism and environmental taxes, with special reference to the "Balearic ecotax. Tourism Management 24 (6), 665–674.

Revilla, G., Dodd, T.H., Hoover, L.C., 2001. Environmental tactics used by hotel companies in Mexico. International Journal of Hospitality and Tourism Administration 1 (3/4), 111–127.

Scanion, N.L., 2007. An analysis and assessment of environmental operating practices in hotel and resort properties. International Journal of Hospitality Management 26 (3), 711–723.

Schultz, W.P., Khazian, A.M., Zaleski, A.C., 2008. Using normative social influence to promote conservation among hotel guests. Social Influence 3 (1), 4–23.

Shiming, D., Burnett, J., 2002. Energy use and management in hotels in Hong Kong. International Journal of Hospitality Management 21 (4), 371–380.

Stipanuk, D.M., 1996. The US lodging industry and the environment. Cornell Hotel and Restaurant Administration Quarterly 37 (5), 39–45.

Swarbrooke, J., 1999. Sustainable Tourism Management. CAB International, Wallingford, UK.

Tzschentke, N., Kirk, D., Lynch, P., 2008. Ahead of their time? Barriers to action in green tourism firms. Service Industries Journal 28 (1/2), 167–178.

Tzschentke, N., Kirk, D., Lynch, P., 2008. Going green: decisional factors in small hospitality operations. International Journal of Hospitality Management 27 (1), 126–133.

Warnken, J., Bradley, M., Guilding, C., 2005. Eco-resorts vs. mainstream accommodation providers: an investigation of the viability of benchmarking environmental performance. Tourism Management 26 (3), 367–379.

Wei, S., Ruys, H., 1999. Managers' perceptions of environmental issues in Australian hotels. Australian Journal of Environmental Management 6 (2), 78–85.

White, C., Hill, N., 2002. How green are your guests? Hospitality Review 4 (2), 50–55.

Zhong, L.S., Buckley, R., Xie, T., 2007. Chinese perspectives on tourism eco-certification. Annals of Tourism Research 34 (3), 808–811.

USEFUL INTERNET RESOURCES

Ecotel Certification: http://www.concepthospitality.com/ecotel/ECOTEL.htm
Environmentally Friendly Hotels: http://environmentallyfriendlyhotels.com/
'Green' Hotels' Association: http://www.greenhotels.com/grntrav.htm
International Ecotourism Society: http://www.ecotourism.org
Rues Ecofriendly Hotels Worldwide: http://www.ecofriendlyhotelsrhs.com/
The Green Restaurant Association: http://www.dinegreen.com/
U.S. Green Building Council: http://www.usgbc.org/DisplayPage.aspx?CategoryID=19

CHAPTER 7

Safety and Security Issues in a Globalizing World

INTRODUCTION

In today's frenetic and unpredictable world, people's concerns about personal safety are becoming more acute; this is especially the case in the context of travel. Tourism is one of the most volatile economic sectors in the world today. Even the slightest reference to political unrest, crime, sickness, natural calamities, or economic decline sends tourist arrivals plummeting, puts thousands of people out of work, and puts a grinding halt on the economic engines of many small or developing countries and tourism-dependent destinations.

Safety and security are paramount in the minds of the traveling public and therefore also in the minds of destination planners and lodging managers. From a destination perspective, tourists' most pressing and consistent concerns relate to general feelings of safety in the destination, food and drinking water hygiene, access to emergency care if needed, feeling secure at attractions and night spots, not being harassed by vendors or prostitution touts, being able to drive safely in a place that is different from home, feeling secure in their accommodations, and safely traveling to, within, and from the destination.

From a lodging perspective, guests' primary concerns focus on theft from their rooms while they are out (by employees, other guests, or outsiders), a property secured from ill-willed intruders, insecure balconies, elevators breaking down, inadequate fire escapes and exits, smoking in non-smoking rooms, prostitution and drugs, bathroom and toilet hygiene, muggings or armed robberies, pool safety, wet floors, food security, and terrorist attacks—primarily in the context of large hotel or resort properties.

The issue of security and safety has grown in importance for property managers in recent years as urban crime rates have grown, rumors spread about the potential for deadly air-borne diseases in enclosed spaces, such as

CONTENTS

Introduction

Accidents

Sickness and Disease

Terrorism

Crime

Disasters

Destination Responses

Institutional Responses

Summary and Conclusion

References

Further Reading

Useful Internet Resources

hotels and resorts, and threats of terrorism have become more of a reality, sometimes targeting tourism, such as the November 2008 terrorist attacks on two hotels in Mumbai, India, and other recent tourist-centered attacks at hotels and restaurants in Indonesia and Egypt.

This chapter examines some of the issues related to tourist safety in the context of accommodation and looks at how destinations and properties respond to various crises to protect their guests and employees.

ACCIDENTS

Accidents involving tourists are a common scenario in destinations and typically involve car accidents, adventure-related incidents (e.g. skydiving, river rafting, mountain climbing, and skiing), and personal mishaps (e.g. falling). When accidents happen too often, the image of a destination can be tainted and labeled as unsafe. The most common type of accommodation involved in the most serious accidents is the ski resort. Ski resort managers have for a long time had to deal with skiing accidents and the emergency responses that go along with them. In cases like this, the general public realizes that mishaps are more the fault of the guest him/herself and typically do not blame the resort. However, when accidents happen in non-ski establishments, such as beach resorts, hotels, motels, and guesthouses, the property is often blamed and suspicion develops related to safety code violations and structural unsoundness. At non-ski lodging facilities the most common accidents include people falling down stairs, tumbling from balconies or rooftops, slipping on wet floors, or being hurt in pool and dining areas. Novelty lodging, discussed later in Chapter 15, faces unique problems, such as ice hotels dealing with slippery surfaces and cold air temperatures, wild creatures intruding in ecolodges, or guests falling from tree house lodges.

SICKNESS AND DISEASE

As already noted, sicknesses can easily spread through lodging facilities because of their enclosed nature and the close proximity of guests. Cruise ships are especially prone to this problem because of people's inability to leave the ship away from ports of call and the relatively crowded spaces involved. Many accounts exist of illnesses spreading through cruise ships quickly, ruining hundreds of people's vacation experience and smearing the image of the cruise company. Lodging facilities, including cruise ships, take special care in sanitizing rooms and common areas, but there is always a chance for sicknesses to develop and spread from room to room and from guest to guest. Unfortunately, isolated instances of illness in hotels or cruise ships often defiles an otherwise hygienic establishment, requiring extra counter-marketing efforts to re-establish a previous image. Due to incubation periods of some illnesses, it is possible for some guests to actually bring conditions to hotels and cruise ships and transmit them to others. The Center for Disease Control and Prevention (CDC) of the United States works closely with cruise lines to monitor such outbreaks. Guests dining in restaurants at destinations have also been known to have been exposed to health conditions outside their hotels but actually attributing their conditions to their lodging facilities.

One of the more pressing concerns today is food safety, which can range from properly washed and cooked foods to food-related terrorism. Until the 1990s, global security was concerned mostly with nuclear weapons and war. However, with the end of the Cold War and increased threats of terrorism in the world today, security concerns have broadened considerably into what Hall et al. (2003) refer to as the New Security Agenda. This new agenda encompasses a far more inclusive view of security, arguing that poverty, economic instability, human rights, the environment, food, and water are equally crucial security concerns as are wars and nuclear proliferation. Of particular concern here is food and water security. While this can refer to broad concepts like sustainable development and draught, it can also include matters such as bioterrorism and food poisoning.

There are many examples of hotels and restaurants being shut down permanently or temporarily because of health code violations. On a broader scale, however, it is now fairly common to see regional problems in the hospitality sector related to food security. In the United States in recent years, there have been some serious health-related concerns in the hospitality and tourism sectors in relation to food. In the late 1990s, severe outbreaks of Hepatitis A in people who ate strawberries imported from Mexico created a flurry of controversy and a lot of sick supermarket and restaurant customers. In 2003 and 2006, dozens of cases of *E. coli* illnesses were reported in more than half of the US states. The sickness, apparently, originated in raw spinach. More recently, in May–June 2008, contaminated tomatoes caused a rapid spread of salmonella poisonings in the United States. Restaurants and supermarkets throughout the country refused to sell or serve tomatoes for several weeks out of fear of poisoning their customers.

On a more mundane level, tourists regularly experience travelers' diarrhea, particularly when they travel to places where hygiene conditions are different from those at home and where their immune systems are unable to cope with the bacteria associated with certain foods and drinking water. According to one study (Torres and Skillicorn, 2004), one third of travelers to Cancun, Mexico, reported experiencing diarrhea. The study also recommends that relationships should be created with local farmers to produce a supply of fresh products that are suitable for international tourist consumption. Other studies have demonstrated where this has been done successfully, benefiting local farmers and fishermen, but also protecting the hotel guests and hotels. Training is also important, and most lodging establishments need to train their staff regarding food handling and preparation techniques.

TERRORISM

Terrorism, or the use of intimidation and fear to force a group's political will, is unfortunately becoming more commonplace in the modern world. Hostage-taking, murders, and mass destruction of property and people are common manifestations today. Tourism is powerfully affected by terrorism in a number of ways. With acts of terrorism comes a halt to nearly all tourist activity in the destination where the violence took place. This can vary from place to place, however, depending on the public perception about the temporariness or rarity of the attack. In some cases, such as September 11, 2001, immediately following the attacks on the World Trade Center, tourists began arriving, hoping to catch a glimpse of the destruction. It is unlikely that in places more prone to terrorism would experience this type of response.

Another way terrorism affects tourism is a general halt in international travel. Violence in one country affects tourist arrivals in neighboring countries and in fact reduces international travel overall for temporary periods of time. This is so for two reasons: a general fear among the public for their safety and a reluctance to spend money on leisure pursuits like travel, as terrorism usually spells economic problems as well. While there is a general avoidance mentality associated with tourists and terrorism, many people simply change their destinations or elect to stay in their own home countries for their holidays.

Perhaps the most urgent issue for this book is terrorist attacks that target tourism, especially hotels and resorts. In general, the intension of terrorists is not to strike small-scale accommodation such as bed and breakfasts, youth hostels, or rural motels, although this is known to have happened. Instead, their declared objective is to destroy as many people as possible, which means that they tend to target large hotels or resorts and busy restaurants, although campgrounds have in the past also been targets for terrorists. Egypt appears to be particularly prone to terrorist attacks on tourists (because of its economic dependence on tourism), as several mass assails against tourists have taken place there since the 1990s. In October 2004, 34 people were killed and 171 were injured in attacks on the Taba Hilton, in Egypt, and at a nearby campground where Israelis were staying. In July 2005, 88 people were killed and 150 wounded in the Egyptian resort town of Sham al-Sheikh, where terrorists bombed one hotel directly and the car park of another nearby hotel. In 2006, bombs also exploded in a busy restaurant area of the Egyptian resort town of Dahab where 23 people were killed and some 80 people wounded.

The terror assaults on the tourism infrastructure of Mumbai, India, during November 26–29, 2008, are particularly remarkable and recent. Approximately 173 people were killed, including many foreign tourists, and more than 300 were hurt when Pakistani terrorists stormed the Taj Mahal Hotel and the Oberoi Trident Hotel with machine guns and grenades. Hostages were taken and many were shot or killed by the exploding grenades. Months later, the city and all of India are trying to recover. The hotel properties are being repaired.

CRIME

In more everyday situations, travelers are concerned about their own personal security and the security of their possessions. Most lodging-related crimes are associated with theft of money and valuables from guest rooms by employees, other guests, or intruders. Many accounts have been recorded about this situation, which ruins holiday trips for tourists and again paints a negative picture of an accommodation property. Pick pocketing and other petty crimes are not uncommon either, particularly purse-snatching in busy common areas, such as restaurants or entertainment venues.

Violent crimes are also an unfortunate part of lodging life and managers must be trained about how to deal with rapes, murders, and armed robbery. Front-desk robberies in large establishments take place, although they are diminishing with general knowledge that stays are typically paid online or by credit card rather than cash. Smaller establishments, which might have more cash on hand, in some cases, are more prone to robbery. Prostitution is another concern for many hotel managers, but such behavior is very difficult to monitor, prove, and report.

One form of crime threat that is becoming more important in today's technologically advanced world is computer hacking and Internet fraud.

Many lodging properties, particularly smaller ones, lack sufficient security mechanisms to protect their own systems and those of their guests.

DISASTERS

Natural disasters tend not to have the same long-term negative implications for destinations the way human-induced crises do. Recovery from natural calamities is much quicker, and tourists realize that Mother Nature is very different from intentional acts targeting tourists specifically. Of course, this can vary for the residents who can endure the impacts of natural disasters long after the hotel guests have left their holiday destination.

One of the most notorious disasters in recent years was the tsunami of December 26, 2004, which killed more than 230 000 people in South Asia, Southeast Asia, and Africa. Many of the dead were foreign tourists spending their December holidays at beach resorts. It was reportedly the worst tsunami in recorded history, caused by one of the worst earthquakes in history. Unfortunately, many of the coastal hotels and resorts in countries like Thailand, Indonesia, and Sri Lanka were ill-prepared for a disaster of such a magnitude. Safety and rescue plans were lacking, and many were structurally unsound.

Hurricanes are also prevalent in the Caribbean, one of the most tourism-dependent regions of the world. Every year, thousands of homes and buildings, including hotels and resorts, are destroyed or damaged by onslaughts of these storms, causing millions of dollars in damage to the countries' infrastructure and to the tourism infrastructure, including ports, airports, and hotels. Hurricanes are especially devastating in the Caribbean region owing to the small size of the islands and their economies and populations. Their overdependence on tourism often leads to additional unemployment and struggles to recover from the devastation of the storms. In September 2004, Hurricane Ivan, one of the most devastating in Caribbean history, hit the small island country of Grenada, killing 39 people and causing more than a billion dollars in damage. Much of the harm included hotels, resorts, and guesthouses. Tourism to Grenada essentially ceased for the next year, thereby perpetuating the underdeveloped nature of the island country even further. It has taken Grenada several years to recover from Hurricane Ivan, although it still has not fully recovered.

Fires are another type of disaster, but are often human induced. For instance, a passenger cigarette started a fire in 2006 that destroyed 100 cabins on a cruise ship before it was extinguished on the Caribbean Sea between the Cayman Islands and Jamaica. The fire exacted approximately

$400 million in damage, and one person was killed. Fires on cruise ships occasionally appear in the media; most are caused by mechanical malfunctions, although human error is not an uncommon trigger. Fires are always a potential danger at lodging facilities everywhere, and it is crucial that sound emergency plans, employee training, and fire escapes are in place to assure the safety of guests and employees.

DESTINATION RESPONSES

Unfortunately, it typically takes a disaster to make destinations disaster-ready, resulting in emergency situations that are more reactive than proactive. Even then, many do not learn from previous mistakes. Extensive research shows that the type of government and destination response to crises of every form will influence the recovery rate. Immediate government responses usually include maintaining order and rule of law, implementing security controls, offering disaster relief, and trying to reduce negative images of the destination. In the long term, disaster responses almost always include adopting or changing policies that address security and provide monetary help to the people most affected by the conflict or disaster. Tourist destinations and lodging establishments that have crisis plans in place are more able to recover quickly by re-establishing their image and restoring customer confidence.

Various scholars and security specialists have identified strategies that assist destinations in managing crises. The most common approaches to recovery are information dissemination, publicity and marketing, public relations endeavors, and post-crisis analysis (Timothy, 2006). Efforts should be made to counteract the negative and often over-exaggerated media reports, which often depict situations more direly that they actually are. Information dissemination is key in allowing destinations to give accurate and honest reports about what has happened. Likewise, aggressive marketing is useful to help console potential visitors and promote image recovery. Post-crisis promotions often include special prices and package deals, familiarization tours for travel professionals, financial support for the industry, product reorienting, and intense advertising campaigns to mitigate negative images. Many destinations have undergone these types of promotional campaigns to counteract the effects of diseases, natural disasters, and human-induced crises. It is a mistake, however, to assume that all problems and all destinations should be treated the same; each situation requires different rates of recovery and different marketing sensitivities. Public relations actions should be implemented during and immediately following the crisis to inform the public that life will go on and that the destination is an attractive holiday option that is open for business. Finally, understanding the emergency, how it impacts the destination, and how responses were handled are critical in evaluation the success of the recovery scheme. From this assessment, lessons can be learned about improving policies and action plans in case of future emergencies.

INSTITUTIONAL RESPONSES

Traditionally, accommodation businesses have dealt with guarding property, preventing loss, and safeguarding guests. In recent years, however, as already noted, the security responsibilities of hotels and other lodgings have broadened considerably to include health, information technology security, fire safety, insurance claims, legal issues, and employee disciplinary actions. Responses to safety and security risks have been spotlighted more prominently since the 1990s, accentuated even further by the terrorist attacks of 2001 and those that have followed, with the result that hotels and other establishments have had to adapt appropriately. At one extreme is the issue of emergency response during times of terror. While it is difficult to predict terror attacks on hotels or other disasters, escape plans and security mechanisms should be in place, particularly in large institutions.

Some hospitality specialists have also called for a general requirement that qualifications of accommodation managers should include crisis preparation and management skills and training. Large properties usually have a security department with a trained security manager who oversees building safety, fire safety, Internet security, first aid, law enforcement, emergency drills and training, insurance claims and legal matters, and safety budgets. In motels, bed and breakfasts, and other small businesses, security duty typically falls under the direction of the owner or general manager.

During mega-disasters, such as September 11, 2001, there is a typical pattern and set of expectations of service sector businesses, because they are valued members of the community where they are located. The first response of hotels and restaurants usually is, and ought to be, to take immediate actions that would be most beneficial in caring for victims of the crisis. New York in 2001 provides a good example of ways that sudden large-scale disasters can be handled by the service industries. Appropriately, hoteliers' and restaurateurs' first response was to provide shelter, water, toilets, food, telephones, and personal comfort to people in shock or physically injured. This included fire fighters and police officers. Their responses to employees were to assure them that their jobs were secure; many companies even operated at a loss or at a very low profit margin to enable their staff members to remain employed. Other positive responses included reducing prices and rates, donating meals, changing menu selections, altering the indoor ambiance, and evaluating the needs of the community. To remain operational, many hotels and restaurants lowered their prices to encourage the public to continue supporting their services.

Given the plethora of media-engaging disasters of recent years in tourism destinations, there has been additional scrutiny on the part of communities and hotels regarding planning and permitting for construction. Design flaws, as many disasters illustrate, can lead to significant loss of life in disaster situations, as they did during the 2004 tsunami in Southeast Asia. Design flaws not only sacrificed the structural integrity of the buildings, they also impeded rescue efforts in some places for many days. Unfortunately, many places in the world have overly relaxed building codes and safety requirements, and even more unfortunate is international companies' taking advantage of these relaxed laws to construct less-than-secure hotels and resort buildings that probably would not pass inspection in the countries where the companies are based. Nonetheless, many large multinationals are adopting standardized policies regarding structural design and safety features. More of these standardized systems need to be adopted worldwide.

Concerns about the safety of guests and their possessions, as well as liability for mishaps and thefts, are causing many properties to install new forms of security systems that aim either to deter criminal actions or to assist in solving cases once an action has occurred. It is in fact the responsibility of the property to ensure the security of its guests. To augment security, many hotels and cruise companies have installed safes in individual rooms to help guests secure their belongings. This has helped decrease the loss of personal property of tourists and elevated the security status of the companies involved.

As well, electronic card keys have become commonplace during the past 25 years in the lodging sector, because they are seen as more secure than traditional keys. Biometric locks on doors are also being considered by large hotel companies. These mechanisms, which require fingerprints, eye scans, or voice recognition, provide extra security in that only validated users can enter guest rooms or certain common areas. For guests who understand the technology, this is seen as providing an extra sense of security; some of the usual key cards have credit card and personal information programmed in them, which biometrics would eliminate. There is also a convenience factor in that people do not have to worry about losing their key or key card. Critics of these types of locks argue that most guests do not understand the safety capabilities of such technology and do not trust them.

Other security measures that have been operationalized and that are being considered these days include security cameras placed in corridors, parking garages, and common areas; verifying guest IDs at check in; placing first aid kits in guest rooms; requiring guests and visitors to walk through metal detectors and place bags in X-ray machines; hiring more uniformed security guards; safety training for guests; extra safety training for employees; and doing background checks of guests. Not surprisingly, background checks are the most extreme and unpopular suggestion, which security cameras, checking IDs, and providing first aid kits are seen as positive moves in the right direction (Feickert et al., 2006). With child molestations receiving more widespread public exposure in recent years in North America and Europe, most campgrounds, resorts, and cruises are rightfully requiring thorough background checks for all employees that work with children, such as recreation programmers and nursery workers.

Recent research indicates that many guests would be willing to pay more, even substantially more in some cases, for added security measures at their place of accommodation. Thus, there is a calculable economic value attached to margins of safety in the hospitality sector, which is important in evaluating return on investment.

During times of food-based disease crises, such as those mentioned earlier in the chapter, restaurants and hotels should simply elect not to sell the types of foods that are reported to be contaminated, such as spinach, tomatoes, or strawberries. This is a wise action in today's litigious western society, for even if the supplier/grower is at fault, the vendor or seller (i.e. restaurant or supermarket) is the one responsible for the ensuing epidemic. To avoid food-based illnesses, many resorts and large hotels in the developing world order food from overseas because it is considered more sanitary than locally produced vegetables, fruits, meats, and fish. This approach has received considerable criticism from a sustainable development perspective, suggesting the more local products need to be used rather than relying on imports.

SUMMARY AND CONCLUSION

This chapter has examined some of the safety and security issues that relate to tourism. While the focus is on the accommodations and lodging sector, the issues permeate the whole tourism industry. Safety and security issues can affect the perception, motivation, decision-making process, and travel outcome of potential visitors. For example, psychocentric visitors (those that are more inclined to desire the comforts of home and who are less adventuresome) may avoid tropical or developing destinations that require vaccinations, or that have mosquitoes and other insects, even if the hotels provide mosquito nets. Similarly, they may avoid areas with high incidence of HIV/AIDS since the blood supply may not be secure, in case they were involved in an accident, get sick, or need a blood transfusion. In most developed countries, workers in food and beverage establishments are tested for medical conditions such as TB and are required to wear gloves during food preparation, and the establishments are inspected regularly. Those in violation are penalized or closed down. Such is not the situation in many tourism destinations in the developing world. This can also limit the economic linkages that could be developed between tourism and the agricultural sector. For example, cruise lines that operate in the Caribbean, Central and South America stop at destinations in countries that cultivate produce fruits, vegetables, sugar, coffee, and seafood that are consumed on the ships. They also manufacture fruit and alcoholic beverages. However, the cruise companies operating in the Caribbean region purchase between 80 and 95% of their food supplies from the United States in an effort to meet the standards established by the US Food and Drug Administration (FDA) for food safety. Ironically, some of the pineapples, bananas, oranges, coffee, and rum served on the ships are produced and imported from the countries being visited.

There is always an element of danger involved in travel: transportation accidents, and those from bungee jumping, sky or scuba diving, natural disasters, and many others that have been discussed in this chapter. Travelers can purchase comprehensive travel insurance to protect themselves against any unforeseen and unfortunate incidents and accidents. But as this chapter has shown, destination governments and accommodation service providers need to have policies and strategies in place to prevent, minimize, and manage these critical safety and security issues that can affect or even debilitate their tourism industries.

REFERENCES

Feickert, J., Verma, R., Plaschka, G., Dev, C.S., 2006. Safeguarding your customers: the guest's view of hotel security. Cornell Hotel and Restaurant Administration Quarterly 47 (3), 224–244.

Hall, C.M., Timothy, D.J., Duval, D.T., 2003. Security and tourism: towards a new understanding? Journal of Travel and Tourism Marketing 15 (2/3), 1–18.

Timothy, D.J., 2006. Safety and security issues in tourism. In: Buhalis, D., Costa, C. (Eds.), Tourism Management Dynamics: Trends, Management and Tools. Butterworth-Heinemann, Oxford, pp. 19–27.

Torres, R., Skillicorn, P., 2004. Montezuma's revenge—how sanitation concerns may injure Mexico's tourist industry. Cornell Hotel and Restaurant Administration Quarterly 45 (2), 132–144.

FURTHER READING

Beirman, D., 2003. Restoring tourism destinations in crisis: a strategic marketing approach. Allen & Unwin, Sydney.

Bently, T.A., Page, S.J., 2001. Scoping the extent of adventure tourism accidents. Annals of Tourism Research 28, 705–726.

Blake, A., Sinclair, M.T., 2003. Tourism crisis management: US response to September 11. Annals of Tourism Research 30, 813–832.

Canally, C., Timothy, D.J., 2007. Perceived constraints to travel across the US-Mexico border among American University Students. International Journal of Tourism Research 9 (6), 423–437.

Carlsen, J.C., Hughes, M., 2007. Tourism market recovery in the Maldives after the 2004 Indian Ocean tsunami. Journal of Travel and Tourism Marketing 23 (2), 139–149.

Čavrak, V., 2004. Traffic safety and tourism development. Acta Turistica 16 (1), 31–63.

Chen, J.S., Ekinci, Y., Riley, M., Yoon, Y., Tjelflaat, S., 2001. What do Norwegians think of US lodging services? International Journal of Contemporary Hospitality Management 13 (6), 280–284.

Chesney-Lind, M., Lind, I.Y., 1986. Visitors as victims: crimes against tourists in Hawaii. Annals of Tourism Research 13, 167–191.

Cheung, C., Law, R., 2006. How can hotel guests be protected during the occurrence of a tsunami? Asia Pacific Journal of Tourism Research 11 (3), 289–295.

Coles, T., 2003. A local reading of a global disaster: some lessons on tourism management from an annus horribilis in south west England. Journal of Travel and Tourism Marketing 15 (2/3), 173–197.

de Albuquerque, K., McElroy, J., 1999. Tourism and crime in the Caribbean. Annals of Tourism Research 26 (4), 968–984.

Duncan, T., 2005. Current issues in the global hospitality industry. Tourism and Hospitality Research 5 (4), 359–366.

Enz, C.A., Taylor, M.S., 2002. The safety and security of U.S. hotels: a post-September 11 report. Cornell Hotel and Restaurant Administration Quarterly 43 (5), 119–136.

Faulkner, B., 2001. Towards a framework for tourism disaster management. Tourism Management 22, 135–147.

Feickert, J., Verma, R., Plaschka, G., Dev, C.S., 2006. Safeguarding your customers: the guest's view of hotel security. Cornell Hotel and Restaurant Administration Quarterly 47 (3), 224–244.

Floyd, M.F., Gibson, H., Pennington-Gray, L., Thapa, B., 2003. The effect of risk perceptions on intensions to travel in the aftermath of September 11, 2001. Journal of Travel and Tourism Marketing 15 (2/3), 19–38.

Fujii, E.T., Mak, J., 1980. Tourism and crime: implications fro regional development policy. Regional Studies 14, 27–36.

Garcia, R., Lau, S.Y.S., Chau, K.W., Kanitpun, R., Shimatsu, Y., Grunder, P., Koo, R., Baharuddin, 2006. Sustainable resorts: learning from the 2004 tsunami. Disaster Prevention and Management 15 (3), 429–447.

Gill, M., Moon, C., Seaman, P., Turbin, V., 2002. Security management and crime in hotels. International Journal of Contemporary Hospitality Management 14 (2), 58–64.

Goodrich, J.N., 2002. September 11, 2001 attack on America: a record of the immediate impacts and reactions in the USA travel and tourism industry. Tourism Management 23, 573–580.

Goh, C.K.L., Law, R., 2007. Applying the "cloak of invisibility" technology to security and privacy in the hotel industry. International Journal of Contemporary Hospitality Management 19 (7), 600–605.

Green, C.G., Bartholomew, P., Murrmann, S., 2003. New York restaurant industry: strategic responses to September 11, 2001. Journal of Travel and Tourism Marketing 15 (2/3), 63–79.

Groenenboom, K., Jones, P., 2003. Issues of security in hotels. International Journal of Contemporary Hospitality Management 15 (1), 14–19.

Hall, C.M., 2002. Travel safety, terrorism and the media: the significance of the issue-attention cycle. Current Issues in Tourism 5 (5), 458–466.

Hall, C.M., Timothy, D.J., Duval, D.T., 2003. Safety and security in tourism: relationships, management and marketing. Haworth, New York.

Hughes, D., 1984. Guide to hotel security. Ashgate, Aldershot.

Ioannides, D., Apostolopoulos, Y., 1999. Political instability, war and tourism in Cyprus: effects, management and prospects for recovery. Journal of Travel Research 38 (1), 51–56.

Kim, J.S., Brewer, P., Bernhard, B., 2008. Hotel customer perceptions of biometric door locks: convenience and security factors. Journal of Hospitality and Leisure Marketing 17 (1/2), 162–183.

Knowles, T., 2001. Trends in food safety: implications for European hotels. International Journal of Contemporary Hospitality Management 13 (4/5), 176–182.

Lazarus, B.I., Kaufman, J.E., 1988. Five hotel safety procedures and special guests. Hospitality Education and Research Journal 12 (2), 215–222.

MacLaurin, T.L., 2003. The importance of food safety in travel planning and destination selection. Journal of Travel and Tourism Marketing 15 (4), 233–257.

Mansfeld, Y., Pizam, A., 2006. Tourism, security and safety: from theory to practice. Butteworth-Heinemann, Oxford.

Mariner, T., 1995. Facing the security challenge. Bottomline 10 (4), 36–41.

McKercher, B., Hui, E.L.L., 2003. Terrorism, economic uncertainty and outbound travel from Hong Kong. Journal of Travel and Tourism Marketing 15 (2/3), 99–115.

Ogle, J., Wagner, E.L., Talbert, M.P., 2008. Hotel network security: a study of computer networks in U.S. hotels. Cornell Hospitality Report 8 (15), 4–20.

Olsen, M.D., 1996. Events shaping the future and their impact on the multinational hotel industry. Tourism Recreation Research 21 (2), 7–14.

Palmer, R.A., 1989. The hospitality customer as crime victim: recent legal research. Hospitality Education and Research Journal 13 (3), 225–229.

Peters, M., Pikkemaat, B., 2005. Crisis management in Alpine winter sports resorts—the 1999 avalanche disaster in Tyrol. Journal of Travel and Tourism Marketing 19 (2/3), 9–20.

Pinhey, T.K., Iverson, T.J., 1994. Safety concerns of Japanese visitors to Guam. Journal of Travel and Tourism Marketing 3 (2), 87–94.

Pizam, A., 1999. A comprehensive approach to classifying acts of crime and violence at tourism destinations. Journal of Travel Research 38 (1), 5–12.

Pizam, A., Mansfeld, Y., 1996. Tourism, crime and international security issues. Wiley, Chichester.

Pizam, A., Tarlow, P., Bloom, J., 1997. Making tourists feel safe: whose responsibility is it? Journal of Travel Research 36 (1), 23–28.

Poon, W.C., Low, L.T.K., 2005. Are travellers satisfied with Malaysian hotels? International Journal of Contemporary Hospitality Management 17 (3), 217–227.

Prideaux, B., 2003. The need to use disaster planning frameworks to respond to major tourism disasters: analysis of Australia's response to tourism disasters in 2001. Journal of Travel and Tourism Marketing 15 (4), 281–298.

Ritchie, B.W., Dorrell, H., Miller, D., Miller, G.A., 2003. Crisis communication and recovery for the tourism industry: lessons from the 2001 foot and mouth disease outbreak in the United Kingdom. Journal of Travel and Tourism Marketing 15 (2/3), 199–216.

Saied, J., 1990. Approaches to risk management. Cornell Hotel and Restaurant Administration Quarterly 31 (2), 45–55.

Santana, G., 2003. Crisis management and tourism: beyond the rhetoric. Journal of Travel and Tourism Marketing 15 (4), 299–321.

Sharma, A., Upneja, A., 2005. Factors influencing financial performance of small hotels in Tanzania. International Journal of Contemporary Hospitality Management 17 (6), 504–515.

Sheridan, S.B., Ellis, R.C., 1996. Current and future trends of security and fire protection technologies in the hospitality industry. Tourism Recreation Research 21 (2), 45–51.

Soemodinoto, A., Wong, P., Saleh, M., 2001. Effect of prolonged political unrest on tourism. Annals of Tourism Research 28, 1056–1060.

Sönmez, S., 1998. Tourism, terrorism, and political instability. Annals of Tourism Research 25 (2), 416–456.

Sönmez, S., Apostolopoulos, Y., Tarlow, P., 1999. Tourism in crisis: managing the effects of terrorism. Journal of Travel Research 38 (1), 13–18.

Stutts, A.T., Wortman, J., 2005. Hotel and lodging management: an introduction. Wiley, Chichester.

Tarlow, P., 2006. Disaster management: exploring ways to mitigate disasters before they occur. Tourism Review International 10 (1/2), 17–25.

Teye, V.B., 1988. Coups d'etat and African tourism: a study of Ghana. Annals of Tourism Research 15, 329–356.

Timothy, D.J., 2006. Safety and security issues in tourism. In: Buhalis, D., Costa, C. (Eds.), Tourism Management Dynamics: Trends, Management and Tools. Butterworth-Heinemann, Oxford, pp. 19–27.

Tranter, M., 2004. Occupational health and safety risks and management issues in the hotel and fast-food sectors. In: D'Annunzio-Green, N., Maxwell, G.A., Watson, S. (Eds.), Human Resource Management: International Perspectives in Hospitality and Tourism. Cengage Learning, Boston, pp. 174–185.

Weaver, P.A., Heung, C.O., 1993. Do American business travellers have different hotel service requirements? International Journal of Contemporary Hospitality Management 5 (3), 16–21.

Wilks, J., Page, S., 2003. Managing tourist health and safety in the new millennium. Elsevier, Amsterdam.

Wilks, J., Pendergast, D., Leggat, P.A., 2006. Tourism in turbulent times: towards safe experiences for visitors. Elsevier, Amsterdam.

World Tourism Organization, 1996. Tourist safety and security: practical measures for destinations. UNWTO, Madrid.

USEFUL INTERNET RESOURCES

Arizona Tourism Safety and Security Conference: http://www.aztourismsafety.com/displayconvention.cfm.

Centers for Disease Control and Prevention, Travelers' Health: http://wwwn.cdc.gov/travel/default.aspx.

Food Safety and Tourism: http://www.4hoteliers.com/4hots_fshw.php?mwi=3446.

Global Risk Management Services: http://www.airsecurity.com/.

Hotel Motel Security: http://www.crimedoctor.com/hotel.htm.

Travel Health Online: https://www.tripprep.com/scripts/main/default.asp.

CHAPTER 8

Food and Beverage Services, Gaming, and Conferences

INTRODUCTION

There are several ancillary services associated with lodging establishments that make a significant contribution to the guest's experience. Among these are food services, gaming, and conferences. These services and their related facilities have become an integral part of the lodging experience in many parts of the world. Cuisine is often cited as one of the highlights of people's holiday experiences, and there are many well-established gastronomical destinations where food not only contributes to the dining experience but underlies much of the region's cultural heritage.

Legalized gambling is becoming more widespread, even in places where it traditionally has been outlawed. Conferences, conventions, and other meetings-related tourism are also on the increase, with many hotels and resorts beginning to cater more specifically to the needs of this sector. While the most common popular tourist destinations have long been important venues for meetings, incentives, conferences, and exhibitions (MICE) tourism, newer destinations are in the process of becoming important conference venues, and many older destinations are re-inventing themselves through conferences and other MICE-based tourism initiatives. This chapter aims to address some of the issues and trends surrounding the food and beverage aspects of the tourism and accommodations experience, as well as the ways in which gaming and conference-based tourism affect the lodging sector.

CONTENTS

Introduction

Food and Beverages

Gaming

Conferences and Conventions

Summary and Conclusion

References

Further Reading

Useful Internet Resources

FOOD AND BEVERAGES

Although typically less than one quarter of all restaurant revenues derive from tourists' spending (the majority of earnings come from local residents), one of the most important components of a tourist trip is dining. In some cases, such as on cruises or in all-inclusive resorts, food is one of the main attractions. Often the quality of food and drinks can make or break a holiday experience; research studies show that quality of food service is also a direct indicator of visitor satisfaction, with hotel guests being most concerned about food quality, variety, number of dishes available, and value for money. Some destinations in their own right have become well known for local or regional cuisine and utilize gastronomical heritage in their marketing and branding campaigns. Accommodation establishments play a critical role in providing food and beverage (F&B) services to tourists through room service, cafés, restaurants, bars, pubs, and lounges. Many properties rely on the sale of food and beverages for as much as a third of their revenue. Several dining-related issues have risen to prominence in recent years and will be discussed below.

Over the years, various meal plans have evolved to serve different market segments in various parts of the world. For example, the Continental Plan (CP), which was popular in European hotel establishments, is now common in hotels in the United States and other parts of the world. This meal plan provides light breakfast, which includes bread, jam or butter served with tea or coffee for mostly business travelers or overnight guests in transit. The American Plan (AP) provides all three meals for hotel guests who may be on vacation, while the Modified American Plan (MAP) provides two meals, usually breakfast and dinner. This serves the needs of guest such as those on motor coach tours who prefer a good breakfast and relaxing dinner after a day of organized tours or sightseeing. There are other meal plans such as Bed and Breakfast (BB) and the Bermuda Plan (BP), which have all become core product offerings that link hotel room divisions with the food and beverage department. There are a number of benefits to the industry, tourists, and the destinations. First, meal plans provide opportunities for hotels to earn additional revenue. Since tour operators earn commissions on total services booked, they also benefit from the purchase of these plans. Second, meal plans can be convenient for hotel guests, since they can order their meals in advance and request special menus or diets. Finally, meal plans can provide direct linkages with a destination's agricultural sector. This is very important to all destinations but especially so in destinations that offer unique ethnic or traditional cuisine as part of the total tourism experience. For example, a stay at a hotel or resort in Fiji will include a traditional Meke dance with a Lovo dinner that involves cooking a variety of dishes wrapped in leaves underground, similar to a Maori Hangi dinner in New Zealand.

Food services are, together with inns and other age-old lodging establishments, among the earliest elements of travel, as most early inns offered lodging and food and beverages to weary travelers for refreshment and sustenance. Marco Polo, in his thirteenth-century travel accounts, described the Chinese propensity to dine out as early as the thirteenth century in noodle shops, inns, tea houses, and taverns, and early English and European tea houses were often established in conjunction with inns along well-traveled routes and popular coastal areas.

Food services in the tourism sector range from haute cuisine (luxury foods) in expensive restaurants to low-cost street vendors. In between is a wide range of dining options, such as fast-food restaurants, ice cream and coffee shops, bars and pubs, sidewalk cafés, and bakeries. Today, there are millions of food service establishments throughout the world, not including even more very small-scale street vendor-type offerings. In the United States alone, there are more than 945 000 restaurant locations, with sales amounting to approximately $566 billion in 2008 (Table 8.1). Especially relevant to this book is the fact that approximately 5.4% of all restaurant sales took place in lodging-based food service establishments.

Fast food has developed rapidly since the mid-1900s, particularly with the global spread of large companies like McDonalds, Wimpy Burgers, Kentucky Fried Chicken (KFC), Subway, and Burger King (branded as Hungry Jack in Australia). Many American and British fast-food brands have diffused throughout the world, and most tourist destinations boast several of these, not only for residents but also to meet the demands of tourists who often desire the familiar tastes of home. Many international fast-food chains have learned to adapt to local tastes and flavors in an effort to draw customers beyond the tourist crowds. Pizza Hut in Indonesia, for example, offers pizza flavored with peanut sauce and chicken satay. KFC in China has a variety of sweet and sour and spicy chicken options unavailable elsewhere. Israel's

Table 8.1	Restaurant Facts in the United States, 2008–2009
Number of restaurants	More than 945 000
Restaurant sales	Approximately $566 billion
Number of people employed	Approximately 13 million
Number of meals served	More than 70 billion
Percent of commercial restaurant sales in lodging-place restaurants	5.4%
Percentage of the US GDP comprising restaurant sales	4%
Average daily restaurant sales	$1.5 billion

Source: National Restaurant Association (2009).

McDonalds restaurants do not offer cheese on hamburgers because of kosher restrictions on eating meat with dairy products.

Ethnic cuisines have also become popular in the catering mix. Among the most popular ethnic foods throughout the world are Chinese, Italian, Mexican, Thai, French, and Middle Eastern cuisines. It is not uncommon to find popular Thai or Mexican restaurants in remote locations such as Greenland, the Faeroe Islands, Swaziland, or Sierra Leone. While such ethnic restaurants appeal to tourists visiting certain areas, they are also a popular dining option for local residents. Many hotels and resorts have integrated ethnic foods into their menus and buffet tables to add variety to what could otherwise be a fairly mundane assortment of food.

Food trends and issues

Recent decades have seen a growing global concern over healthy eating and sustainable agriculture. Organic foods have become very popular in people's personal lives and in their dining choices while on vacation. As part of this broader movement, in North America, Australia, and Western Europe, a variety of health food stores and organic markets have turned up, and some restaurant menus have been modified to provide healthier alternatives to meet the demands of an increasingly more health-conscious public. Nonetheless, recent research shows that restaurant atmosphere, attractive food displays, eating habits, and personal lifestyle still determine people's dining choices and are still more influential than concerns about personal health (Chen et al., 2008), which has led many food service managers to choose not to include health food options on their menus because of a concern that guests would be critical of such options.

An important part of this notion of sustainable food and healthy eating is the Slow Food movement, which began in the 1980s in Italy in response to the pervasiveness of fast food, which is commonly seen as unhealthy and unsustainable. The movement's goals include producing and preserving heirloom, organic varieties of vegetables and fruits, celebrating indigenous foods, highlighting cuisines that are part of a region's culinary heritage, encouraging ethical buying and growing, producing small-scale and family-operated farms, and discouraging fast-food consumption. The Slow Food movement has become especially popular in Europe and is becoming more so in the United States, Canada, Mexico, Japan, Taiwan, Australia, Argentina, and South Africa. There are many Slow Food groups in these countries, and others are catching on to this unique trend as well. Slow Food restaurants have cropped up in Europe, and many hotel establishments are beginning to offer this alternative cuisine on their restaurant menus.

The focus on food in modern-day tourism has resulted in the establishment of gastronomy/food trails in many areas of the world, as well as wine routes that cater to wine connoisseurs. Places that have become well-established wine destinations, such as California (USA), Ontario (Canada), Australia, Chile, France, Italy, Portugal, Spain, South Africa, and a multitude of other locations, have designated wine routes that involve long distance, but connected, travel between wineries and vineyards, with dining and accommodation facilities highlighting the connectedness of the routes. Food trails have similarly been developed to connect places where food heritage is important and where unique cuisines have developed, such as the Taste of the Tropics Food Trail in Queensland, Australia, and the Isle of Arran Taste Trail in Scotland. Along these trails are bed and breakfast facilities and other lodging businesses that provide traditional foods associated with the cuisine routes of which they are a part.

Although these broader issues are important to the food services sector, other issues also exist on the institutional scale that are equally important. One pressing concern for food service managers is purchasing volume or cover; this must be examined from at least two perspectives: sustainability and budget. One of the primary concerns associated with F&B is how much food and beverage to order to avoid waste and spoilage. This is an especially important task on cruise ships and in resorts where food is always available to consumers. In these situations there is a constant concern regarding the projected amounts of food needed to satisfy the demands of guests and employees, and new ways are constantly being considered by the industry to manage waste and purchasing. While historical food-use data are often used to project future needs, one of the best techniques, as outlined by Thompson and Killam (2008), is to utilize occupancy data. In their study, forecast accuracy improved by more than 11% by using occupancy data rather than historical trends.

Another institutional trend is food outsourcing by hotels. This is very common in the context of national park lodges, where catering services are often operated by non-park entities that have been contracted to provide meals and refreshments to park visitors. Many hotels do essentially the same. It is even becoming more common to find fast food (e.g. McDonalds and Burger King) inside large hotels and casino resorts. Hotels outsource food because it is more cost effective than purchasing food supplies and preparing meals onsite. The practice also allows hotels to focus on their core mission of providing lodging services without the distractions and management implications associated with an additional F&B department. Some hotels that previously offered meals are beginning to abandon dining services entirely because of management challenges, lack of cost effectiveness, and other logistical problems.

GAMING

Gambling in various forms is becoming more commonplace throughout the world as a tool for economic development. Many communities provide gaming opportunities as a tourist attraction, and several important tourist destinations have developed during the past half century as important gaming destinations, including Las Vegas, Atlantic City, the former independent homelands of South Africa (Bophuthatswana, Transkei, Ciskei), Australia's Gold Coast, Macau, and Monaco. These well-established gambling destinations are home to famous resort casinos, such as the MGM Grand, the Excalibur, Mandalay Bay, the Luxor, and the Bellagio in Las Vegas; the Taj Mahal, Bally's, Tropicana, Ceasers, and the Showboat in Atlantic City; and Le Grand Casino de Monte Carlo and the Monte Carlo Sporting Club and Casino, Monaco. In some gaming destinations, particularly Las Vegas, slot machines can be found in nearly all lodging facilities, not only in resort complexes, including low-budget motels, inexpensive hotels, and even in campgrounds. Aside from these traditional locations, casino resorts are being developed in non-traditional destinations such as Cambodia, Laos, Indonesia, Malaysia, Myanmar, Singapore, Thailand, Vietnam, and Cyprus, which in several instances is quite remarkable given the dominant religious conservatism and socialist political slant in several of these countries.

Many hotel companies became involved in casino gaming during the 1980s and 1990s as a way of capturing high-end markets and offsetting the shortfalls in occupancy rates associated with low tourist season. In theory, casinos are appealing to hotel companies because they provide additional revenues that are by most counts recession resistant. Hilton, Sheraton, and Promus have become involved in the casino aspects of the hotel industry, lending well-established brand names to attract customers.

A number of salient gaming trends should be highlighted in this regard. In the American context, Indian gaming has become popular since the late 1980s, when the Indian Gaming Regulatory Act was passed by the US Congress. Similar legislation exists in Canada, where gaming is permitted on First Nations lands, even in provinces where gambling is not otherwise permitted. These legislation actions have led to the development of hundreds of casinos on native reservations throughout the United States and Canada. In the United States, revenues from Indian gaming grew from $10.96 billion in 2000 to an astonishing $26.02 billion in 2007 (National Indian Gaming

Commission, 2009) (Table 8.2). There are currently 425 Indian gaming facilities and 230 tribes operating casinos in 28 states in the United States.

Riverboat casinos have also become important in recent years with the liberalization of gaming laws in the United States. Several states that border navigable rivers, such as the Mississippi, Missouri, and Ohio rivers, have allowed riverboat gaming since the early 1990s as an economic development tool. Iowa, Illinois, Indiana, Louisiana, Missouri, and Mississippi are established riverboat casino destinations. Several other states, including Massachusetts, Florida, Georgia, and South Carolina have established similar boat-based casinos that cruise beyond the US territorial waters and once there open their casino operations.

Both of these trends—Indian casinos and riverboat gaming—have major implications for the lodging sector. As will be noted later in this book, several Native American casino resorts have developed into extremely popular tourist destinations in their own right, and have evolved into major anchor attractions in their respective regions. Foxwoods Casino and the Mohegan Sun, both in Connecticut, are two prime examples, but many more exist throughout the United States, with a preponderance of Indian casino resorts in Arizona, California, Minnesota, Oklahoma, Wisconsin, and Michigan, and 17 Canadian native casinos in Alberta, Manitoba, New Brunswick, Ontario, and Saskatchewan, most of which offer hotel or resort-type accommodations.

The riverboat gaming experiences are unique in that they are essentially day-gaming destinations. Most boats set sail, open their casinos, and arrive back to port on the river within a few hours. Several river cruise companies, however, offer overnight packages on casino riverboats. This is especially popular along the southern portions of the Mississippi River.

An interesting lodging perspective related to casino hotels and resorts is pricing. In the past, accommodation costs in gaming destinations, Las Vegas for instance, were exceptionally low compared to other leisure destinations. In the 1980s and even into the 1990s, for example, it was not uncommon to find hotel rooms on the Las Vegas Strip for less than $35 per night, or to purchase buffet meals for under $5. The rationale behind these

Table 8.2 Indian Gaming Revenues in the United States, 2000–2007 ($ billions)

2000	2001	2002	2003	2004	2005	2006	2007
10.96	12.82	14.72	16.83	19.48	22.58	24.89	26.02

Source: National Indian Gaming Commission (2009).

inexpensive prices was that customers' primary activity was gambling; food and lodging were secondary, and properties were bound to earn most of their profits from gaming revenues. Low lodging and food costs would, in theory, encourage more spending on slot machines and other games. While this is still the case to a degree in secondary gaming destinations, casino resorts in Las Vegas, Atlantic City, and other large-scale gambling destinations have begun to charge more for lodging and meals, seeing these as additional revenue sources rather than simple services provided for gambling visitors. Nonetheless, there is still a tendency for casino resort lodging to be less expensive than accommodations at similar properties on tropical islands or mountain areas.

Casino resorts are often looked upon as economic saviors for struggling communities, and many tourism communities that are facing decline turn to casino gaming as a way of rejuvenating their tourism economies. As already noted in Chapter 4, the economic implications of accommodations, including casino hotels, are remarkable. Considerable research has been done in recent years to understand the economic effects of gaming resorts on the communities that host them, with most findings suggesting that casinos provide significant boosts in employment levels, but do not necessarily affect per capita earnings, primarily because most jobs associated with casinos are low-skill positions that pay at or near minimum wage. Nonetheless, the spillover effects of casino employment are quite impressive in terms of other services that are connected to the gaming establishments themselves. Nevertheless, many communities are loathe to accept the social implications often associated with casinos and casino resorts (e.g. addiction, crime, etc.).

CONFERENCES AND CONVENTIONS

Conferences and conventions are one of the fastest growing forms of tourism in the world today, and many destinations have been decisive in the growth of convention-based tourism, with places throughout Europe, Asia, North America, the Pacific, and the Caribbean becoming important venues for thousands of conferences and business meetings each year. Table 8.3 illustrates some interesting patterns and facts associated with the conferences sector of tourism in the United States. Table 8.4 shows the top ten countries in terms of the number of conventions/meetings organized in 2007. While food services are not always a lucrative option for increasing a hotel's revenue, conferences, meetings, and conventions typically are. As a result, many resorts and hotels, as well as cruise ships and casinos, compete for this lucrative market and provide meeting spaces to supplement their incomes

Table 8.3	Recent Facts and Figures Associated with MICE Tourism in the United States	
Value of total direct spending in 2004		$122.31 billion
Number of jobs		1.7 million
Proportion of the hotel industry's revenue (including stays and meeting rooms) attributed to conferences and other MICE tourism		36%
Convention dollars spent on hotels		35%

Source: Adapted from Convention Industry Council (2005).

and as a way of filling rooms with conference attendees. Conventions and business meetings are seen as a good way of filling rooms during off season, and large hotel companies work hard to increase yield through conferences during seasons of low demand. Although large-scale conference and convention centers, many also offering some form of lodging and catering services, are becoming more commonplace in urban areas worldwide, hotels and resorts are attempting to capture much of the conference market and increase their bottom line by providing board rooms, conference space, catering services, and renting out various instructional media.

Table 8.4	Top 15 Countries for Conferences and Meetings in 2007	
Ranking	**Country**	**Number of Conferences**
1	United States	467
2	Germany	429
3	Spain	303
4	United Kingdom	281
5	France	255
6	Italy	250
7	Japan	215
8	Brazil	209
9	Austria	204
10	Canada	197
11	Netherlands	195
12	China	195
13	Australia	194
14	Switzerland	175
15	Portugal	153

Source: Adapted from International Congress and Convention Association (2008).

Weddings and family reunions are a specialized form of meeting and event that are becoming more appealing to hotels and resorts as an additional income source. Weddings, especially, are viewed as a particularly lucrative addition to hotel sales as they contribute significantly to food and beverage sales, meeting room rentals, and overnight stays.

It is common knowledge that the attractiveness of the destination determines in large part the level of attendance at national and international conventions and conferences. As a result, conferences being held in interesting cultural and natural areas, or in locations where there is a wide range of recreational opportunities, typically see the highest attendance rates. Such destinations usually experience the highest level of growth in MICE tourism, and communities compete aggressively for this form of business travel because of the potential economic outcomes.

SUMMARY AND CONCLUSION

This chapter has highlighted three ancillary attractions associated with lodging facilities, namely food and beverage services, gambling, and conferences/conventions, as well as several trends affecting each one. These elements of accommodation operations are important economically for both communities and individual properties. They draw people to a community, can transform what otherwise might be considered simply lodging into a tourist attraction, and cause guests to stay longer and increase individual expenditures.

The lodging sector is inextricably linked to food services, gaming, and MICE-based tourism. It plays a central role in the success of these sectors and vice versa. The provision of these services by hotels, resorts, convention centers, and cruise ships can result in huge capital earnings, but managed badly, they can also become a liability. There appears to be a dichotomous trend at present. Many hotels have ceased providing food to guests, or have opted to outsource it, while others are adopting dining as a supplementary revenue stream. Scale appears to be important in this regard in that larger hotels and resorts—those that also have convention facilities and food services—are the ones expanding most rapidly into the realm of dining.

REFERENCES

Chen, J.S., Legrand, W., Sloan, P., 2008. Managers' perspectives on the provision of healthy meals in resort hotels. FIU Hospitality and Tourism Review 26 (2), 19–25.

Convention Industry Council, 2005. Meetings industry is 29th largest contributor to the gross national product. Online < http://www.conventionindustry.org/aboutcic/pr/pr_091305.htm>

International Congress and Convention Association, 2008. Press release: ICCA publishes top 20 country and city rankings 2007. The International Congress & Convention Association, Amsterdam.

National Indian Gaming Commission, 2009. Government performance and results act, strategic plan for fiscal years 2009–2014. National Indian Gaming Commission, Washington, DC.

National Restaurant Association, 2009. Restaurant industry—facts at a glance. Online <http://www.restaurant.org/research/ind_glance.cfm> Accessed January 15.

Thompson, G.M., Killam, E.D., 2008. Forecasting covers in hotel food and beverage outlets. Cornell Hospitality Quarterly 8 (16), 4–20.

FURTHER READING

Adler, H., Chien, T.C., 2004. The wedding business: a method to boost food and beverage revenues in hotels. Journal of Foodservice Business Research 7 (1), 117–125.

Ahmed, Z.U., Heller, V.L., Hughes, K.A., 1999. South Africa's hotel industry. Cornell Hotel and Restaurant Administration Quarterly 40 (1), 74–86.

Bai, B., Brewer, K.P., Sammons, G., Swerdlow, S., 2006. Job satisfaction, organizational commitment, and internal service quality: a case study of Las Vegas hotel/casino industry. Journal of Human Resources in Hospitality and Tourism 5 (2), 37–54.

Baker, R., Ottenbacher, M., 2007. Indian gaming at the 20-year mark: hospitality's fastest-growing industry? FIU Hospitality and Tourism Review 25 (2), 58–65.

Barrows, C.W., Giannakopoulos, E., 2006. An exploratory study of outsourcing of foodservice operations in Canadian hotels. Tourism 54 (4), 375–383.

Benar, H., Jenkins, G.P., 2008. The economics of regulation and taxation policies for casino tourism. Tourism Economics 14 (3), 483–510.

Braunlich, C.G., 1996. Lessons from Atlantic City casino experience. Journal of Travel Research 34 (3), 46–56.

Brown, G., Raedler, S., 1994. Gold Coast hotels: examining the prospects for growth. International Journal of Contemporary Hospitality Management 6 (4), 16–24.

Cabañas, B., 1992. A marketing strategy for resort conference centers. Cornell Hotel and Restaurant Administration Quarterly 33 (3), 45–49.

Carmichael, B.A., Peppard, D.M., Boudeau, F.A., 1996. Megaresort on my doorstep: local resident attitudes toward Foxwoods Casino gambling on nearby Indian reservation land. Journal of Travel Research 34 (3), 9–16.

Chhabra, D., 2007. Estimating benefits and costs of casino gambling in Iowa, United States. Journal of Travel Research 46 (2), 173–182.

Chhabra, D., 2008. Social exchange theory in resort and non-resort casino settings. Anatolia 19 (1), 155–160.

Cho, M.H., 2002. Tourism redevelopment strategy: the case of he Kangwon Land Resort Casino. Anatolia 13 (2), 185–197.

Corr, F., 2007. Selling the 'Food Island'. Hotel and Catering Review 40 (7), 33–35.

Cotti, C., 2008. The effect of casinos on local labor markets: a county level analysis. Journal of Gambling Business and Economics 2 (2), 17–41.

DeFranco, A., Wortman, J., Lam, T., Countryman, C., 2005. A cross-cultural comparison of customer complaint behavior in restaurants in hotels. Asia Pacific Journal of Tourism Research 10 (2), 173–190.

D'Hauteserre, A.M., 2001. Representations of rurality: is Foxwoods Casino Resort threatening the quality of life in southeastern Connecticut? Tourism Geographies 3 (4), 405–429.

Elson, J.M., Muller, C.C., 2002. Including the "restaurant mix" in vacation ownership and resort development planning. International Journal of Hospitality Management 21 (3), 277–284.

Gu, Z., 2003. Analysis of Las Vegas Strip casino hotel capacity: an inventory model of optimization. Tourism Management 24 (3), 309–314.

Gu, Z., 2004. Macau gaming: copying the Las Vegas style or creating a Macau model? Asia Pacific Journal of Tourism Research 9 (1), 89–96.

Henderson, J., 2006. Betting on casino tourism in Asia: Singapore's integrated resorts. Tourism Review International 10 (3), 169–179.

Hsu, C.H.C., 2006. Casino industry in Asia Pacific: development, operation and impact. Howarth, New York.

Jackson, D., 1984. Destination restaurants. Independent Restaurants 46, 39–45.

Kochak, J.W., 1984. Fast food operators: more than just chicken. Restaurant Business 83 (3), 104–114.

Lattin, G.W., 2002. The lodging and food service industry. American Hotel and Lodging Association, Lansing, MI.

Lee, D.R., 1984. Hotel casinos: strong odds for growth. Cornell Hotel and Restaurant Administration Quarterly 25 (3), 21–29.

Lee, M.J., Back, K.J., 2007. Effects of destination image on meeting participation intensions: empirical findings from a professional association and its annual convention. Service Industries Journal 27 (1/2), 59–73.

Lord-Wood, E.H., 1982. The casino resort hotel. Cornell Hotel and Restaurant Administration Quarterly 22 (4), 54–60.

Lundberg, D.E., 1994. The hotel and restaurant business. Wiley, New York.

MacLaurin, D.J., Wolstenholme, S., 2008. An analysis of the gaming industry in the Niagara region. International Journal of Contemporary Hospitality Management 20 (3), 320–331.

McMahon, L., Lloyd, G., 2006. 'Rien ne va plus.' Casino developments and land use planning? Planning Practice and Research 21 (2), 257–266.

Miller, A., 1986. Food at the hostelry. Leisure Management 6 (5), 35–40.

Mill, R.C., 2007. Resorts: management and operation. Wiley, New York.

Mills, I., 2008. Innovation in the lifestyle hotel sector. Hospitality Review 10 (2), 22–27.

Mohsin, A., Lockyer, T., 2008. Hamilton, New Zealand: divergent attitudes when the casino came to town. Cornell Hospitality Quarterly 49 (2), 163–176.

Morrison, A.M., Braunlich, C.G., Cai, L.A., O'Leary, J.T., 1996. A profile of the casino resort vacationer. Journal of Travel Research 35 (2), 55–61.

Morrison, A.M., Yang, C.H., O'Leary, J.T., Nadkarni, N., 2003. Comparative profiles of travellers on cruises and land-based resort vacations. Journal of Tourism Studies 14 (1), 99–111.

Nield, K., Kozak, M., LeGrys, G., 2000. The role of food service in tourist satisfaction. International Journal of Hospitality Management 19 (4), 375–384.

Norman, E.D., Mayer, K.J., 1997. Yield management in Las Vegas casino hotels. Cornell Hotel and Restaurant Administration Quarterly 39 (5), 28–33.

O'Mahony, B., 2006. The challenge for hotel food and beverage delivery. Hospitality Review 8 (4), 11–14.

Ramdeen, C., Santos, J., Chatfield, H.K., 2007. Measuring the cost of quality in a hotel restaurant operation. International Journal of Contemporary Hospitality Management 19 (4), 286–295.

Rogerson, C.M., 1990. Sun International: the making of a South African tourism multinational. GeoJournal 22 (3), 345–354.

Sammons, G., 1997. The casino hotel and the internet: what's on-line? Bottomline 12 (1), 6–9.

Sheffield, E.A., Guthrie, R., Penland, D., Myers, K., 1993. Resort recreation programs for conference groups: programs and pricing. Visions in Leisure and Business 12 (3), 42–54.

Simpson, A., 1984. The pub food boom. Hospitality 55 (13), 16–17.

Stutts, A.T., 2006. Hotel and lodging management: an introduction. Wiley, New York.

Swerdlow, S., Strate, L., Brown, F.X., 1987. Fast-food franchises: an alternative menu for hotel/casinos. Hotel and Casino Law Letter 4 (1), 68–71.

Tannahill, R., 1989. Food in history. Three Rivers, New York.

Thompson, W.N., Pinney, J.K., Schibrowsky, J.A., 1996. The family that gambles together: business and social concerns. Journal of Travel Research 34 (3), 70–74.

Turner, M., 2008. Puzzles, problems and messes: food and beverage management on cruise ships. Hospitality Review 10 (3), 40–46.

Urbanowicz, C.F., 2001. Gambling into the 21st century. In: Smith, V.L., Brent, M. (Eds.), Hosts and guests revisited: tourism issues of the 21st century. Cognizant, New York, pp. 69–79.

Vallen, G., Cothran, C.C., Combrink, T.E., 1998. Indian gaming—are tribal employees being promoted to management positions in Arizona casinos? Cornell Hotel and Restaurant Administration Quarterly 39 (4), 56–63.

Waddoups, C.J., 2001. Unionism and poverty-level wages in the service sector: the case of Nevada's hotel-casino industry. Applied Economics Letters 8 (3), 163–167.

Walker, D.M., Jackson, J.D., 2007. Do casinos cause economic growth? American Journal of Economics and Sociology 66 (3), 593–607.

USEFUL INTERNET RESOURCES

Academic Conferences International: http://www.academic-conferences.org/.

FoodRoutes: http://www.foodroutes.org/.

Green Restaurant Association: http://www.dinegreen.com/.

Indian Casinos.com: http://www.indiancasinos.com/.

Indian Casinos Supersite: http://500nations.com/Indian_Casinos.asp.

International Congress and Convention Association: http://www.iccaworld.com.

International Association of Conference Center Administrators: http://www.iacca.org/.

International Council on Hotel, Restaurant and Institutional Education: http://www.chrie.org/i4a/pages/index.cfm?pageid=1

Meeting Professionals International: http://www.mpiweb.org/cms/mpiweb/default.aspx.

National Indian Gaming Commission: http://www.nigc.gov/.

National Restaurant Association: http://www.restaurant.org/.

Riverboat Casinos: http://www.riverboatcasinos.com/.

Slow Food: http://www.slowfood.com/.

Tourist Lodging Types and Forms

CHAPTER 9

Hotels, Motels, and Resorts

INTRODUCTION

Perhaps the most pervasive form of accommodation and most commonly utilized by the traveling public are hotels, motels, and resorts. These have received more attention than other forms of accommodation in public circles, academic discourse, and business commentaries. Indeed hotels have become an integral element of the urban landscape in all parts of the world today, resorts are permanent fixtures in mountains and on coastlines everywhere, and even the most remote communities boast some kind of lodging known as a hotel or motel.

The custom of opening one's home to travelers dates back many centuries. A couple of millennia ago, inns of various sorts were established along the Roman highway system throughout Europe. During the Middle Ages, lodging establishments developed in the burgeoning cities of Europe and Asia because of a demand for business travel (i.e. trade) and emerging forms of pleasure travel. Likewise, monasteries and religious orders provided lodging for religious pilgrims, but in most cases, travelers relied on the kindness of strangers to take them in and provide a bed for the night. Some stagecoach inns provided accommodations for weary sojourners along regular routes and were associated with taverns and places to eat. Inns and hotels became more commonplace after the advent of the railroad in the early 1800s. Large hotels were built in European cities near railway stations in the city centers, and many mega-hotels were constructed along rail lines in the United States and Canada, most notably in scenic areas that were to become important stop-overs on cross-country trips. With the introduction of the automobile and long-distance highways (particularly the interstate highway system) in the United States in the early twentieth century, motels developed to serve the sleeping needs of road-based travelers. Similar developments occurred along European highways such as the Motorways of the United Kingdom, the

CONTENTS

Introduction

Hotels, Motels, and Resorts Magnitude

Development and Management Dimensions

Resort and Hotel Challenges

Discussion and Conclusion

References

Further Reading

Useful Internet Resources

Autobahn of Germany, and Autostrada of Italy. During the colonial period, European administrations including the British, French, Portuguese, and Dutch built homes at strategic locations for their local representatives or governors. Many of these structures have become guesthouses that support the tourism industry, especially in developing countries in the Caribbean, Africa, and Asia. Large-scale resorts began as hotels and have since developed into much more. With the rapid development of international tourism following the Second World War, more places in the world today have been touched by tourism than ever before, resulting in many different types of resorts in a variety of environmental contexts. The advent of the jet engine in particular aided resort development in warm destinations of southern Europe, the Caribbean, Hawaii, Southeast Asia, and the South Pacific.

This chapter briefly traces the emergence of motels, hotels, and resorts, examines their broad classifications, and discusses their challenges and broad relationships with various aspects of the tourism field.

HOTELS, MOTELS, AND RESORTS MAGNITUDE

The global distribution of accommodations and similar establishments shows that Europe has about 45% of global hotel and resort room inventory, followed by North America, accounting for about 27%, giving the two regions a combined total of about 72%. The Asia Pacific region has about 14%. The industry profile in the United States in 2006 consists of about 47 135 motel, hotel, and resort properties, 4.4 million rooms, $133 billion in sales, with about $26.6 billion in pre-tax profits. While domestic travelers constitute the primary market, foreign visitors make a significant contribution to these lodging sectors as well. For example, in 2006 17 million international guests stayed in motels, hotels, or resorts in the United States, with a significant average length of stay of 7.5 nights, according to the American Hotel & Lodging Association (AH&LA, 2007).

Hotels

Broadly speaking, hotels are businesses that supply paid lodging on a short-term and temporary basis. A hotel typically has a large number of rooms and provides basic accommodation, including en-suite bathrooms. Traditionally hotel rooms have included a bed, bathroom, a television, and a small refrigerator, stocked with drinks and snacks that may be purchased. In recent years, in an ever-changing business climate and in the face of shifting demand, hotels have had to compete against one another and against other lodging alternatives, so they have added a large number of amenities and extras, such as swimming pools, saunas, spas, exercise rooms, concierge services, business centers, valet parking, conference centers, hot drink makers en-suite, and Internet links to individual rooms or common areas. Many hotels provide various meal plans as a room and board package, offering hot breakfasts or simple coffee and doughnuts.

There is no global standard for the use of the term 'hotel', so many variations of hotels exist throughout the world and can range from small bed and breakfast-like establishments in Asia and the Middle East to mega-resorts in the Caribbean, Hawaii, and the Mediterranean. Although a standard definition and grading system

Holiday Inn Express is part of the InterContinental Hotels Group

have been attempted, such efforts have been unsuccessful owing to the difficulty of trying to assimilate so many varying qualities and characteristics in so many different locations. However, some countries and individual states or provinces have devised their own definitions of hotel for statistical and marketing purposes, and to set a standard to distinguish themselves from businesses that simply elect to call themselves hotels. For example, Florida, the most visited state in the United States, has an official definition that helps in its tourism business efforts. Hotels according to Florida's view are public lodging establishments that contain sleeping room accommodations for 25 or more guests, provide the services commonly provided by a hotel, and is recognized as a hotel in the community and by the hospitality industry.

The star rating system, where the higher the number of stars, the more luxurious the quality, is the closest effort to a global standard, but even this varies from place to place and hotel to hotel. Some countries have standardized star ratings and specific criteria, but in many countries, the

A mid-range hotel in a beautiful setting in Paro, Bhutan

Istanbul, Turkey, is home to several popular historic hotels such as these

This historic hotel is reminiscent of cattlemen and frontier settlement in Australia

ratings are left to the individual properties without oversight from any central organization or monitoring agency. This results in many low-grade lodging establishments claiming to be four or five-star hotels, when clearly they would hardly be classified as one or two stars in countries where the ratings are more systematically controlled. However, standardized systems also have problems, for example where high-quality older hotels might be downgraded because they lack certain amenities (e.g. elevators) that would be more typical of newer establishments, even though all else should be graded higher.

Several different general types of hotels exist depending on location and primary market: resort, commercial, airport, conference, business, gaming, and residential. Resort hotels are typically luxury hotels with many other added amenities. Airport hotels are, as the title suggests, located at or near major airports and are usually geared toward business travelers or transit passengers, offering comfortable rooms, cable TV, Internet access, and complementary coffee and/or breakfast, shuttles to and from the airport, and a business center so clients can access Internet, faxes, and other work-related conveniences. Commercial hotels are more generic and situated in a wide variety of locations, including city centers, near airports, by famous attractions, and in natural areas. Residential hotels cater to long-term guests who pay either by the week or by the month. Guests at residential hotels are often long-distance commuters, or people looking to rent or purchase a more permanent home.

Similar to residential hotels are extended stay hotels. These are usually owned by major hotel and resort companies, such as the InterContinental Hotels Group (e.g. Holiday Inn and Candlewood Suites) but cater to people who want to stay for longer periods of time than just one or a few nights. The market for extended stays is long-term vacationers, people moving or between homes, people who need temporary housing while their homes are being remodeled, extended business travelers, temporary project workers or teachers and researchers, or people visiting relatives. The units resemble condominiums, often with multiple bedrooms, living rooms, and furnished kitchens. In most cases, people using extended stay facilities prefer to cook at least some of their own meals rather than dine out frequently. Extended stay companies, such as Candlewood Suites, Staybridge Suites, Amerisuites, and Studio 6, actively promote the idea that ordinary hotels are lackluster and lonely, while extended stay suites provide the 'comforts of home'. Extended stay hotels are originally an American idea, but are beginning to spread to the United Kingdom and other parts of Europe as more mobile and budget conscious travelers begin to see the value of renting self-catering units that might be cheaper by the week than by the night.

There is significant demand for hotels around the entire world. In the United States, more than half of all tourist trips taken in 2006 included a stay in a hotel or motel, which translated to more than 500 million overnight person trips in hotels or motels (and bed and breakfasts) in 2006. In the US, on the domestic front then, hotels and motels are very important, more so than approximately 34% of the traveling public who stayed at someone else's home or camped (4%) (Travel Industry Association, 2007).

Historic hotels

An interesting perspective on hotels is the idea of historic hotels, which typically have played an important role in the historical development of a place, which have become famous through TV and film, or which represent a unique architecture or period of history. The Raffles Hotel in Singapore, for instance, is not only an architectural work of art, it also played a crucial role in the invasion by Japan and the Japanese surrender in the Second World War. The Waldorf Astoria Hotel in New York City gained part of its fame as the place where the Waldorf salad was initially created. Many other famous and historic hotels are an important part of the attractiveness of destinations (Table 9.1). Many of these historic hotels have become national monuments or otherwise officially designated heritage sites and are thus in themselves important tourist attractions, not just for tenants, but also for tourists in general.

Table 9.1	Examples of Famous Historic Hotels	
Hotel	**Location**	**Year Opened**
Oriental Hotel	Bangkok, Thailand	1876
Raffles Hotel	Singapore, Singapore	1887
Goldener Hirsch	Salzburg, Austria	1671
Grand Hotel Europe	St Petersburg, Russia	1875
Hotel D'Angleterre	Copenhagen, Denmark	1755
Grand Hotel du Louvre	Paris, France	1855
Mena House	Cairo, Egypt	1886
Grand Hotel Royal Budapest	Budapest, Hungary	1896
Banff Springs	Banff, Canada	1888

Motels

Motels are different from hotels, although some of the differences between higher-end motels and hotels are hard to distinguish. Essentially a motel is a lodging establishment with an exit to the outside from each individual unit with ample parking. Most often, the rooms are organized in linear rows or in an L or U shape, facing a central courtyard or parking area. Motels are usually small (usually between six and 100 units), have a bathroom in each unit, and are rarely more than two or three stories in elevation. The rooms tend to be rather small, and they are considered a high-value, low-budget, no-frills accommodation option with limited amenities and services. In most cases they offer daily and weekly rates and are therefore seen as a viable extended stay option, although they do not typically have kitchenettes and living space.

Motels are originally an American phenomenon, but they have since spread to other parts of the world, including Australia and New Zealand. They originated in the 1920s with the construction of long-distance highways, and grew quickly in the 1950s and 1960s with the development of the Eisenhower Interstate Highway System. The motel, which is an abbreviation of 'motor hotel', was built along the emerging highways as a well-situated lodging option for

A traditional roadside motel in the USA

car-based travelers. They provide free parking and were located conveniently by major roads and highways, typically on the outskirts of cities or in rural areas. The private automobile had become the primary mode of transportation in America by the mid-1900s, so the number of motels continued to grow well into the end of the millennium.

The immediate precursor to motels typically appeared as a set of separate or connected roadside cabins or tents, which was often referred to as an auto camp, tourist camp, motor camp, motor court, or cabin camp, until the term 'motor hotel' was

Motel 6 is a popular and inexpensive lodging brand in the USA

conceived in 1925 by the Milestone Interstate Corporation, which planned to build a number of these along the new highway from San Diego to Seattle. These roadside cabins, or auto courts as they were commonly known, continued in popularity even beyond the day of the motel. Some of these are still discernable in the highway landscapes, although most of these cabin-based places were eventually connected and renamed motels. Through the years,

'motor hotel' evolved into motel, which eventually became the accepted and most common vernacular term.

There are two sets of negative connotations associated with motels. The first is that motels are low quality, dingy, and otherwise of a very low standard. While motels of this nature do still exist, most have been remodeled since their initial construction earlier in the twentieth century, and some newer motels have been built to a much higher standard. Several brand-name chains, such as Motel 6 (part of the Accor group) and Super 8 (part of the Wyndham hotel company), are among the top-end motels that defy the traditional

This roadside motel in Arizona, USA, is one of the few remaining 'motor courts'

A luxury beachfront resort in Aruba

reputation of motels and are sought out because of their clean atmospheres, family-friendly setups, and low rates ($35–$85, depending on location and time of year); most Motel 6s also have swimming pools. The second negative connotation derives from Latin America, where the term refers to a seedy lodging option that can be rented by the hour or in three-hour blocks for sexual encounters. These are also referred to cheekily as 'love motels'. In many areas, sincere tourists needing a place to sleep for eight or nine hours would hardly lay their head in a Latin American motel.

Resorts

A Fijian resort compound with an attractive beachfront

In the English-speaking world there are two meanings of resort. The first is more common in Britain and former British colonies. From this perspective a resort is a tourist destination, a community, or region where leisure tourism is an important part of the local economy and cultural landscape. Some prominent examples include Brighton, England; Whistler, British Columbia (Canada); Vale, Colorado (USA); Orlando, Florida (USA); Phuket, Thailand; Nice, France; Agadir, Morocco; Tenerife, Spain; Paphos, Cyprus; Goa, India; and Kuta, Bali (Indonesia). In other parts of the world (e.g. North America and Asia) such a place is referred to as a resort community or simply a resort destination. A resort from the second perspective is a self-contained, individual vacation establishment owned by a single company. This latter meaning is the focus of this section.

Resorts include guest rooms and suites, just as hotels or timeshare complexes do, and in fact many timeshare units are located in elaborate resort complexes. However, there is considerably more to a resort than just hotel rooms. Self-contained resorts typically include a wide range of recreational services, including: swimming pools, spas, exercise rooms, game rooms and theaters, golf courses, ski slopes, a wide range of dining options, gift shops, barbeque pits, hairdressers, water sport equipment rentals, dance halls, and conference centers.

Properties that offer these activities, a room, and all the food guests can consume for a fixed price are known as all-inclusive resorts. Some inclusive resorts include room, food, and certain activities but charge

This pool is only one of many amenities at this five-star resort in Fiji

additional fees for extra activities like spa treatments or cooking classes. Often such enterprises are referred to as mega-resorts or luxury resorts because of the wide range of entertainment and leisure options they provide, their large size, high-quality customer service and individual attention, interesting locations, and architectural grandeur. Club Med popularized the all-inclusive resort concept in the 1960s and 1970s, and today resort chains such as Barcelo, based in Spain, have all-inclusive properties in Europe and several Latin American countries. All-inclusive properties characteristically try to get their guests to spend as much time as possible inside the resort by providing a wide range of recreational activities and dining options. This has resulted in several important criticisms in recent years, which will be discussed in more detail later.

To meet the needs of an ever-changing global market and increasingly sophisticated and specialized tourist demands, many resorts have geared themselves toward certain population segments. For example, many resort properties are now pet-friendly, as many people see pets as part of the family and choose to take them on family vacations. Some resort properties specialize in family holidays, providing a wide assortment of child-friendly activities and sleeping arrangements. Others focus attention and marketing efforts on young guests, under 30, who desire a more entertainment and party-like atmosphere, to older adults who prefer solitude and relaxation, to couples, or to homosexual guests, providing activities and services that meet their demands.

There are several different kinds of resorts that can be classified by their location and the primary attraction or region they represent. Perhaps the

Beachcomber is a self-contained island resort in Fiji

This ski resort in Canada is popular among local and regional tourists

most common is *beach and island resorts*. The most salient feature of these, of course, is their location on or near beaches. While some of these exist in more temperate climates and on rugged coastlines, the most sought after beach resorts are located in the tropics where the weather is consistently warm year-round and where the beaches are sandy. Activities at beach resorts focus almost exclusively on water-based pursuits, such as snorkeling, scuba diving, water skiing, parasailing, fishing, swimming and sunbathing, and boating. Many beach resorts are beginning to include more land-based activities, such as golf. Among the most popular destinations for this type of resort attraction are the Caribbean, the Pacific Islands, Southeast Asia, and parts of Africa and its Indian Ocean islands, although thousands more exist in places either as isolated resorts or in resort communities with a conglomeration of other properties. Some of the oil-rich states in the Gulf region have recently developed high-end beach resorts, including some on man-made islands.

Ski resorts are located near ski areas and are often clustered in ski villages in mountainous areas. In addition to downhill skiing and snowboarding, ski resorts typically offer other attractions associated with snow and ice, including cross-country skiing, dog sledding, snowmobiling, ice-skating, and hot tub and spa treatments. During the summer months, ski resorts often try to offset the effects of seasonality by providing non-snow-based attractions like hiking, camping, alpine sliding, dog shows, summer theater, and art exhibitions. Many ski resorts exist all over the world, but among the most popular are those in the Rocky Mountains of the US and Canada, and in the alpine areas of Europe.

At the center of *theme park resorts* are of course theme parks, or amusement parks. Some of the larger theme park companies, such as Disney, offer family-oriented resorts at their amusement properties around the world. These typically provide fewer recreational pursuits in the hotel area, since their focus is the park, but they do offer high levels of lodging services in conjunction with park admissions.

Casino resorts have become fairly commonplace since the 1970s. Their concentration is casino gaming and are usually attached to a well-known casino. They are different from the commonplace hotel-casinos in many places around the globe in that they are functioning resorts with the same types of amenities described above in other resort contexts. Foxwoods Resort Casino in Connecticut (USA) claims to be the largest casino in the world and offers golf, gaming, spa treatments, and many other services. Sun International, based in southern Africa, operates a large number of casino resorts in several countries, including South Africa, Lesotho, Namibia, Swaziland, Botswana, and Chile. Harrah's is one of the largest casino resort developers in the United States and Canada and is continuing to expand its

The Mohegan Sun, USA, is one of the world's largest casino resorts

This casino resort in Myanmar was built near the border of Thailand to attract Thai visitors

holdings in interesting and good-weather locations throughout North America.

Golf resorts are another important type of property. Their primary appeal lies in the climate where they are located, which makes golfing and other outdoor sports a lucrative and promising option year-round. Scottsdale, Arizona (USA); Palm Springs, California (USA); Denarau Island, Fiji; Maui,

Suites overlooking the greens of a golf resort in the southwestern USA

Hawaii (USA); Port Douglas, Australia; and the Gold Coast, Australia; Sharm El Sheikh, Egypt; Marrakech, Morocco; Aruba; Montego Bay and Ocho Rios, Jamaica; Bermuda; and Providenciales, Turks and Caicos Islands, are good examples of large clusters of golf resorts and are well-established golf destinations. While some of the golf resorts in these destinations also fit the definition of a beach resort, they often choose to market themselves as golf properties.

Finally, one of the more popular types of resorts is *health spas*. Spa resorts are known for healthy living, and their primary purpose is to get people to think about their health and change unhealthy practices. People also travel to health resorts for treatment of various diseases and ailments. Activities include healthy eating, exercise, outdoor activities, alternative medicine, spiritual healing, and cooking classes. Spa resorts often grow around natural hot springs, or water with healing qualities, and have been popular since ancient Greek and Roman times. Spa, Belgium, is sometimes seen as the epitome of healing water spa towns and was known throughout the Roman Empire for its healing waters. Many other spa resorts and resort communities have developed throughout the world. The former communist countries of Eastern Europe are important spa destinations. Before 1990, it was common for western Europeans to travel to Eastern Europe to undergo treatments and to enjoy the relaxing atmospheres of spa resorts in East Germany, Yugoslavia, Hungary, Romania, and Czechoslovakia. These are still popular attractions in the countries of Eastern Europe; many spa resorts have also developed in North America, New Zealand, and Australia. For example, New Zealand's geothermal region around the town of Rotorua is an important health spa resort destination in the South Pacific.

A study by Keri et al. (2007) identified several influential variables in the growth of spa resorts in recent years. First is changing markets and demand, with an increasing number of men and teenage girls being attracted to spa venues and more spa tourists desiring an 'experience' rather than just a 'treatment'. Second, there is an increased social movement that focuses on health and wellness. More people now than ever before are exercising regularly, eating organic and healthier foods, and undertaking de-stressing exercises. These translate into more patronage at health resorts. Another trend is the combination of physical beauty, health, and medicine now being a focus of less traditional spas. Many spa resorts now have dieticians, nurses, and physicians on staff to assist in designing programs for individual guests. Such a concept is evident in the 'plastic surgery resorts' of Asia and Latin America, which are discussed in greater depth in Chapter 15. Technological advancement related to exercise and healthy eating is another important variable, as is the adoption of more Asian traditional medicine, wellness services, and architectural design.

There are other widely accepted ways of classifying resorts besides the primary purpose or attraction associated with it. One such way is seasonal or climatic in nature and includes summer resorts, warm winter resorts, cold winter resorts, and year-round resorts. Year-round resorts are the most stable of all of these, as seasonal resorts face the vagaries and temperament of nature. Ski resorts, for example, suffer huge losses when warm weather extends too far into the winter season or when there is insufficient moisture to produce snow. Likewise, warm winter resorts in the Caribbean face seasonal problems associated with hurricanes between July and November that not only dissuade people from visiting but also cause expensive damage to the resorts' physical structure.

DEVELOPMENT AND MANAGEMENT DIMENSIONS

As illustrated in Table 9.2, hotel and resort classification can be based on a set of criteria that include size, location, services and amenities, guest profile, price tier, and corporate structure.

Table 9.2 Hotel and Resort Classification

Criteria	Descriptors
Size	Square footage, number of rooms, number of beds
Location	Urban, rural, mountain, airport, beach, lake, island, highway
Amenity & service	Full or limited service, all-suite, golf, spa
Guest profile	Leisure, corporate, family, gaming, conventions
Price Tier	Budget, standard, deluxe, luxury
Star ranking	5 to 1 star, unranked
Corporate structure	Independent, chain, franchise, management contract

Significant consolidation in the hotel and resort industry has taken place in the last 20 years. The trend has seen a shift away from independently owned and operated hotels. This trend has produced very large hotel chains and has also globalized the industry. Based on total rooms, Table 9.3 shows the top ten hotel chains in the world in 2006 with their share of 3.9 million rooms.

The hotel and resort sectors of the tourism and hospitality industry have evolved to become highly complex and sophisticated in operations. There are companies that specialize in providing funding for private investment such as Fortress Investment Group in the United States. There is also an array of sources for public domestic and international investment including some aid agencies as well as those that secure and underwrite loans for resort development, including the World Bank's Multi-lateral Investment Guarantee Agency (MIGA). Developing countries in particular have difficulties in securing domestic or foreign investment capital for even small hotel projects without such guarantees. For example, in October 2008, MIGA issued a guarantee for the construction of the Tamboho Hotel in Madagascar by developers from Mauritius.

Some hotel and resort companies develop, as well as manage, lodging properties as in the case on Intrawest with its headquarters in Vancouver, Canada. It has developed several resort destinations, while managing several mountain, lake and beach resorts in Hawaii, California, Nevada, Florida, Ontario, British Columbia, and France. Other companies specialize in managing hotels and resorts that are developed or owned by other investors. The Jumeirah Group, based in Dubai, is an example of a luxury international

Table 9.3	Top Ten Hotel Chains in 2006			
Rank	**Hotel Chain**	**Base Country**	**Rooms**	**Hotels**
1	InterContinental Group	England	556 246	3 7141
2	Wyndham Hotel Group	United States	543 234	6 473
3	Marriott International	United States	513 832	2 832
4	Hilton Hotels	United States	501 478	2 935
5	Accor Group	France	486 512	4 121
6	Choice Hotels International	United States	435 000	5 376
7	Best Western International	United States	315 401	4 164
8	Starwood Hotels & Resorts	United States	265 600	871
9	Carlson Hospitality	United States	145 331	945
10	Global Hyatt Corporation	United States	140 416	749

Source: Cahners 2007.

hospitality management group. Hotels under its management include the world-renowned and iconic Burj Al Arab, the Jumeirah Beach Hotel in Dubai, and the Jumeirah Carlton Tower in London. In late 2008, it was appointed by Timbers Resorts to manage its luxury multi-use resort property in the US Virgin Islands.

RESORT AND HOTEL CHALLENGES

Although resorts are among the most popular accommodation options in the world today and are seen as an ultimate vacation experience by many, they are not without controversy and challenges; neither are hotels. The most divisive issues today in the resort sector deal with social and economic impacts of resort-based tourism.

As noted in Chapter 4 one of the most notable debates surrounds economic leakage, or how much money spent by tourists actually remains in the destination economy to help augment the local economy through job creation, a growing tax base, regional income, health care, and education. There is significant evidence to suggest that in the less-developed parts of the world especially, a relatively small proportion of the money spent by holiday makers remains in the destination economy, thereby benefiting foreign-owned companies and local elites, while the destination residents themselves suffer from poverty and high levels of unemployment. Leakage occurs most often when foreign transportation and foreign-owned resorts and hotels are utilized, sending most of the money spent back to the headquarters and home countries of the transport and accommodation companies. Another cause of leakage is the hiring of foreign 'experts' or skilled staff, such as construction supervisors, chefs, and hotel managers from abroad. It is very common for the best-paying jobs to be given to outsiders. Too often, even most of the food served to tourists in the developing world is imported, so that local fishers and farmers are unable to earn a living through tourism. There have been some innovative programs established, however, by individual chefs at some resorts in Indonesia and elsewhere that have attempted to purchase products from local markets, local farmers, and local fishermen. Tourism in most cases is very import dependent, but one of the principles of sustainable tourism development is to use local resources, including labor, building materials, and agricultural products, rather than import them. Some resort properties are making great strides in this direction, while many of them have not yet achieved this important goal.

Some observers also argue that resorts, particularly all-inclusive resorts, are tourist bubbles, or tourist enclaves, that provide all the comforts of home and more, and where relatively few guests wander outside the confines of the resort to explore the destination. Sometimes cultural shows are brought to guests at the hotels and resorts. These trends give way to thinking such as 'people have been to a resort in Jamaica, but they have not really been to Jamaica'. This leads to the notion of placelessness, in that all resorts therefore become generic and sterilized versions of an elite landscape, wherein the location of the resort is irrelevant. Any resort could just as well be located anywhere.

Questions also arise about why tourists would want to leave home for another destination and still expect all the same comforts of home. 'Why not stay home then' is often the reaction. Instead of tourists seeking cultural demonstrations, local foods, historic sites, and natural scenery on the outside, they remain in the resort complex, eating, sunbathing, parasailing, and gambling. This is good for the resort owners, but not so good for the local economy and society. Visitor spending outside the resort is often one of the only ways in which local people and local economies can realize benefits from tourism. One complaint among destination residents is that the construction of large hotels and mega-resorts threatens the survival of small tourism businesses, particularly food services, guesthouses, souvenir shops, and taxis, which depend on tourists as customers, thereby exacerbating the economic leakages discussed above and creating significant discontent in the local community.

The tourist enclave phenomenon is a demonstration of cultural arrogance, and destination residents become dismayed that their culture is not good enough for tourists but that the beaches (which locals themselves are often unable to gain access to) are. Even when visitors do venture outside the resorts, there is often a significant disconnect between the values of tourists and the values of destination residents. For example, one of the most upsetting issues related to tourists visiting traditional societies is their assumption that their dress and behavior inside the resort are acceptable outside the resort. Unfortunately, resort-based tourism often epitomizes the negative socio-cultural and economic impacts of tourism that have been discussed for several decades in the realm of tourism studies. The conspicuous consumption by resort guests (on food, alcohol, merchandise, entertainment, etc.) can also have both economic and social demonstration effect on those residents they encounter, particularly among resort employees.

On the opposite side, the Maldives, a small island country in South Asia, has used island resorts as a tool for preventing widespread negative social impacts. The Maldives model is based on the principle of 'one island, one resort'. Many of the country's nearly 2000 islands are self-contained, segregated, all-inclusive resorts. Tourists are encouraged to remain on their resort island and may only visit inhabited, non-tourist islands with restrictions and special permission, including that they behave and dress appropriately. This works well in the Maldives context, as this requirement minimizes contact between hedonistic tourists and the country's conservative Muslim population.

Seasonality is another major challenge. Like all forms of accommodation, resorts and hotels face severe seasonal changes in demand. However, for resorts, seasonality is especially acute, since the attractiveness of most resorts is based on climate and nature, and other forms of accommodation might be more business oriented rather than just leisure oriented and therefore do not experience the same degree of seasonal variations. As a result, during low seasons, resorts are required to offer special deals or find alternative ways of filling rooms, as was noted earlier in this chapter in the case of ski resorts. Some of the golf and good winter weather-based resorts of Scottsdale-Phoenix, Arizona, for example, offer special prices and package deals during the hot summer months. As well, they offer specials to 'local' tourists as well in an effort to get Arizona residents to spend a night or two away from home and enjoy everything the resort has to offer.

DISCUSSION AND CONCLUSION

Motels, hotels, and resorts have evolved from simple beginnings to become very diverse, ranging from basic accommodation facilities to ultra-luxury, mega-resorts that cost over a billion dollars to construct, as in the case of some resort properties in Las Vagas. Others may cost more but the amounts are not disclosed as in the case of the Burj Al Arab in Dubai and the Emirate Palace in Abu Dhabi. There is an ever-increasingly wide range of hotel-like accommodation options all around the world that meet the lodging needs of tourists.

While hotels and resorts are responsible for several negative socio-economic impacts noted earlier in this chapter, they can produce positive backward economic linkages during the construction period. The MGM Resort cost about one million dollars each day over an 18 month period to build. Half of this amount went to construction worker wages. Local building materials are also purchased, while architects and interior decorators also benefit. The construction of even small hotel and resort properties in developing countries can produce significant economic benefits.

While not discussed in great depth in this chapter, technology is incredibly important and has served the lodging industry well in many aspects of its development, operations, management, and marketing. Prospective travelers can compare properties, view rooms and amenities, see space availability, and make their reservations on-line from the comfort of their homes, offices, or even in travel status. In recent years, several electronic marketing intermediaries have also emerged marketing hotels exclusively (Hotels.com) or as part of other travel products and services including airline and car rentals (Orbitz, Travelocity, Expedia, etc.). Technological applications in the hospitality industry have provided convenience and cost savings to both guests and hoteliers. Many guests now want Internet access in their rooms. They can also view their accounts or check out interactively on the television in their rooms. Management also benefits from electronic card keys, water and energy management, as well as ensuring guests' safety from electronic security installations. Technological advances will continue to affect the design, operations, management, and marketing of the motel, hotels, and resort sector.

REFERENCES

AH&LA, 2007. 2007 Lodging Industry Profile. American Hotel and Lodging Association, Washington, D.C.

Cahners, 2007. Hotels Magazine. Cahners Publications, Oak Brook, Illinois, USA (July 2007).

Keri, K., Ottenbacher, M., Baker, R., 2007. The growth trends in North America. Hospitality Review 9 (2), 21–27.

Travel Industry Association, 2007. Domestic travel market report. TIA, Washington, DC.

FURTHER READING

Agarwal, S., Shaw, G. (Eds.), 2007. Managing Coastal Tourism Resorts: A Global Perspective. Channel View, Clevedon, UK.

Ahmed, Z.U., Heller, V.L., Hughes, K.A., 1999. South Africa's hotel industry: opportunities and challenges for international companies. Cornell Hotel and Restaurant Administration Quarterly 40 (1), 74–85.

Andriotis, K., 2008. Integrated resort development: the case of Cavo Sidero, Crete. Journal of Sustainable Tourism 16 (4), 428–444.

Arbel, A., Pizam, A., 1977. Some determinants of urban hotel location: the tourist inclinations. Journal of Travel Research 15 (3), 18–22.

Belasco, W.J., 1979. Americans on the road: from autocamp to motel. MIT Press, Cambridge.

Bergen-Seers, S., Jago, L., 2007. Performance measurement in small motels in Australia. Tourism and Hospitality Research 7 (2), 144–155.

Bicknell, S., McManus, P., 2006. The canary in the coalmine: Australian ski resorts and their response to climate change. Geographical Research 44 (4), 386–400.

Brey, E.T., Lehto, X., 2008. Changing family dynamics: a force of change for the family-resort industry? International Journal of Hospitality Management 27 (2), 241–248.

Broome, S., Hall, L., 2007. Extended stay hotels: a US model whose time has come in the UK? Hospitality Directions European Edition, 15: n.p.

Clark, T.A., Gill, A., Hartmann, R. (Eds.), 2006. Mountain Resort Planning and Development in an Era of Globalization. Cognizant, New York.

Cope, R., 2003. All-inclusives—the major players. Travel and Tourism Analyst 3, 1–25.

Cser, K., Ohuchi, A., 2008. World practices of hotel classification systems. Asia Pacific Journal of Tourism Research 13 (4), 379–398.

Curry, S., 1992. Economic adjustment policies and the hotel sector in Jamaica. In: Johnson, P., Thomas, B. (Eds.), Perspectives on Tourism Policy. Mansell, London, pp. 193–213.

Deng, W.J., 2007. Using a revised importance-performance analysis approach: the case of Taiwanese hot springs tourism. Tourism Management 28 (5), 1274–1284.

Devas, E., 1997. Hotels in the Caribbean. Travel and Tourism Analyst 2, 57–76.

D'Hauteserre, A.M., 2001. Representations of rurality: is Foxwoods Casino Resort threatening the quality of life in southeastern Connecticut? Tourism Geographies 3 (4), 405–429.

Dinçer, F.I., Ertuğral, S.M., 2003. Economic impact of heritage tourism hotels in Istanbul. Journal of Tourism Studies 14 (2), 23–34.

Domroes, M., 2001. Tourism in the Maldives: the advantages of the resort island concept. Tourism 49 (4), 369–382.

Fockler, S., 1998. Extended stay hotels in the USA. Travel and Tourism Analyst 2, 57–75.

Gee, C.Y., 1988. Resort development and management. Educational Institute of the American Hotel and Motel Association, Lansing, MI.

Gordon, Y., 1994. Hotels report good tourist season. Hotel and Catering Review 24 (9), 22–23.

Haden, L., 2007. Spa tourism. Travel and Tourism Analyst 9, 1–48.

Hart, W.A., 1994. Elegant survivors: historic hotel renovation in Oregon. Cornell Hotel and Restaurant Administration Quarterly 35 (4), 38–61.

Henderson, J.C., 2006. Betting on casino tourism in Asia: Singapore's integrated resorts. Tourism Review International 10 (3), 169–179.

Inbakaran, R., Jackson, M., 2005. Understanding resort visitors through segmentation. Tourism and Hospitality Research 6 (1), 53–71.

Jackson, L.A., Naipaul, S., 2008. Isadore Sharp and four seasons hotels and resorts: redefining luxury and building a sustained brand. Journal of Hospitality and Tourism Education 20 (2), 44–50.

Jakle, J.A., Keith, A.S., Jefferson, S.R., 1996. The motel in America. Johns Hopkins University Press, Baltimore.

Jordan, F., 2008. Performing tourism: exploring the productive consumption of tourism in enclavic spaces. International Journal of Tourism Research 10 (4), 293–304.

Keri, K., Ottenbacher, M., Baker, R., 2007. The growth trends in North America. Hospitality Review 9 (2), 21–27.

King, B., 2001. Resort-based tourism on the pleasure periphery. In: Harrison, D. (Ed.), Tourism and the Less Developed World: Issues and Case Studies. CAB International, Wallingford, UK, pp. 175–190.

King, B., McVey, M., 1996. Accommodation: resorts in Asia. Travel and Tourism Analyst 4, 35–50.

Lasanta, T., Laguna, M., Vincente-Serrano, S.M., 2007. Do tourism-based ski resorts contribute to the homogenous development of the Mediterranean mountains? A case study in the central Spanish Pyrenees. Tourism Management 28 (5), 1326–1339.

Leonard, S.F., 1987. Hotel chains in the USA: review of an industry in transition. Travel and Tourism Analyst 3, 43–53.

Lord-Wood, E.H., 1982. The casino hotel resort. Cornell Hotel and Restaurant Administration Quarterly 22 (4), 54–60.

Margolies, J., 1987. Home away from home: motels in America. Little, Brown, Bulfinch Press, Boston.

Matzler, K., Füller, J., Faullant, R., 2007. Customer satisfaction and loyalty to Alpine ski resorts: the moderating effect of lifestyle, spending and customers' skiing skills. International Journal of Tourism Research 9 (6), 409–421.

McGuffie, J., 1987. UK hotel industry: revival for the chains at home and abroad. Travel and Tourism Analyst 3, 15–31.

McGuffie, J., 1996. Franchising hotels in Europe. Travel and Tourism Analyst 1, 36–52.

McMorran, C., 2008. Understanding the 'heritage"in heritage tourism: ideological tool of economic tool for a Japanese hot springs resort? Tourism Geographies 10 (3), 334–354.

Mbaiwa, J.E., 2005. Enclave tourism and its socio-economic impacts in the Okavango Delta, Botswana. Tourism Management 26 (2), 157–172.

Mill, R.C., 2007. Resorts: management and operation. Wiley, New York.

Morrison, A.M., Yang, C.H., O'Leary, J.T., Nadkarni, N., 1996. Comparative profiles of travelers on cruises and land-based resorts. Journal of Tourism Studies 7 (2), 15–27.

O'Neill, J.W., Hanson, B., Mattila, A.S., 2008. The relationship of sales and marketing expenses and hotel performance in the United States. Cornell Hospitality Journal 49 (4), 355–363.

Ormiston, D., Gilbert, A., Manning, R.E., 1998. Indicators and standards of quality for ski resort management. Journal of Travel Research 36 (3), 35–41.

Pacaud, L., Vollet, D., Angeon, V., 2007. Impact of tourism infrastructure on regional development: the implantation of a Center Parcs resort in northern France. Tourism Economics 13 (3), 389–406.

Pearce, D.G., 1987. Motel location and choice in Christchurch. New Zealand Geographer 43 (1), 10–17.

Rogerson, C.M., 1990. Sun International: the making of a South African tourism multinational. GeoJournal 22 (3), 345–354.

Shanahan, K.J., 2003. The degree of congruency between roadside billboard advertisements and sought attributes of motels by US drive tourists. Journal of Vacation Marketing 9 (4), 381–395.

Simpson, P., Wall, G., 1999. Consequences of resort development: a comparative study. Tourism Management 20 (3), 283–296.

Smith, R.A., Henderson, J.C., 2008. Integrated beach resorts, informal tourism commerce and the 2004 tsunami: Laguna Phuket in Thailand. International Journal of Tourism Research 10 (3), 271–282.

Stein, M., Berman, S., 1987. The hotel industry in the Caribbean. Travel and Tourism Analyst 7, 29–39.

Stern, E., 1987. Competition and location in the gaming industry: the 'casinos states' of Southern Africa. Geography 72 (2), 140–150.

Telfer, D.J., Wall, G., 2000. Strengthening backward economic linkages: local food purchasing by three Indonesian hotels. Tourism Geographies 2 (4), 421–447.

Toda, M., Makino, H., Kobayashi, H., Morimoto, K., 2006. Health effects of a long-term stay in a spa resort. Archives of Environmental and Occupational Health 61 (3), 131–137.

Wall, G., 1996. Integrating integrated resorts. Annals of Tourism Research 23 (3), 713–717.

Wise, B., 1993. Hotels/accommodation. Travel and Tourism Analyst 4, 57–73.

Wöber, K.W., Zins, A.H., 1995. Key success factors for tourism resort management. Journal of Travel and Tourism Marketing 4 (4), 73–84.

Yavas, U., Babkus, E., 2003. What do guests look for in a hotel? A multi-attribute approach. Services Marketing Quarterly 25 (2), 1–9.

USEFUL INTERNET RESOURCES

American Hotel and Lodging Association: www.ahla.com/.

Barcelo Hotels and Resorts: www.Barcelo.com.

Caribbean Hotel Association: www.caribbeanhotelassociation.com.

Council on Hotel, Restaurant and Institutional Education: www.chrie.org.

Extended Stay Hotels: www.extendedstayhotels.com/.

Green Hotels Association: www.greenhotels.com/.

Hotel Online: www.hotel-online.com.

Hotel, Motel and Accommodation Association of Australia: www.hmaa.com.au/hmaa/website/.

International Hotel and Restaurant Association: www.ih-ra.com/.

Intrawest: www.intrawest.com.

Jumeirah Hospitality Management Group: www.jumeirah.com.

Multilateral Investment Guarantee Agency: www.miga.org.

National Accommodation Association of South Africa: www.naa.co.za/.

The Most Famous Hotels in the World: www.famoushotels.org/.

Thrifty Motel Group (Australia): www.thriftymotels.com.au/.

CHAPTER 10

Second Homes and Timeshares

INTRODUCTION

There is a growing trend in the world of accommodation that has received considerable attention by industry observers, researchers, entrepreneurs, and tourists themselves: second homes and timeshares. What distinguishes these two forms of accommodation from others discussed in this book are ownership and self-catering. Second homes, also known as recreational properties, summer cottages, or holiday/vacation homes, are an owner-occupied phenomenon, which is at the center of so-called residential tourism or amenity migration. These often take the form of cabins or beach homes but might also include high-rise apartments in large cities, or single-family homes in suburban areas. Some people rent out their recreational homes to tourists when they are not occupying the property themselves. From the timeshare perspective, while guests do not own timeshare properties outright, they do own shares and a period of time associated with a specific property, and thus partial ownership is involved.

Holiday homes and timeshares are the two most notable self-catering forms of accommodation, which means that tourists are able to prepare their own meals in the comfort of a well-stocked kitchen in a condominium or summer cottage setting. These circumstances are particularly favorable for families, because dining in restaurants everyday becomes unhealthy, expensive, monotonous, and inconvenient. Self-catering options are gaining importance as people are becoming more budget and health conscious. This chapter examines the evolution of recreational second homes and timeshares, some of the factors affecting their preference by owners, their spatial dimensions, as well as some of the global aspects of their location. The chapter concludes by focusing on the timeshare sector in the United States.

CONTENTS

Introduction

Recreational Second Homes

Timeshares

Conclusion

References

Further Reading

Useful Internet Resources

RECREATIONAL SECOND HOMES

Second homes have long been a part of everyday life and one of the most commonly inherited properties in some parts of the world, most notably in the Nordic countries of Europe. While second home ownership in places like North America and Asia is considered the exclusive domain of the wealthy and socially privileged, in Nordic Europe it has long been a part of ordinary living, with even the poorest families owning summer cottages to which they withdraw on holidays and during the summer months. In the five Nordic countries alone (e.g. Norway, Finland, Denmark, Iceland, and Sweden) there are more than 1.5 million second homes. Amazingly, there is one vacation home for every 16 people in the population (Table 10.1). Summer cottages are also one of the most significant elements of domestic and regional tourism in all the Nordic states. In addition to being getaway venues from the pressures of urban life, second homes in Scandinavia and Finland have played an important role in the development of the region's folklore and cultural history. For example, in Finland, where approximately half the population owns or has access to a rural second home, Finnish traditional identity and national folklore are intrinsically linked to the country's multitude of forests and lakes, and the summer cottages that adorn them. Such settings have produced romanticized landscapes of idealized habitats, and are often associated with natural living, including activities such as sauna bathing, swimming, fishing, hunting, hiking, and gathering wild berries and mushrooms.

This small house is located in a recreational second-home subdivision in Manitoba, Canada

While not as prevalent as in the Nordic countries, second homes are an important part of the gamut of tourist accommodations in other parts of Europe as well, especially lakeside locations in Central Europe (e.g. Lake Balaton, Hungary), in the alpine region of Switzerland, Austria, Germany, Italy, and France, and along the Mediterranean coast in Spain, Greece, and Italy. North America, New Zealand, Australia, the Caribbean, Southeast Asia, South Africa, and Latin America have also seen a growth in second home

Table 10.1	Second Homes and Populations in the Nordic Countries		Population Per
Country	Population (2006)	Second Homes	Second Home
Denmark	5 427 400	202 500	27
Finland	5 255 600	450 600	12
Iceland	304 400	10 450	29
Norway	4 640 200	379 200	12
Sweden	9 047 800	469 900	19
Nordic total	24 371 000	1 502 200	16

Source: After Hall et al. (2008).

ownership during the past 50 years. Table 10.2 shows the growth of vacation homes in the United States since 1965.

Several trends can be attributed to the growth of second homes in countries such as the United States, South Africa, and Mexico, where the phenomenon is not as well rooted in tradition as it is in parts of Europe. The low cost of land and property during the past half century has provided a significant appeal, although rising real estate costs during the 1990s and early 2000s saw a significant change in this pattern. Increased mobility through transportation innovations and mega-highway systems enables people to purchase land further from home. Increased family incomes because both parents have jobs outside the home have become the norm in most of the developed world, which in theory at least, increases a family's disposable income. This additional income has been spent in many instances on recreational amenities, such as second homes. In the United States there are also lucrative tax incentives associated with buying a second home; they can act as a tax shelter or a tax-deductible investment expense. These trends have enabled a broader spectrum of the population to acquire a recreational home and have taken the phenomenon from the sole domain of the wealthy and made it more accessible to the masses.

There are some unique spatial patterns associated with second home development. In most cases, vacation homes are located in environments of very high amenity, with the most common being lakes, ocean or sea beaches,

Table 10.2	Seasonal Housing in the United States by Year (in thousands)							
1965	1970	1975	1980	1985	1990	1995	2000	2007
1860	1746	1694	2106	2046	2931	3099	2931	4376

Source: US Census Bureau (2008).

islands, and mountains. Research in Sweden suggests that there is a strong inclination for mountains that cannot easily be explained by traditional distance-decay models of demand.

There is also a propensity in most parts of the world for second homes to be located relatively close to large urban areas. However, increased suburbanization between the 1950s and 2000s has forced holiday homes further away from cities. The pressures of urban living cause people to need to get away for recreation and leisure purposes, but time constraints require recreational properties to be located relatively near the home base. Research shows that most second homes are used primarily as weekend retreats, so that use is constrained by distance and time.

Summer homes on the coast at Portrush, Northern Ireland

A growing number of research studies have reported the reasons for people to own and use second homes. The primary motive for second-home tourism is escape—the opportunity to get away from the place of primary residence and all of its pressures, such as work and school, and to relax and regenerate oneself. There appears to be an element of psychological rejuvenation associated with second homes, much as there is with other forms of tourism. Some observer have suggested that, despite second homes being a respite from the everyday pressures of life, there is a simultaneity of place wherein second homes become both an escape and a home.

Another common reason is to get back to nature, a place and state of mind devoid of the hustle and noise of city life. This relates to the first point in that being in nature has repercussions for mental well being, but it also includes an expression of being able to appreciate the natural environment when one's surroundings are so often comprising cityscapes.

A third common motive is to spend time with family and friends, to enhance relations with loved ones, and to create lasting memories. Fourth, pursuing hobbies and other interests are popular reasons for getting away to the holiday home. Many people feel constrained by frenetic schedules at their primary place of residence, whereas visiting the cottage puts them more in a leisure state of mind, which allows them to feel more at ease and able to justify their hobbies and leisure pursuits.

Continuity is another important motive. This concerns people who have long visited certain destinations because they enjoy the place and desire to move back permanently or purchase a seasonal home there. This is a very common situation in the context of amenity migration, which will be described later. It also refers to people who grew up visiting the family's summer home and desire to continue that tradition in their own families. In this way, attachment to place, or relationship with place, is developed. Several studies have been done to understand the notion of sense of place and attachment to places associated with second homes.

Trends and issues

Several issues are currently facing second home owners, destination managers, and permanent residents who live in or near second home areas. Often as regards the impacts of tourism, researchers refer to the concept of social carrying capacity. This can be viewed from two perspectives: the residents of the destination and the tourists themselves. For many second home owners, the attractiveness of the holiday home and its broader location are enhanced by isolation and an absence of other cottages. For these people, solitude and nature are crucial, and if their 'social carrying capacity' is exceeded, their residential tourism experiences will become much less enjoyable. On the other hand, there are significant cohorts of consumers who intentionally purchase second homes in recreational subdivisions in cities and suburbs, where rows of holiday properties dominate the landscape. For these people, the socialization aspects and simple getaways are more important than getting back to nature.

Most research in the area of social carrying capacity deals with the attitudes of permanent residents toward second homes and their absentee owners. Second homes are not without controversy in the communities where they are located. While the majority of full-time community members are ambivalent about second home development in their communities, many have salient concerns. Security concerns are paramount. Many second home proprietors rent out their properties when they are unoccupied by the owners. This is popular everywhere but is an especially popular way of paying for the property and its taxes in places such as the Caribbean, Hawaii, Europe, and Mexico.

Locals often voice trepidation over second home owners renting out their properties, because they see this as an open invitation to transient outsiders who have little connection to place and therefore may have little respect for the destination and its people. Crime, public mischief, violence, and drunkenness have all been voiced as concerns related to seasonal homes being rented out by absentee owners. Even if they are not hired out to holi-daymakers, homes sitting empty for large portions of the year are seen as an open invitation to burglars and vandals. According to one study in the Czech Republic (Vaněček et al., 1997), approximately one third of second homes in that country had been vandalized or burgled at the time of writing.

Conflicts also ensue between recreational home owners and local residents, when second home development is blamed for inflated prices and higher property taxes. Some observers have argued that the existence and development of recreational second homes are causing a displacement of permanent residents in some parts of Europe. Studies from Sweden, however, have refuted these claims and found that property values and increased property taxes were a result of the building of permanent homes and that some popular second home areas have experienced repopulation rather than depopulation.

Environmental carrying capacity is also crucial and has come to the fore of scholarly debates about second homes since the 1970s. Concerns linger about the negative ecological impacts of cottages and other recreational homes. Among these are forest clear cutting, overcrowding and over-development of recreational subdivisions, the construction of larger homes, seasonal overload on public infrastructure (e.g. sewer systems, roads, water supplies, etc.), and demand for year-round access, which can result in the construction of new access routes. In some well-established vacation home areas, such as Finland, there is a push to enhance second home-based tourism as a tool for rejuvenating a declining countryside, creating substantial concerns in that country about the conflict between rural development and environmental protection.

Many of these negative social and environmental connotations in the United States resulted from 1960s and 1970s unscrupulous second home area developers who took advantage of consumers by selling low quality properties that were not properly deeded and surveyed, and to which utility services could not be extended. As a result of such dishonest practices, and to stem growing ecological concerns, many municipalities and counties have down-zoned, or de-zoned land, to inhibit the growth of second home estates.

The internationalization of second home ownership is a fairly recent and interesting turn of events. While second-home tourism is typically viewed as being in the domestic tourism realm, this is changing in some contexts as property ownership regulations are relaxing with increased cross-border cooperation (e.g. European Union) and liberalization of laws that formerly prohibited foreign ownership of land and buildings. Favorable exchange rates between currencies are also an important push factor in the global real estate market.

Many examples exist of people crossing borders to purchase recreational second homes. Among the best documented are Americans building apartments and homes in popular Mexican resorts such as Acapulco, Lake Chapala, Mazatlan, Cancun, Puerto Penasco, and San Carlos. The latter two are relatively recent resort destinations and easily accessible by car from the United States. Second home condominiums in Puerto Penasco and San Carlos are particularly popular among Americans from Arizona, Texas, and California.

With a weak Canadian dollar and strong US dollar in the late 1990s, Americans also flocked north to buy recreational properties along the lakeshores and in the mountains of Canada. Today, however, the tides have turned. With the economic recession and real estate crisis in the United States in 2007–2009, and a much stronger Canadian dollar, affluent Canadians by the thousands are buying up relatively inexpensive homes in Florida, Arizona, Texas, and California to use as winter residences.

The practice of purchasing houses or apartments overseas is not as new in Europe, where British and northern Europeans have long purchased second home units along the Costa del Sol and Costa Brava in Spain, and Germans have purchased summer cottages on the lakes of Sweden. This leads to another important issue—amenity migration, where people move, or migrate, permanently or semi-permanently because of climate or other desirable amenities.

There are countless instances of people vacationing in a certain destination, enjoying it so much that they purchase a second home in that destination, and eventually move there permanently. The Spanish cases above are good examples of this as well. Most often, ethnic groups or nationalities do not integrate well into the local community and culture; instead, they tend to commune with people of their own ethno-linguistic group, creating 'ethnic islands' or 'ethnic enclaves', where languages and cultural practices are transplanted from the visitors' homeland, differing significantly from those of the communities that surround them. There are many British and German enclaves on the Spanish Mediterranean coast where very little Spanish is spoken. Likewise, in Florida, USA, there are several tourism-induced ethnic islands, such as Floribec (where French is spoken and where the majority population originates in Quebec, Canada) and Lantana/Lake Worth, where Finnish language and traditions overshadow English or Spanish. In communities like these, second home proprietors or permanent migrants can own vacation properties in areas of high amenity (primarily climate) and live every aspect of daily life (e.g. medical services, school, church, shopping) in their native language.

This amenity migration also occurs on a domestic basis in the United States and is one of the most important elements of tourism in Florida, Texas and the southwestern states (e.g. Arizona, Nevada, California, and New Mexico). Distinctive social networks, the promotion of retirement communities, and good climate encourage the development of this form of amenity migration. For example, hundreds of thousands of 'snowbirds' (retirees) travel to central and southern Arizona each winter to enjoy the mild winters of the desert climate. This has resulted in the development of huge camper/RV parks, whose populations are more than double each winter. Many of the mobile homes in the caravan parks are absentee owned and lay dormant over the long, hot summer months. However, between November and March each year, these RV complexes flurry with activity. In most cases, the 'snowbirds' are best connected to their first home and the social networks there. In the Sunbelt, however, their behaviors change. Wintertime becomes a vacation period for them as they renew friendships with neighbors, sightsee, dine, dance, bowl, and undertake leisure lifestyles they would otherwise not be able to do in their places of primary residence with the family, church, volunteer, and community-based constraints there.

A winter retirement ('snowbird') community in Mesa, Arizona

There has been some debate in some destinations related to whether or not second home-based tourism should be considered tourism at all. This concern comes primarily from an economic viewpoint, with destination residents, business owners, and public officials suggesting that recreational property owners spend relatively little in the local economy, given that they typically prepare their own food, furnish their own accommodations, and spend most of their time relaxing at the cabin. While it is true that most vacation home owners have different spending patterns than traditional tourists (e.g. they typically do not spend much on souvenirs and dining out), they fit every definition of a tourist, and they do have a positive economic impact. Critics sometimes forget to consider the supermarket and gas station purchases made by second-home recreationists, not to mention the utility services they subscribe to, property taxes they pay, and home improvement stores they frequent for home-related items and repairs. In addition to positive economic impacts, second home owners often contribute socially to the community where their holiday homes are located, such as volunteering in community service and museums, or participating in local music groups and choirs.

Recent studies have suggested that in countries such as Norway, Sweden, and Finland, second home use might be diminishing with the current generation in light of modern-day interests in convenience, comfort, and extraordinary tourist experiences. In North America, though, the opposite is true, with more people than ever before having purchased recreational properties during the past quarter century; the current economic crisis in this regard is a double-edged sword. There has hardly been a better time in recent history to purchase a second home, but people are afraid to spend large sums of money on frivolous purchases, including recreational second homes.

In addition to the factors discussed above, many people are attracted to the tax benefits of second homes offered in some countries where the entire amount or a percentage of the interest paid on a mortgage is tax deductible. National laws that encourage residential ownership of foreigners, non-residents, or seasonal residents also have played important role in island destinations such as Hawaii, Bermuda, the Cayman Islands, and several Caribbean countries, as well as new Central American hotspots including Belize, Costa Rica, and Panama. The Gulf Arab States of Dubai, Bahrain, and Qatar have recently become very popular second home destinations for Europeans, Americans, and wealthy Asians including those from Japan, China, and India.

TIMESHARES

Timeshares can be seen as a type of second home ownership. Timeshare resorts are typically developed by large companies or private investors, but ownership of individual units is divided by shareholders and time is allotted to be used in the property by individual holders, depending on how much time they purchase. In this sense, these can also be seen as a type of second home or recreational property because they entail ownership of a specific time at a specific location. Timeshares are one of the fastest growing lodging options in the world of tourism today, and according to the World Tourism Organization, it is one the most salient tourism-related phenomena altogether. In North America, for example, in recent years, timeshare ownership and construction have grown between 14 and 18% and an average of 15% worldwide. Unfortunately, there is no single authority to keep track of timeshare resorts, ownership data, and shareholder information; it is a highly fragmented sector with properties being owned and operated by numerous national and international companies. Among the largest are Resort Condominiums International (RCI), Interval International (II), and the American Resort Development Association (ARDA). New companies are getting involved in the timeshare sector, including some of the established tourism multinationals such as Marriott, Disney, and Hyatt.

The concept of timeshares originated in the early 1960s with a group of acquaintances who enjoyed skiing in the European Alps. Each of them wanted to purchase an apartment at a ski resort, but individually they could not afford to do so. Pooling their money together was the most obvious solution, as it allowed them to purchase a unit collectively and work out the sharing arrangements by weekly time intervals. The number of weeks at the resort each friend could use was determined by the amount of money he was able to contribute toward the purchase. From these unintentional beginnings, the timeshare notion spread throughout Europe and across the Atlantic to North America, where the first timeshares in the US were developed in Florida in the late 1960s and in Hawaii in the early 1970s. It was in the United States that the timeshare concept accelerated and developed early on.

Timeshares are typically located in areas of very high amenity, such as mountains or beaches and are resort-based condominium units, often referred to as villas, which are fully furnished with appliances, kitchen utensils, furniture, and bedding, ready for use by guests, a situation known as 'turnkey' in the language of hospitality. The units come in a variety of sizes from studio apartments that sleep two, to spacious four-bedroom villas that can accommodate large families. In addition to furnishings and kitchen accoutrements, some units are equipped with clothes' washers and dryers, televisions, wine coolers, and fireplaces. Their resort settings most often provide many added amenities, such as arcades, saunas, swimming pools, exercise rooms, and spas.

The earliest and most common timeshare program is sometimes referred to as fixed week ownership. In this tradition, each shareholder is considered a fractional owner and has the deed to use a unit at a particular property for a specific period of time, typically one or two weeks,

A Marriott timeshare resort in Aruba

depending on the amount of time they purchase. This deeded contract is considered real ownership and can be sold as real estate, rented out, traded for another property, or left to beneficiaries in a will or trust. By the same token, shareholders are required to pay their portion of the property tax. Interestingly, in the United States, where interest and taxes on second homes may, like those of primary residences, be deducted from their taxable income, the expenses associated with some deeded timeshares might create an additional tax incentive.

Since their early beginnings, timeshares have evolved beyond the normative one-week deeded ownership at a specific property into a variety of programs that aim to cater to the demands of an ever changing global market. One such arrangement is 'right to use' in which the client has the right to use the unit for a specified number of years. Once the time limit has been reached, the contract ends and all rights return to the property owner. This is a popular approach in countries where foreign property ownership is heavily restricted or forbidden altogether. Likewise, some of the newcomers to vacation properties, such as Disney Vacation Club, sell on a right-to-use basis. Within the framework of deeded versus right to use, there are several sub-programs available to consumers.

One model, and perhaps the most popular today, are the points or credit systems. Here, guests can purchase a certain level of points equal to a level of property ownership, but typically it is not at a specific property. Purchasers can use the points to arrange stays and other forms of travel within the resort group, based on a wide array of destinations. If the desired destination is costlier than the points available to a person, he or she can purchase the difference. Likewise, if the destination of choice is less expensive than the level of ownership points, the points can be banked for future travel arrangements. Like the cost of more traditional timeshares, the point value of a given property is based on several factors, including location, season, size of unit, day of week, and length of time. This program is more flexible than many of the other programs, although as with all timeshare exchanges, fees are levied for bookings, trades, dues, and upgrades. These can also be purchased with deeded or right-to-use contracts.

Rotating and floating arrangements can also be made in the timeshare sector. Rotating approaches move forward or backward through the calendar so that all owners will have a chance to 'own' the best weeks of the year at some point in time. Floating contracts mean that purchasers can request any week during a set period of time, such as the summer or winter months, although this is based on a first-come, first-served basis, so reservations are typically made quite far in advance. Banked points can be used for other travel-related activities such the purchase of cruise vacations.

A timeshare information booth near the beach in Aruba

Another of the most flexible programs are vacation clubs, which are now being operated by large lodging companies such as Marriott, Starwood Resorts, Hyatt, and Disney. These companies own units in various locations, and intervals are sold as deeded or right to use. Club members are permitted to reserve holiday time at any of the properties, which allows them to experience new places in different seasons.

Magnitude and measure

Across the globe there are thousands of vacation ownership properties in more than 175 countries. This is a significant number, but international data are difficult to acquire. The timeshare sector in the United States, however, is strictly regulated and well documented. Owing to a lack of international data and the availability of US-based data, the focus of the numbers that follow is the US timeshare sector. At the beginning of 2008, 6.5 million US timeshare intervals or point equivalents were owned by some 4.7 million households. As Table 10.3 demonstrates, at the beginning of 2008, there were 1641 timeshare resorts in the United States, totaling 180 200 units. In 2007, more than half a million timeshares were sold in the United States for a value of approximately $10.6 billion (Table 10.4). More than one third of the world's timeshare resorts are located in the United States alone, and more than 50% of the world's timeshare owners are Americans.

The majority of timeshare owners purchase their units or intervals from the resort developers, but there are a number of other ways people come to own timeshare intervals. According to the American Resort Development

Table 10.3	Timeshare Characteristics in the United States, as of January 1, 2008				
Number of Timeshare Resorts	Number of Units	Average Resort Size (in units)	Intervals Owned	Number of Households Owning Timeshares	Top Three Timeshare Destination States
1 641	180 158	110	6.5 million	4.7 million	Florida, California, South Carolina

Source: American Resort Development Association (2008).

Table 10.4	Economics of Timeshares in the United States, 2008			
Total Number of Timeshares Sold in 2007	Total Sales Volume in 2007	Average Selling Price in 2007	Average Occupancy	Average Maintenance Fee Per Unit/Interval
551 457	$10.6 billion	$19 216	80.1%	$575

Source: American Resort Development Association (2008).

Association's (2008) research office, 57.4% of buyers purchase intervals directly from developers, 25.9% from a home owners' association, and 7.2% from a previous owner. Some 10.5% of owners acquired their timeshares as an inheritance, gift, or some other source.

Timeshare prices range from a few thousand to hundreds of thousands of dollars. This depends on several variables, including location, time of year of the interval being purchased, length of time (i.e. one or two weeks), size of unit, etc. Annual fees, which include property tax levies and maintenance costs, range between a couple of hundred dollars per year to upwards of a thousand. As Table 10.4 notes, the average annual fee for interval owner-ship is $575. Several research studies have shown that most timeshare buyers are affluent and well-educated members of the baby-boomer genera-tion. They purchase intervals because of their exchange possibilities and because of perceived savings on future vacations.

On the international scene, timeshare ownership is growing and becoming a more salient part of the tourism economy. The notion of interval ownership has far-reaching cultural and political implications around the world. In China, for instance, and a few other communist countries, the idea of interval ownership is gaining in popularity partly because it resembles a socialist-type approach to collective property ownership. A rapidly growing middle class, a growing form of socialized capitalism, and a stable economy are contributing to the expansion of the timeshare industry in China.

Timeshare issues

After their initial debut, timeshares faced some important challenges during the 1970s and 1980s that reduced their popularity considerably. Perhaps the most significant of these were the deceitful practices of many salespeople (Table 10.5). Problematic management methods, high-pressure sales, and negative media exposure tainted the timeshare reputation, and word spread quickly. This is particularly the case as regards false sales claim that time-shares were guaranteed to appreciate as a real estate investment, which they rarely did, or that renting out the week one owned could pay off the initial

Table 10.5	Problems/Issues Facing the US Timeshare Industry
Tainted industry reputation	New financing
High-pressure sales tactics	Accounting standards
Individual company reputations	Product flexibility
Questionable business ethics	Legal costs
Employee training	Lack of nationwide regulations
Human resource management	Internet marketing
Employee shortages	Stock market problems
Marketing costs	Lost tax incentives
Sales costs	Industry consolidation
Owner relations	Resale issues
Marketing practices	
Heavy-handed and complex regulations	
Costs of capitalization	
Management development	
Independent developments versus brands	
Illegality of selling timeshares as investment in most states	
State laws and regulations in conflict with one another	

Source: Compiled from Woods (2001).

investment in a short time. As the negative word spread, these unscrupulous tactics came under fire by state and national governments to the point that today in many places, promoting timeshares as a real estate investment is illegal. In nearly all cases, timeshares either remain static or, like automobiles, depreciate beginning at the time of purchase. Unscrupulous practices are still rampant in Asia and Africa. Given this negative history, to protect the interests of consumers in their own countries, the governments of Australia, New Zealand, and South Africa have decided to keep a close regulatory eye on the timeshare sector. Likewise, the European Commission adopted a Timeshare Directive that set out rules and regulations for the timeshare sector in the EU member states. These include:

- Giving buyers the right to information in a prospectus before signing a contract and requirements for the content of the contract.

- Once the contract is signed, the consumer is allowed to have a cooling-off period of at least 10 days, during which time he or she can withdraw from the contract without identifying a reason.

- A ban on advance payments during the cooling-off period.

Fortunately, with government intervention and widespread word of mouth, the tarnished timeshare picture is improving now in all parts of the world.

Some industry specialists suggested early on that selling intervals might be a solid alternative for resort and hotel properties that were suffering low occupancy rates. The advice was heeded, and now there are hundreds, if not thousands of hotels whose owners have converted a certain portion of the rooms into vacation ownership suites. For most of these mix-use properties, this has improved occupancy (timeshares have an average occupancy of 80–90%) and revenues, and it also helps mitigate the negative effects of seasonality.

One of the most pressing concerns in the new millennium is an over-supply of timeshares. While construction of new properties and the percent of growth in timeshare purchases continue to grow, there is still an over-supply of weeks and units. Many people are unable to utilize the intervals they purchased, for a variety of reasons, such as the rising cost of air transportation, increased levels of unemployment, and the overall bad economy of 2007–2009. In addition to the cost of traveling, there are, as already noted, annual maintenance fees, which must be paid regardless of whether or not one's interval is used in any given year. Those who elect to finance their purchase (as most people do), end up with high interest rates that are comparable to those of some credit cards. These issues combined often result in people trying to get out of their timeshare agreements. Online auctions, such as ebay, are laden with people selling timeshares, often for a small portion of what they orginally paid.

CONCLUSION

The dark image of timeshares and other second homes during the 1970s and 1980s has given way to a more mainstream phenomenon that has much to offer potential buyers. Owing largely to the renewed image of timesharing and because of the popularity of interval ownership, many new companies are jumping on the timeshare wagon. Companies like Disney, Hyatt, Four Seasons, Ramada, and Hilton have all begun investing extensively in time-share intervals in many parts of the globe. In fact, major hotel chains such as these control over one quarter of all vacation ownership today. Despite the ups and downs associated with timeshares, the phenomenon continues to grow. For example, a few years ago, the Wyndham Hotel chain purchased the Worldmark Timeshare Club, which is the world's third largest vacation program. Its 250 000 timeshare owners have access to resorts mostly in the United States, Canada, and Mexico but also in Fiji.

Large numbers of timeshare and second home owners can have signifi-cant impacts on the economy of a destination. They create employment, spend on purchases for food, gas/petrol, recreational activities, entrance fees, souvenirs, and gifts. They also tend not only to be repeat visitors to the same destination (especially those close to their primary residence) but also frequently sample destinations where their timeshare properties are located. Since timeshares appeal more to people who are retired or semi-retired because they have the flexibility and time to travel, it is expected that as the world's mature population expands, the role of timeshares in the travel and tourism industry will increase.

REFERENCES

American Resort Development Association, 2008. State of the Vacation Time-share Industry. Online http://www.arda.org/AM/Template.cfm?Section= State_of_the_Industry Accessed December 1, 2008.

Hall, C.M., Müller, D.K., Saarinen, J., 2008. Nordic tourism: issues and cases. Channel View Publications, Clevedon, UK.

McHugh, K.E., 2006. Citadels in the sun. In: McIntyre, N., Williams, D.R., McHugh, K.E. (Eds.), Multiple dwelling and tourism: negotiating place, home and identity. CAB International, Wallingford, UK, pp. 262–277.

US Census Bureau, 2008. Housing vacancies and ownership. Online <http://www.census.gov/hhes/www/housing/hvs/annual07/ann07t9.html> Accessed December 5, 2008.

Vaněček, D., Váňa, E., Třicátník, J., 1997. Průzkum využívání chat a chalup (Investigation of usage of weekend houses and village cottages). Ekonomicka Rada 22 (1), 57–62.

Woods, R.H., 2001. Important issues for a growing timeshare industry. Cornell Hotel and Restaurant and Administration Quarterly 42 (1), 71–81.

FURTHER READING

Beck, R.L., Hussey, D., 1989. Politics, property rights, and cottage development. Canadian Public Policy 15 (1), 23–33.

Bieger, T., Beritelli, P., Weinert, R., 2007. Understanding second home owners who do not rent—insights on the proprietors of self-catering accommodation. International Journal of Hospitality Management 26 (2), 263–276.

Butler, R.W., 1985. Timesharing: the implications of an alternative to the conventional cottage. Loisir et Société/Society and Leisure 8 (2), 769–779.

Chaplin, D., 1999. Consuming work/productive leisure: the consumption patterns of second home environments. Leisure Studies 18 (1), 41–55.

Chiang, L.C., 2001. Marketing timeshare in Singapore: an analysis of potential customers and present owners. Asia Pacific Journal of Tourism Research 6 (2), 17–23.

Clout, H.D., 1969. Second homes in France. Journal of the Town Planning Institute 55, 440–443.

Clout, H.D., 1971. Second homes in the United States. Tijdschrift voor Economische en Sociale Geografie 63, 393–401.

Clout, H.D., 1974. The growth of second-home ownership: an example of seasonal suburbanization. In: Johnson, J.H. (Ed.), Suburban Growth: Geographical Processes at the Edge of the Western City. Wiley, London, pp. 101–127.

Coppack, P.M., 1977. Second Homes: Curse or Blessing? Pergamon, Oxford.

Crotts, J.C., Aziz, A., Upchurch, R.S., 2005. Relationship between machiavellianism and sales performance. Tourism Analysis 10 (1), 79–84.

Crotts, J.C., Ragatz, R.L., 1998. Resort timeshare development: trends and future prospects for the East Asia and ANZSA regions. Pacific Tourism Review 1 (3), 257–265.

Crotts, J.C., Ragatz, R.L., 2002. Recent US timeshare purchases: who are they, what are they buying, and how can they be reached? International Journal of Hospitality Management 21 (3), 227–238.

Damon, A.J., 1991. Vacation homes in South East Asia. Travel and Tourism Analyst 5, 24–41.

de Haan, J., 1983. How exchange works. Chartered Surveyor Weekly 4 (7), 333.

Dean, P., 1993. Timesharing opportunities for the hotel sector. Travel and Tourism Analyst, 74–94. August.

Dean, P., 1997. The timeshare industry in the Asia-Pacific region. Travel and Tourism Analyst 4, 38–57.

Deller, S.C., Marcouiller, D.W., Green, G.P., 1997. Recreational housing and local government finance. Annals of Tourism Research 24 (3), 687–705.

Dingsdale, A., 1986. Ideology and leisure under socialism: the geography of second homes in Hungary. Leisure Studies 5 (1), 35–55.

Domke-Damonte, D., Damonte, L.T., Loftus, G., 2008. Are timeshares really different from hotels? Comparative assessment of public service demands by timeshares vs. hotels. International Journal of Tourism Policy 1 (4), 299–314.

Ferreira, S.L.A., Hanekom, F., 1995. Tourism and the local economy of Warmbaths, Northern Transvaal. Development Southern Africa 12 (2), 249–257.

Flognfeldt, T., 2002. Second home ownership: a sustainable semi-migration. In: Hall, C.M., Williams, A.M. (Eds.), Tourism and migration: new relationships between production and consumption. Kluwer, Dordrecht, pp. 187–203.

Gallent, N., Mace, A., Tewdwr-Jones, M., 2005. Second homes: European perspectives and UK policies. Ashgate, Aldershot.

Gallent, N., Tewdwr-Jones, M., 2001. Second homes and the UK planning system. Planning Practice and Research 16 (1), 59–69.

Garnock, D., 1983. Timeshare in our time. Chartered Surveyor Weekly 4 (7), 327.

Gartner, W.C., 1987. Environmental impacts of recreational home developments. Annals of Tourism Research 14, 38–57.

Girard, T.C., Gartner, W.C., 1993. Second home second view: Host community perceptions. Annals of Tourism Research 20, 685–700.

Go, F., 1988. Holiday homes in Europe. Travel and Tourism Analyst 3, 20–33.

Goodall, B., Stabler, M., 1990. Timeshare—An all year round contribution to the local economy? In: Hardy, S., Hart, T., Shaw, T. (Eds.), The Role of Tourism in the Urban and Regional Economy. Regional Studies Association, London, pp. 26–31.

Goodall, B., Stabler, M., 1992. Timeshare: the policy issues. In: Johnson, P., Thomas, B. (Eds.), Perspectives on Tourism Policy. Mansell, London, pp. 175–191.

Gosar, A., 1989. Second homes in the alpine region of Yugoslavia. Mountain Research and Development 9 (2), 165–174.

Groves, D.L., Timothy, D.J., 2001. Festivals, migration, and long-term residency. Téoros: Revue de Recherche en Tourisme 20 (1), 56–62.

Haldrup, M., 2004. Laid-back mobilities: second-home holidays in time and space. Tourism Geographies 6 (4), 434–454.

Hall, C.M., Müller, D.K. (Eds.), 2004. Tourism, mobility and second homes: between elite landscape and common ground. Channel View Publications, Clevedon, UK.

Hall, C.M., Müller, D.K., Saarinen, J., 2008. Nordic tourism: issues and cases. Channel View Publications, Clevedon, UK.

Halseth, G., 1998. Cottage country in transition: a social geography of change and contention in the rural-recreational countryside. McGill-Queen's University Press, Montreal.

Haylock, R., 1991. Prospects for the European timeshare market. Travel and Tourism Analyst 2, 55–77.

Haylock, R., 1994. The European timeshare market: the growth, development, regulation and economic benefits of one of tourism's most successful sectors. Tourism Management 15 (5), 333–341.

Haylock, R., 1995. Developments in the global timeshare market. Travel and Tourism Analyst 4, 38–52.

Hecock, R.D., 1993. Second homes in the Norwegian mountains: cultural and institutional contexts for continuing development. Tourism Recreation Research 18 (1), 45–50.

Hiltunen, M.J., 2007. Environmental impacts of rural second home tourism— case of Lake District in Finland. Scandinavian Journal of Hospitality and Tourism 7 (3), 243–265.

Hopper, M., 1984. Australian resort timesharing. International Journal of Hospitality Management 3 (1), 3–10.

Irvine, C., Cunningham, B., 1990. Second homes. Bantam Books, New York.

Jaakson, R., 1986. Second-home domestic tourism. Annals of Tourism Research 13 (3), 367–391.

Kaltenborn, B.P., 1997. Recreation homes in natural settings: factors affecting place attachments. Norsk Geografisk Tidsskrift 51 (4), 187–198.

Kaltenborn, B.P., 1998. The alternate home: motives of recreation home use. Norsk Geografisk Tidsskrift 52 (3), 121–134.

Lawton, L.J., Weaver, D.B., Faulkner, B., 1998. Customer satisfaction in the Australian timeshare industry. Journal of Travel Research 37 (1), 30–38.

Lengfelder, J.R., Timothy, D.J., 2000. Leisure time in the 1990s and beyond: Cherished friend or incessant foe? Visions in Leisure and Business 19 (1), 13–26.

Liu, J., Pryer, M., Roberts, A., 2001. Timeshare opportunities in China: an evaluation of the conditions for market development. Journal of Vacation Marketing 8 (1), 88–98.

Lundmark, L., Marjavaara, R., 2005. Second home localizations in the Swedish mountain range. Tourism 53 (1), 3–16.

Marjavaara, R., 2007. The displacement myth: second home tourism in the Stockholm Archipelago. Tourism Geographies 9 (3), 296–317.

Massey, J.C., Maxwell, S., 1993. Second houses and summer homes. Old House Journal 21 (4), 28–34.

McHugh, K.E., Hogan, T.D., Happel, S.K., 1995. Multiple residence and cyclical migration: a life course perspective. Professional Geographer 47 (3), 251–267.

McHugh, K.E., Mings, R.C., 1992. Canadian snowbirds in Arizona. Journal of Applied Recreation Research 17 (3), 255–277.

McIntyre, N., Williams, D.R., McHugh, K.E. (Eds.), 2006. Multiple dwelling and tourism: negotiating place, home and identity. CAB International, Wallingford, UK.

Mendoza, L., 1986. A decade of timeshare. Leisure Management 6 (2), 41–42.

Miner, S.S., 1987. Timesharing in the USA. Travel and Tourism Analyst 4, 15–27.

Mings, R.C., McHugh, K.E., 1995. Wintering in the American Sunbelt: linking place and behaviour. Journal of Tourism Studies 6 (2), 56–62.

Moss, L.A.G. (Ed.), 2006. The amenity migrants: seeking and sustaining mountains and their cultures. CAB International, Wallingford, UK.

Mottiar, Z., 2006. Holiday home owners, a route to sustainable tourism development? An economic analysis of tourist expenditure data. Journal of Sustainable Tourism 14 (6), 582–599.

Moule, C., 2002. Pointing the way to the future of timeshare: a treatise on the emergence of points clubs. Marketing Papers 1, 51–65.

Müller, D.K., 2004. Reinventing the countryside: German second-home owners in southern Sweden. Current Issues in Tourism 5 (5), 426–446.

Müller, D.K., 2006. The attractiveness of second home areas in Sweden: a quantitative analysis. Current Issues in Tourism 9 (4/5), 335–350.

Murphy, P.A., 1985. Development of strata units in New South Wales north coast resorts. Australian Geographer 16 (4), 272–279.

Peisley, T., 2002. The international timeshare market. Travel and Tourism Analyst 3, 2.1–2.25.

Pitkänen, K., 2008. Second-home landscape: the meaning(s) of landscape for second-home tourism in Finnish Lakeland. Tourism Geographies 10 (2), 169–192.

Pitkänen, K., Vepsäläinen, M., 2008. Foreseeing the future of second home tourism: the case of Finnish media and policy discourse. Scandinavian Journal of Hospitality and Tourism 8 (1), 1–24.

Pryce, A.H., 2002. Timeshare industry structure and competitive analysis. International Journal of Hospitality Management 21 (3), 267–275.

Ragatz, R.L., 1970. Vacation homes in the north eastern United States: seasonality in population distribution. Annals of the Association of American Geographers 60, 447–455.

Ragatz, R.L., Gelb, G.M., 1970. The quiet boom in the vacation home market. California Management Review 12, 57–64.

Scottish Tourist Board, 1986. A survey of timeshare owners in Scotland. Scottish Tourist Board, Research Section, Edinburgh.

Skak, M., 2004. Restricting ownership of vacation homes. Tourism Economics 10 (4), 435–447.

Sparks, B., Butcher, K., Bradley, G., 2008. Dimensions and correlates of consumer value: an application to the timeshare industry. International Journal of Hospitality Management 27 (1), 98–108.

Sparks, B., Butcher, K., Pan, G., 2007. Understanding customer-derived value in the timeshare industry. Cornell Hotel and Restaurant Administration Quarterly 48 (1), 28–45.

Strapp, J.D., 1988. The resort cycle and second homes. Annals of Tourism Research 15 (4), 504–516.

Stroud, H.B., 1995. The promise of paradise: recreational and retirement communities in the United States since 1950. Johns Hopkins University Press, Baltimore.

Suffron, R.V., 1998. Perceived impacts of outdoor recreation development on benefits of cottage owners at Aylesford Lake: A test of the social exchange theory. Journal of Applied Recreation Research 23 (1), 23–41.

Terry, G.A., 1994. Resort timesharing: growth and situation analysis. Journal of Travel and Tourism Marketing 3 (1), 99–113.

Timothy, D.J., 2002. Tourism and the growth of urban ethnic islands. In: Hall, C.M., Williams, A.M. (Eds.), Tourism and migration: new relationships between production and consumption. Kluwer, Dordrecht, Netherlands, pp. 135–151.

Timothy, D.J., 2006. Supply and organization of tourism in North America. In: Fennell, D. (Ed.), North America: a tourism handbook. Channel View Publications, Clevedon, UK, pp. 53–81.

Tremblay, R., 2006. NonEn Floribec: Espace et Communauté. University of Ottawa Press, Ottawa.

Tuulentie, S., 2007. Settled tourists: second homes as a part of tourist life stories. Scandinavian Journal of Hospitality and Tourism 7 (3), 281–300.

Upchurch, R.S., Gruber, K., 2002. The evolution of a sleeping giant: resort time-sharing. International Journal of Hospitality Management 21 (3), 211–225.

Visser, G., 2004. Second homes and local development: issues arising from Cape Town's De Waterkant. GeoJournal 60 (3), 259–271.

Visser, G., 2006. South Africa has second homes too! An exploration of the unexplored. Current Issues in Tourism 9 (4/5), 351–383.

Vitterso, G., 2007. Norwegian cabin life in transition. Scandinavian Journal of Hospitality and Tourism 7 (3), 266–280.

Walter, C., 1997. Timeshare is reborn. Ski Area Management 36 (5), 66–67, 79.

Woods, R.H., 2001. Important issues for a growing timeshare industry. Cornell Hotel and Restaurant and Administration Quarterly 42 (1), 71–81.

Woodside, A.G., Moore, E.M., Bonn, M.A., Wizeman, D.G., 1985. Segmenting the timeshare resort market. Journal of Travel Research 24 (3), 6–12.

World Tourism Organization, 1996. Timeshare: the new force in tourism. UNWTO, Madrid.

USEFUL INTERNET RESOURCES

American Resort Development Association: www.arda.org.

An Updated Guide for Second-Home Owners: http://articles.latimes.com/2008/jun/15/realestate/re-book15.

Association of Second Home Owners: www.associationofsecondhomeowners.co.uk.

Interval International: www.intervalworld.com.

North American Recreational Properties Association www.narpaonline.org

RCI: www.rci.com/RCI.

WorldMark Timeshare: www.worldmarktheclub.com.

CHAPTER 11

Small-Scale Boutique Accommodations: Inns, Bed and Breakfasts, Lodges, Farm Stays, and Pensions

INTRODUCTION

There is a category of lodging that caters to travelers who seek a cozy experience in elegant and high-amenity settings, where the lodging establishment is an important part of the holiday experience, proprietors are hands-on workers and become personally involved in the services and experiences of guests, and is sometimes, though not always, costlier than hotels and motels. We have chosen to call this category of accommodation 'boutique accommodations', although such a designation could be equally applied to other lodging forms that have already been discussed and that will be discussed later in this book (e.g. ecolodges, lighthouse hotels, resorts, etc.).

BED AND BREAKFASTS, INNS, GUESTHOUSES, PENSIONS, AND HOMESTAYS

In addition to smallness, what unites bed and breakfasts, inns, guesthouses, pensions, and homestays is that they are predominantly family owned and operated, and are in most cases part of the home of the proprietary family. Humans have a long history of welcoming traveling strangers into their homes. Historical records suggest that more than 2000 years ago, the people of ancient Israel/Palestine opened up their homes for people undertaking pilgrimages, attending festivals, and traveling to be taxed, or counted in national censuses. There are several Biblical references to this phenomenon. Likewise, some thirteen centuries ago the Prophet Mohammed taught his Muslim followers that hospitality is a holy attribute and that all Muslims should treat strangers with respect and provide food and accommodations when needed. Many very old examples exist in the Middle East, Europe, Asia, and Africa of people letting out spare rooms in their homes to pilgrims and

CONTENTS

Introduction

Bed and Breakfasts, Inns, Guesthouses, Pensions, and Homestays

Farm Stays and Guest Ranches

Lodges

Summary and Conclusion

References

Further Reading

Useful Internet Resources

other travelers, so the notion of homestays, guesthouses, and bed and breakfasts is of ancient origins.

Hotels and motels were built primarily because of long-distance rail travel in the 1800s and more recently with the advent of the automobile and the emergence of road and highway networks in the early and mid-1900s. During the Middle Ages and prior to the widespread development of railway lines, homestays (i.e. a bed with breakfast in people's homes) were the primary form of accommodation in many parts of the world. With the exception of a few scattered taverns with rooms, inns were scarce and relatively expensive; in the seventeenth and eighteenth centuries lodging in people's homes was a more popular alternative. During the Second World War and the Great Depression of the 1930s, which affected the entire world, North Americans and Europeans began letting out rooms in their homes for extra income. Later, drawing on the idea of guesthouses and B&Bs in Europe and the UK, this idea of more formalized home-based tourist accommodation caught on in the USA, Canada, Australia, and New Zealand.

Probably the best-known form of this boutique accommodation is the ubiquitous bed and breakfast, variously known as B&B, bed 'n' breakfast, or bed and breakfast inn. Inns, homestays, pensions, and guesthouses fall within this same general category, in that rooms are provided in private or semi-private homes where guests share the quarters of the person or family who owns it. They all are also small in scale, with anywhere from 1 to 20 rooms, although some government bodies and professional associations dictate the maximum number of rooms an inn can have to be considered a B&B. In the United States, B&Bs and inns are generally synonymous. They provide breakfast, whereas pensions and guesthouses do no always include the morning meal in the price. Typically, B&Bs are located in scenic areas with relatively high tourist appeal or along important transportation corridors. The UK-based Bed and Breakfast Association defines B&Bs as 'independent, owner-managed establishments not recognized as hotels, and offering overnight accommodation and breakfast on a "per night" basis to paying guests' (Bed and Breakfast Association, 2008: n.p.).

It should be pointed out that this form of lodging differs somewhat between countries and regions in terms of their characteristics and designs. In the United Kingdom, for example, most B&Bs are seen as low-cost, budget accommodation (although there are deluxe B&B rooms in Britain as well), are typically located in people's homes, are relatively small or have only a few rooms for rent, and are not necessarily located in the most scenic areas. Nonetheless, there is a prevalence of B&Bs in seaside resort communities where the British have traditionally spent their holidays.

In the United States, Canada, and New Zealand, however, they are seen as a more exclusive, high-end accommodation choice, often with more rooms, and most have been structurally remodeled to meet basic standards of a public lodging facility. In fact, to establish their exclusivity, some B&Bs have installed wine bars, spa facilities, and wireless Internet. They are located in areas of high esthetic appeal and are housed in homes that in most cases have some degree of heritage appeal and ambience. Most bed and breakfast inns have 'a character, history and authenticity which is typical of the area in which they are located, and they provide superior standards of decoration, comfort and catering … they are usually found in quiet backwaters in the most picturesque locations and often have spectacular views of the surrounding countryside, providing both pleasure to tourists and inspiration to artists and photographers' (Cazelais 1998: 45). Nearly always in North America, the owners live en suite, but the home is given over more to a business function with only a small portion of the house providing the living quarters of the owners. The majority of B&Bs in the UK cost between USD $30 and $75 per night, while in the USA, relatively few cost less than $80 a night and can easily range upwards of $400–500 per night, depending on location and setting, season, and degree of elegance and sophistication. American and Canadian B&Bs are commonly regarded as romantic getaway options for honeymooners and anniversary celebrations, while they rarely possess this sort of appeal in the UK and Europe.

The modern-day concept of bed and breakfasts originated in the United Kingdom but has spread

An urban bed and breakfast in New Zealand

One of many ubiquitous B&Bs on the coast of Ireland

A small country inn in England provides a few rooms, food and drink

An urban inn in Dublin, Ireland, provides beds and 'traditional Irish food'

throughout the world and is commonplace in Ireland, New Zealand, North America, and the Caribbean. By definition, B&Bs offer a bed and a breakfast but typically no other meals. Some B&Bs have private bathrooms and toilets en suite, while others require guests to share a common bathroom. Breakfast is usually served in a common dining room or in the home's kitchen and is nearly always prepared by the proprietor.

Some B&Bs are very small in scale, being designated 'Zimmer' (room) in German-speaking countries and in Israel, and *chambres d'hotes* in France. *Zimmer* in Europe typically indicates one or two rooms for rent in a home that has not necessarily been remodeled into traditional accommodations. There may not be a common social area, and the majority of the home's square footage serves as the owners' residence. The concept of *Zimmer* in Israel often indicates larger businesses that resemble more the North American concept of B&B, with an historic atmosphere, romantic connotations, and family vacation possibilities. In much of the world, B&Bs and *Zimmer*-like arrangements are sometimes referred to as homestays, which indicates families offering extra bedrooms for rest to guests. It is quite common for people to offer a bedroom for rent to visitors when a son or daughter moves away to work or to attend university. The term 'homestay' is used quite frequently in the developing world, in Southeast Asia for example, much the same way *Zimmer* is used in Germany. Pensions are essentially the same as B&Bs and *Zimmer*s, differing primarily by name and location. Located primarily in the Latin countries of Europe (e.g. Italy, Spain, Portugal, and France), pensions are often seen as inexpensive alternatives to hotels. They are also family-run operations and have limited services other than basic breakfasts.

Guesthouses are nearly identical to B&Bs in many places and resemble them in terms of services, intimacy, and hands-on management by the owners. However, in Germany, Liechtenstein, Austria, Belgium, and Switzerland, these *Gasthäuser* tend to be somewhat larger than *Zimmer*s and might include a bar, tavern, restaurant, or café. They are typically found in small towns and villages, although they do also exist in cities. They are usually family owned and operated, and like the other forms examined in this section, the owners live in the guesthouse or nearby.

Professional associations and organizations

From an administrative perspective there are dozens of professional organizations, or bed and breakfast associations that aim to promote the use of B&Bs. Most associations serve the needs of member properties and assist travelers in making reservations. Members are required to pay a fee and must adhere to certain quality standards related to hospitality and service excellence, management practices, hygiene, security, and adherence to established guidelines. In return, the association assists in marketing efforts and certifies each property as conforming to the required standards of quality. These organizations exist on national and regional levels. Each state in the US, for example, has innkeepers associations, and the American Bed and Breakfast Association is dedicated to promoting B&B accommodation as an alternative to traditional hotel and resort stays. In the UK there are thousands of B&Bs, which are a crucial part of the tourism supply there and seen by many as the archetypal type of lodging in the UK and Ireland and a must-do experience. The objectives of the Bed and Breakfast Association in the United Kingdom are manifold. The first is to represent the interests of members and to lobby on their behalf in government agencies and legislative assemblies. Second, it provides information and support services to members that will enable them to improve their businesses. Third, it aims to establish and promote best practices in the B&B sector. Fourth, it encourages and facilitates the professional development of the independent bed and breakfast sector in the United Kingdom, and finally, endeavors to build public awareness of the benefits of staying in bed and breakfast accommodation (Bed and Breakfast Association, 2008).

According to the Professional Association of Innkeepers International, which keeps statistics on the US bed and breakfast industry, there are approximately 20 000 inns/B&Bs in the United States, providing some 153 000 rooms. The average occupancy rate is around 38–40%, and the average cost per night in the US is $150–165. Most B&Bs are located in small towns and villages (54%), 29% in rural locations, and 17% in urban and suburban settings. Each inn employs about 4.3 people, and 58% of all proprietors are dependent on additional income sources. In the United Kingdom, nearly 1.2 million guests stayed in B&Bs in 2007, compared to 14 million overnights in hotels. Unfortunately, there is relatively little data available about B&B/inn operations at national or international levels. Most statistics are amalgamated with all other lodging data, and the little amount that does exist focuses only on the number of B&B bed nights.

Research has shown that B&B-style lodging in North America is popular for well-educated professional couples, who desire to spend time in the countryside. In other parts of the world, they have a broader market base, appealing to families, couples, and backpacking youth. Private baths, privacy, quiet atmosphere, and involved innkeepers are commonly cited as the most desirable characteristics of B&Bs.

Management issues

There are several current management issues affecting the B&B sector. First is e-commerce and Internet reservation systems. Although the network of B&B-type establishments is growing, and several online reservation systems are in place, there is still a lack of representation in much of the world. Most online systems focus on the UK, USA, and Canada, with other parts of the world being overly neglected by the large booking systems. Many of the smaller properties that might not afford costly memberships still rely heavily on word of mouth, printed promotional materials, and chambers of commerce, although with the decreased cost of building websites, many of them have begun to achieve higher levels of recognition and Internet visibility. Unfortunately, too few proprietors are using secure servers for online reservations. Likewise, several recent studies have found that B&B owners do not use the Internet to its full potential, for communicating with guests or acquiring feedback.

Another crucial management concern today is safety and security. While hotels and resorts can afford staff security officers, most small-scale lodging cannot. This is particularly salient in the less-developed parts of the world, where entrepreneurialism should be encouraged, but security concerns are prevalent. In addition, while there is generally a high level of satisfaction with owning a home-based lodging operation, owners frequently voice their frustration with the lack of leisure time and ability to come and go when they need to. These are highly labor-intensive operations, and most do not employ more than a few immediate family members.

Several management problems and constraints have been identified that keep many entrepreneurs from realizing their ambitions to develop B&Bs

and other boutique accommodations. One of these is zoning regulations and building permits. Because many such businesses are located in towns, villages, and cities, there are strict municipal regulations and policies in place regarding building, remodeling, and reconstructing. Likewise, because many B&B structures are historic in nature, they have a heritage value, which can require additional procedures, permits, and restrictions on what is allowed or not. It is important to note, however, that B&Bs can be seen as an important tool for preserving heritage buildings and historic homes, which might not otherwise be economically or physically possible. A second constraint is a lack of experience in the hospitality sector. Many people feel inadequate to open up such an operation, although there are now many books, websites, and companies that train people how to become B&B or pension entrepreneurs. Third is a lack of financial resources. Often, lending institutions are wary about making loans to small operators.

FARM STAYS AND GUEST RANCHES

Farm stays and guest ranches are another related form of B&B or inn, but they entail much more than just a bed and breakfast. With changing agricultural environments in terms of world markets, demand for produce, increasingly mechanized and expensive production methods, and seasonality and specialized niche products, farmers around the world have begun looking for additional income prospects. Agritourism, or farm-based recreation, is now seen as a viable alternative. Agritourism activities include horseback riding, fishing, hunting, petting zoos, u-pick orchards and gardens, harvest celebrations, farmers' markets, feeding animals, milking cows and goats, cleaning stalls, herding livestock, gathering eggs, sheering sheep, hay rides, and farm tours. For many people, there is a nostalgic element about getting to the countryside. In many urbanites' minds, rural life and agricultural lifestyles symbolize a simpler and more wholesome standard of living, where people assist in earth's creative processes and partake of more holistic foods and atmospheres. Many parents desire to expose their children to landscapes and agrarian values they might have enjoyed as youth, while other guests simply need to get away from the fast-paced pressures of urban living.

There are a number of benefits involved when farmers elect to become involved in tourism. First, as already noted, it provides supplemental income and allows them to meet financial goals, such as paying off the farm early or financing their children's university education. Second, it helps diversify a farmer's revenue sources to guard against the volatilities of weather and climate, global produce markets, technological demands, property taxes, fuel costs, and government policies. As well, it provides jobs for family and community members. Fourth, it has a ripple effect in stimulating the local economy off the farm. This is particularly the case with small-scale establishments, such as these, because in most cases they use local products, local suppliers, and the local workforce. Fifth, it fulfills their dreams of a rural lifestyle. Some entrepreneurs purchase farms and lands with the purpose of establishing working farms and lodging for tourists as a means of achieving their own rural lifestyle goals. Several studies have found that the lifestyle benefits of establishing farm stays and other rural B&Bs far outweigh the risks and costs associated with their establishment. Finally, it can impress upon the farming community the value of preserving pristine lands that can be utilized for leisure pursuits.

According to recent research, one third of all farm operations in the UK maintain tourist activities in addition to farming. The number is even higher in Italy, France, and Germany. In the United States, some 52 000 farms (2.5% of the total) received income from recreation and tourism in 2004–2005, earning an estimated $955 million in additional income.

An important part of this agritourism movement is the establishment of inns or homestays on farms and ranches. Staying at such a property is motivated by a desire to be immersed in an agricultural way of life for a short time or to have ready access to rural trails and hiking opportunities, and farm guests are most satisfied by meeting friendly people, getting value for money, and understanding green issues. Many farm guests have genuine interests in rural living, raising farm animals, riding horses, and growing gardens, but owing to job and family constraints are unable to do so on a daily basis. Farm stays and guest ranches allow them to fulfill this aspect of their lives in a surrogate manner, and many return frequently.

Farm stays are an important component of tourism in nearly all parts of the world, especially in New Zealand, Australia, Israel, Europe, Japan, Taiwan, South America, North America, and a smattering of other countries in Asia and Africa. Agritourism, including farm accommodation, is still more common in Europe and New Zealand than it is in the US and Canada, but the notion is expected to continue gaining in popularity in North America as well.

Farm-based lodging demonstrates some distinct spatial differences in several parts of the word. In Europe, for instance, there are tangible disparities between the cattle- and fruit-based farm stays in the colder north and mountain regions, and the olive and vineyard backdrop of the

Mediterranean. In the USA, farm-based accommodation like that in New Zealand and Europe is based overwhelmingly in the South and secondly in the Midwest. Dude ranches dominate in the western states, predominantly in Arizona, Colorado, Wyoming, Nevada, Utah, New Mexico, and Montana.

Guest ranches, also known as 'dude ranches' in the western United States, are one form of farm stay where the focus is large ranches that specialize in large-scale cattle production and where much of the work is done on horseback. Guest ranches have become an important experiential phenomenon of the Australian outback where cattlemen focus their efforts on sheep and cattle in the harsh environments of the central deserts. In New Zealand, most farm stays are also centered on the sheep and cattle industries but in a much more temperate climate, and can be found scattered through both the North and the South Islands. In Japan, there is an increasing awareness of the Japanese countryside and agrarian heritage. Along with that has come a boom in the growth of farm inns, most of which cater primarily to a domestic market.

Dude ranches

Western American guest ranches began in the 1800s, but with the twentieth century mythological view of the 'disappearance' of the American frontier, they gained more prominence, especially in the wake of post-WWI affluence and the widespread use of automobiles, as easterners began traveling to the western states via railroad and car in search of the illusive western frontier. Popular western movies that glorified the cowboy way of life generated flows of 'dudes' (urban easterners) to the American west in search of the cattlemen's frontier lifestyle.

Today, guest ranches/dude ranches cater primarily to the needs of urban dwellers, who desire to get away from the frenetic lifestyles of the city. Tourism researchers have discussed at length tourist motivations, and a consensus has been reached that people travel to specific destinations to have encounters with the 'other' or to experience something different, beyond their normal environments. Dude ranches are an important illustration of this motive. Thousands of people desire to get back to their agrarian roots or to begin a new hobby, such as horseback riding. Likewise, as with farm-based tourism in general, getting one's 'hands dirty' and helping out on the ranch provide learning opportunities for guests, and their children can experience alternative ways of living outside their urban estates. In Israel, Israelis and foreign tourists spend time working and staying on *kibbutzim*, or communal working farms, to experience this old-fashioned lifestyle, to learn about organics, for altruistic and solidarity reasons, or as a way of experiencing this aspect of Israeli life.

Most dude ranch experiences include more than just riding and taking care of animals; they also include trail rides, hiking, fishing, camping, and country cooking lessons. The Dude Ranchers' Association (2008) appeals to these interests: 'Imagine yourself taking the best vacation of your life at a dude ranch. The cool, fresh mountain air, the open spaces, the feel of a steady horse beneath you as you top the next rise ... the flash of color from the dark pool as the monster trout rises to your offering... luxuriating in the warmth of the setting sun as you wait for the dinner bell's call ... shared time with family and friends'.

Each sub-sector of accommodations has its own associations. Guest ranches are no exception. The Dude Ranchers' Association was founded in 1926, as the phenomenon began to grow in the American west. Today there are over 100 members, all of which have to undergo a strict two-year inspection and approval process. The stamp of approval from the Association demonstrates that a ranch has met basic quality and safety requirements. Several of the western states also have their own dude ranchers' associations with similar required industry standards.

LODGES

There are several different kinds of tourist lodges, but all of them conjure up images of rustic and exotic surroundings whose reason for being is to allow visitors to become immersed in nature and/or outdoor sports. Eco-lodges will be discussed in greater depth in Chapter 15. The most common types of lodges include ski lodges, hunting and fishing lodges, mountain lodges, and national park lodges. Their common characteristics include relatively isolated locations, natural settings (e.g. mountains, lakeside, riverside, and rainforests), rustic construction (e.g. logs and fireplaces) and atmosphere, and on-site meal services. Many older ski resorts are representative of this phenomenon, where guests spend their days on the ski slopes and return to the lodge in the evenings for fireplace-based entertainment, barbeques, and music and dancing. These are often located in far-flung mountain regions where snows last longer at high elevations and where few other signs of human civilization exist. Besides ski resorts, other mountain lodges have been developed in high-altitude areas to cater to the desires of mountain hikers and those who want to escape the busy life of the city. These are especially popular in alpine Europe and in the Rocky Mountains of the US and Canada. Some mountain retreats in South and

Southeast Asia resemble the lodges discussed above. While many of them are not made of logs and are more accessible by car, they are exclusive destinations, many built by British and Dutch colonialists in the eighteenth and nineteenth centuries, to cater to people who want to get away from the sweltering heat of the tropical lowlands by spending time at exclusive lodge-type resorts in the highlands.

Hunting and fishing lodges tend to be more isolated than ski lodges. Many such enterprises exist in remote parts of Canada and the United States and can only be accessed via floatplane, horseback and hiking, or canoe. These secluded lodges, like ski resorts, are expensive and cater to a high-income market that is able to pay considerable sums of money for airplane rides and hunting guide services. Some nights are spent at the lodges, which act as the home base, with other nights being spent in tents in the field. Through the lodges, game animals and fish can be processed, frozen, and sent to the hunter's home address. Game lodges of the North American and European models continue to be developed in southern and eastern Africa as well, where big game hunting has long been an important form of sport tourism. Today in countries such as Namibia, Kenya, Zimbabwe, Botswana, and South Africa, such hunting resorts are becoming more common and are still in high demand. Besides hunting, several of these lodges also cater to other wildlife tourism activities such as photography, walking, and hot air balloon safaris.

North America was the world's forerunner in establishing national parks, with Yellowstone (USA) being the first national park in the world, established in 1872. Aside from camping, accommodations in national parks in the US and Canada are synonymous with lodges. Most of the US National Park Service properties do not offer accommodations within their boundaries, but many of the earliest parks do. During the early 1900s it was fairly common for railway companies and private investors in the United States to build tourist lodges in natural areas and in designated parklands to accommodate park visitors and to promote the use of the railway lines for long-distance travel. Several of these original lodges, including Bryce Canyon Lodge (Bryce Canyon National Park, Utah), Zion Lodge (Zion National Park, Utah), El Tovar Hotel (Grand Canyon National Park, Arizona), Ahwahnee Hotel (Yosemite National Park, California), and Old Faithful Inn (Yellowstone National Park, Wyoming), are still used and have become expensive and romanticized accommodations options for national park visitors. Prices often range upwards of $500 per night, including one or two meals. These lodges were built approximately during the same era and have a similar foundational design, often referred to as National Park Service Rustic architecture, or Parkitecture, for short.

Most of them were built of logs, the most common natural construction resource where they are located.

Several of Canada's western national parks have corresponding lodges, or grand railway hotels, although they differ somewhat in their design (châteauesque) from their American Parkitecture counterparts, and most of them were built slightly earlier (1880s–1890s). These railway hotels were built by the Canadian Pacific and Canadian National Railways in scenic areas serviced by the rail companies. Most were constructed before their surrounding national parks were designated. Well-known examples include Banff Springs Hotel (Banff National Park, Alberta), Chateau Lake Louise (Banff National Park, Alberta), and the Prince of Wales Hotel (Waterton Lakes National Park, Alberta), the Prince of Wales being built by an American, rather than Canadian, rail company.

In both countries, these park lodges and chateaus have a high historic value, because of their association with the railway lines that played such an important role in the settlement of the western states and provinces. Likewise, they are representative of the earliest designation of national parks in North America and stand as testimonies to the importance of tourism in the late nineteenth and early twentieth centuries in the US and Canada. This has established these properties not only as lodging facilities but also as important heritage sites and are in fact, among the most popular tourist attractions in their respective park boundaries. Their heritage value has prompted the US Secretary of the Interior to list several of the American lodges as National Historic Landmarks on its National Register of Historic Places.

Despite their historic elegance, national park lodges are more barebones than traditional hotels. Swimming pools are uncommon, televisions are even absent from some of them, and bathrooms might have to be shared. This is so for a variety of reasons, but primary among them are that the lodges on the historic properties list are required by law to maintain their original structural integrity and that they are meant to feel rustic in their appeal. In the United States, park lodges are typically owned by the National Park Service but operated by private concession companies. Forever Resorts and Xanterra Parks and Resorts operate many of them; in Canada, several lodge properties are operated by Fairmont Hotels and Resorts of Toronto.

SUMMARY AND CONCLUSION

One of the most important principles of sustainable development is appropriate scale. Like hostels and ecolodges, B&Bs, inns, guesthouses, farm stays, and lodges, are operated at a very small scale. As such, they have more freedom to purchase locally produced goods and utilize a local workforce, much more so than large international hotel chains. Thus, the leakage effect with B&B-type lodging is very small. Also, they are extremely important in the tourism industry, because they are not as sensitive to seasonality as large hotels and resorts and are therefore an excellent way to diversify a destination's range of accommodations.

B&B types of development provide more suitable and appropriate options for tourism in developing countries. First, owing to limited domestic investment capital for large hotel and resort projects, B&Bs, guesthouses and agritourism facilities can be developed more easily utilizing local building material and labor. Second, these types of facilities have significant social dimensions that may not be available in regular hotels and resorts. The types of lodging facilities examined in this chapter facilitate a greater degree of host–guest interaction when visitors stay and interact with local owners, service providers, and their families. Personal relationships may be formed that could last a lifetime, thereby accomplishing some of the principal social and cultural objectives of tourism as a peace industry that builds bridges between individuals, societies, and countries. Finally, the educational value of international visitors staying at a rural B&B or on a farm located on a vineyard in France, Austria, Chile, or South Africa goes beyond the general notion of a 'wine-tasting' tour. Visitors have the opportunity to learn about the whole system of land preparation, cultivation, monitoring crops, harvesting, processing, and wine production. Similarly, staying at a B&B or lodge on a coffee plantation in Kenya or Costa Rica, or on a cocoa plantation in Brazil or Ghana provides education about two products (coffee and chocolate) that have a high level of consumption in industrial countries, but many people there have little knowledge of the agricultural requirements. Obviously, there are the economic benefits that have been addressed in this chapter. For example, it is common for visitors to purchase samples of products from their destinations such as coffee, tea, various nuts (Macadamia) and even alcoholic drinks, such as rum, after visiting or staying at a sugar plantation B&B in the Caribbean. Finally, because of their mostly rural locations, B&Bs, lodges, and farm guesthouses help to disperse the economic benefits to rural areas of a tourism destination by providing revenue, employment, foreign exchange, and linkages with other economic sectors, especially the agricultural sector.

REFERENCES

Bed and Breakfast Association, 2008. About the bed and breakfast association. Online <http://www.bandbassociation.org/about.htm> Accessed November 15.

Cazelais, N., 1998. Charlevoix et ses auberges. Téoros, Revue de Recherche en Tourisme 17 (1), 45–47.

Dude Ranchers Association, 2008. Helping people find quality dude ranch and guest ranch vacations since 1926. Online <www.duderanch.org/index.cfm>; Accessed November 15.

FURTHER READING

Alonso Chousa, J., 1984. El parador nacional de Santo Domingo de la Calzada y su entoro. Estudios Turisticos 84, 49–64.

Antolović, J., 1997. Immovable cultural monuments and tourism. Acta Turistica 9 (2), 136–154.

Barrett, P., 1986. Old buildings—new accommodations. Wales Tourist Board, Cardiff.

Borne, L.R., 1983. Dude ranching: a complete history. University of New Mexico Press, Albuquerque.

Bote Gómez, V., 1985. Tourisme rural en Espagne et patrimoine bâti. Tourist Review 40 (1), 21–23.

Brown, D.M., Reeder, R.J., 2007. Farm-based recreation: a statistical profile. US Department of Agriculture, Washington, DC.

Bryan, B., 1991. Ecotourism on family farms and ranches in the American west. In: Whelan, T. (Ed.), Nature Tourism: Managing for the Environment. Island Press, Washington, DC, pp. 75–85.

Busby, G., Rendle, S., 2000. The transition from tourism on farms to farm tourism. Tourism Management 21 (6), 635–642.

Clarke, J., 1999. Marketing structures for farm tourism: beyond the individual provider of rural tourism. Journal of Sustainable Tourism 7 (1), 26–47.

Connolly, L., 1997. Opportunities in rural tourism. Farm and Food 7 (1), 9–11.

Daugherty, C.M., Jaquay, B.G., 1998. The emerging bed and breakfast industry in Costa Rica. Pacific Tourism Review 2 (1), 11–19.

Dawson, C.P., Brown, T.L., 1988. B&Bs: a matter of choice. Cornell Hotel and Restaurant Administration Quarterly 29 (1), 17–21.

Dinçer, F.I., Ertuğral, S.M., 2003. Economic impact of heritage tourism hotels in Istanbul. Journal of Tourism Studies 14 (2), 23–34.

Emerick, R.E., Emerick, C.A., 1994. Profiling American bed and breakfast accommodations. Journal of Travel Research 32 (4), 20–25.

Evans, N.J., Ilbery, B.W., 1992. The distribution of farm-based accommodations in England and Wales. Journal of the Royal Agricultural Society of England 53, 67–80.

Fennell, D.A., Weaver, D.B., 1997. Vacation farms and ecotourism in Saskatchewan, Canada. Journal of Rural Studies 13 (4), 467–475.

Fletcher, K., Johnson, R., 1991. The bed and breakfast in Ontario: a preliminary analysis of an alternative form of tourist accommodation. Journal of Applied Recreation Research 16 (2), 149–164.

Garcia-Ramon, M.D., Canoves, G., Valdovinos, N., 1995. Farm tourism, gender and the environment in Spain. Annals of Tourism Research 22, 267–282.

Getz, D., Petersen, T., 2005. Growth and profit-oriented entrepreneurship among family business owners in the tourism and hospitality industry. Hospitality Management 24, 219–242.

Gladstone, J., Morris, A., 2000. Farm accommodation and agricultural heritage in Orkney. In: Brown, F., Hall, D. (Eds.), Tourism in Peripheral Areas: Case Studies. Channel View, Clevedon, UK, pp. 91–100.

Griffin, R.K., 1998. Small lodging operations in Costa Rica. Cornell Hotel and Restaurant Administration Quarterly 39 (2), 55–63.

Gyimóthy, S., 2002. Nothing like the good old days: myths and realities of Danish inns. Hospitality Review 4 (1), 26–30.

Haines, M., Davies, R., 1987. Diversifying the farm business. BSP Professional Books, Oxford.

Hall, C.M., Rusher, K., 2004. Risky lifestyles? Entrepreneurial characteristics of the New Zealand bed and breakfast sector. In: Thomas, R. (Ed.), Small Firms in Tourism: International Perspectives. Elsevier, Amsterdam, pp. 83–97.

Hart, W.A., 1994. Elegant survivors: historic hotel renovation in Oregon. Cornell Hotel and Restaurant Administration Quarterly 35 (4), 38–61.

Hill, R., Busby, G., 2002. An inspector calls: farm accommodation providers' attitudes to quality assurance schemes in the county of Devon. International Journal of Tourism Research 4 (6), 459–478.

Hjalager, A.M., 1996. Agricultural diversification into tourism: evidence of a European Community development programme. Tourism Management 17 (1), 103–111.

Huang, L., 2006. Rural tourism revitalization of the leisure farm industry by implementing an e-commerce strategy. Journal of Vacation Marketing 12 (3), 232–245.

Huang, L., 2008. Bed and breakfast industry adopting e-commerce strategies in e-service. Service Industries Journal 28 (5/6), 633–648.

Hudson, S., Gilbert, D., 2006. The Internet and small hospitality businesses: B&B marketing in Canada. Journal of Hospitality and Leisure Marketing 14 (1), 99–116.

Ingram, H., 1996. Classification and grading of smaller hotels, guesthouses, and bed and breakfast accommodation. International Journal of Contemporary Hospitality Management 8 (5), 30–34.

Jackson, J.J., 1989. Hunting enterprises for forest farmers. Forest Farmer 48 (9), 24–28.

Jeong, M., 2004. An exploratory study of perceived importance of Web site characteristics: the case of the bed and breakfast industry. Journal of Hospitality and Leisure Marketing 11 (4), 29–44.

Johnston, M., 1983. Historical recreation geography of tourist lodges: the example of Algonquin Park, Ontario. Recreation Research Review 10 (3), 22–33.

Jones, W.D., Green, D.A.G., 1986. Farm tourism in hill and upland areas of Wales. University College of Wales, Aberystwyth, UK. Department of Agricultural Economics and Marketing.

Kaufman, T.J., Weaver, P.A., 1998. Marketing efforts of bed and breakfast operations: do they influence success? Journal of Travel and Tourism Marketing 7 (4), 61–78.

Kaufman, T.J., Weaver, P.A., Poynter, J., 1996. Success attributes of B&B operators. Cornell Hotel and Restaurant Administration Quarterly 37 (4), 29–33.

Kidd, J.N., King, B.E.M., Whitelaw, P.A., 2004. A profile of farmstay visitors in Victoria, Australia and preliminary activity-based segmentation. Journal of Hospitality and Leisure Marketing 11 (4), 45–64.

Kline, S.F., Morrison, A.M., St John, A., 2004. Exploring bed & breakfast web-sites: a balanced scorecard approach. Journal of Travel and Tourism Marketing 17 (2/3), 253–267.

Lanier, P., Berman, J., 1993. Bed-and-breakfast inns come of age. Cornell Hotel and Restaurant Administration Quarterly 34 (2), 14–23.

Lanier, P., Caples, D., Cook, H., 2000. How big is small? A study of bed & breakfasts, country inns, and small hotels. Cornell Hotel and Restaurant Administration Quarterly 41 (5), 90–95.

Lee, S.Y., Reynolds, J.S., Kennon, L.R., 2003. Bed and breakfasts industries: successful marketing strategies. Journal of Travel and Tourism Marketing 14 (1), 37–53.

Lubetkin, M., 1999. Bed-and-breakfasts: advertising and marketing. Cornell Hotel and Restaurant Administration Quarterly 49 (4), 84–90.

Lundberg, D., 1984. How Scottish innkeepers parlay their assets. Hotels and Restaurants International 18 (6), 120–124.

Lynch, P.A., 2000. Networking in the homestay sector. Service Industries Journal 20 (3), 95–116.

Lynch, P.A., Tucker, H., 2004. Quality homes, quality people: the challenge of quality grading and assurance in small accommodation enterprises. In: Thomas, R. (Ed.), Small Firms in Tourism: International Perspectives. Elsevier, Amsterdam, pp. 183–195.

Mahoney, E.M., Holecek, D.F., 1989. 1988 Michigan bed and breakfast guest study. Michigan State University, East Lansing, MI.

Mangan, E., Collins, A., 2002. Threats to brand integrity in the hospitality sector: evidence from a tourist brand. International Journal of Contemporary Hospitality Management 14 (6), 286–293.

McIntosh, A.J., Bonnemann, S.M., 2006. Willing workers on organic farms (WWOOF): the alternative farm stay experience? Journal of Sustainable Tourism 14 (1), 82–99.

McLean, D.D., Hurd, A., 2001. Lodges, resorts and state park systems. Visions in Leisure and Business 20 (4), 41–48.

Millman, C., Martin, L.M., 2006. Small rural hospitality firms: how have bed and breakfast establishments embraced the internet? Journal of Rural Enterprise and Management 2 (2), 5–22.

Monty, B., Skidmore, M., 2003. Hedonic pricing and willingness to pay for bed and breakfast amenities in southeast Wisconsin. Journal of Travel Research 42 (2), 195–199.

Morris, H., Romeril, M., 1986. Farm tourism in England's Peak National Park. The Environmentalist 6 (2), 105–110.

Nickerson, N.P., Black, R.J., McCool, S.F., 2001. Agritourism: motivations behind farm/ranch business diversification. Journal of Travel Research 40 (1), 19–26.

Nilsson, P.Å, 2002. Staying on farms: an ideological background. Annals of Tourism Research 29, 7–24.

Nummedal, M., Hall, C.M., 2006. Local food in tourism: an investigation of the New Zealand South Island's bed and breakfast sector's use and perception of local food. Tourism Review International 9 (4), 365–378.

Nuntsu, N., Tassiopoulos, D., Haydam, N., 2004. The bed and breakfast market of Buffalo City (BC), South Africa: present status, constraints and success factors. Tourism Management 25, 515–522.

Ollenburg, C., 2008. Regional signatures and trends in the farm tourism sector. Tourism Recreation Research 33 (1), 13–23.

Pearce, P.L., 1990. Farm tourism in New Zealand: a social situation analysis. Annals of Tourism Research 17, 337–352.

Roberts, B., 1995. Looking for tourist potential. Ski Area Management 34 (5), 59–61.

Rodnitzky, J.L., 1968. Recapturing the West: the dude ranch in American life. Arizona and the West 10 (2), 111–126.

Rogerson, C.M., 2004. Transforming the South African tourism industry: the emerging black-owned bed and breakfast economy. GeoJournal 60, 273–281.

Shackley, M., 1993. Guest farms in Namibia: an emerging accommodation sector in Africa's hottest destination. International Journal of Hospitality Management 12 (3), 253–265.

Stevens, L.B., 1983. B and Bs: a booming market. Cornell Hotel and Restaurant Administration Quarterly 24 (3), 49–51.

Stringer, P.F., 1981. Hosts and guest: the bed and breakfast phenomenon. Annals of Tourism Research 8 (3), 357–376.

Sutton, M., 1993. From five star hotel to intimate homestays. Information on Human Development 19 (7/8), 6.

Takada, T., Sato, Y., Ishikawa, M., 2000. The present condition and problems of the farm inns in Hokkaido: cases of Shikaoi town and Shintoku town. Journal of the Rural Planning Association 19 (2), 289–294.

Turner, J.C., Davies, W.P., 1995. Farm-based tourism and recreation in the United Kingdom. Agricultural Progress 70, 21–43.

Upchurch, R.S., 1997. Conduct of midwestern bed and breakfast operations in the USA. International Journal of Contemporary Hospitality Management 9 (1), 39–43.

Vallen, G., Rande, W., 1997. Bed and breakfasts in Arizona. Cornell Hotel and Restaurant Administration Quarterly 38 (4), 62–75.

Vallen, G., Rande, W., 2002. The incidence of burnout among bed-and-breakfast owner/operators. Journal of Human Resources in Hospitality and Tourism 1 (2), 41–56.

Walford, N., 2001. Patterns of development in tourist accommodation enterprises on farms in England and Wales. Applied Geography 21, 331–345.

Warnick, R.B., Klar, L.R., 1991. The bed and breakfast and small inn industry of the Commonwealth of Massachusetts: an exploratory survey. Journal of Travel Research 29 (3), 17–25.

Zane, B., 1997. The B&B guest: a comprehensive view. Cornell Hotel and Restaurant Administration Quarterly 38 (4), 69–75.

USEFUL INTERNET RESOURCES

American Bed and Breakfast Association: www.abba.com/.

Arizona Dude Ranch Association: www.azdra.com.

B&B and Farmstay Owners Association: www.bbfassociation.com.au.

B&B Association: www.bandbassociation.org/.

BedandBreakfast.com: www.bedandbreakfast.com/.

Bed and Breakfast Network: www.bedandbreakfastnetwork.com/.

B&B Club: www.bandbclub.com/.

British Columbia Guest Ranchers Association: www.bcguestranches.com.

Colorado Dude Ranch Association: www.coloradoranch.com.

Dude Ranchers' Association: www.duderanch.org.

DudeRanches.com: www.duderanches.com.

European Inns: www.europeaninns.com.

Fishing Lodges Network: www.fishinglodges.net.

Hunting Lodges Directory: www.huntinglodges.net.

Hunting Top 10 Lodges: www.huntingtop10.com/lodges/index.html.

Montana Dude Ranch Association: www.montanadra.com.

National Ski Areas Association: www.nsaa.org/nsaa/home.

Professional Association of Innkeepers International: www.paii.org.

Worldwide Fishing Guide: www.worldwidefishing.com.

CHAPTER 12

Mobile Lodging

INTRODUCTION

People are always on the move, and many travel experiences involve mobile forms of lodging. It is not uncommon for people to travel to a single destination and spend their vacation time there. However, millions of others appreciate being on the move, visiting more than one place during their holidays, and perhaps being more economical in their lodging decisions. This chapter examines several forms of itinerant lodging that are popular today throughout the world, including recreation vehicles (RVs), houseboats, yachts, canal barges, trains, and cruise ships. These forms of mobile lodging facilities have several unique attributes that appeal to different market segments. First, the very mobile nature of this category of lodging facilities sometimes places them more in the domain of the transportation sector of the tourism industry. Second, they are most likely to include amenities and facilities that range from the basic to the more elaborate but considered essential to the itinerant traveler. For example, RVs, houseboats, and yachts have kitchens, living room space, or quarters, and a range of appliances to provide convenience, comfort, and recreation while in motion, in transit, or at rest. Third, unlike traditional hotels, ownership of some of these mobile itinerant lodgings can range from rental, leasing, to outright ownership. Finally, improved technology continues to transform the mobile lodgings and has implications for service providers, tourists' experiences, destinations, and the environment.

CONTENTS

Introduction

Recreational Vehicles and Caravans

Houseboats and Yachts

Trains

Cruises

Summary and Conclusion

References

Further Reading

Useful Internet Resources

RECREATIONAL VEHICLES AND CARAVANS

Recreational vehicles (RVs) combine transportation and temporary living quarters for recreation, travel, sightseeing, and camping, and include campers, trailers, motor homes, and caravans. During the 1980s and 1990s, recreational vehicles became very popular, and this popularity continued to grow into the new millennium. RVs are especially popular forms of mobile lodging in North America, Europe, Australia, and New Zealand, although in Europe, Australia, and New Zealand, more people rent them than own them. In the US and Canada, while renting RVs is popular, most people who use them own them. In 2001, some 10% of all American vehicle-owning households also owned an RV. Today, approximately eight million US households own a recreational vehicle, representing an increase of over 58% since 1980. Some forecasts suggest that by 2010 approximately 8.5 million US households will own an RV, although this estimate might be overly optimistic given the current dire economic situation, which is forcing many families to reduce spending on non-essential luxury items like RVs. Nonetheless, according to a 2005 study, almost one quarter (23%) of all US households intended to purchase an RV sometime in the future (Curtin, 2005).

Caravans/trailers for sale in the USA

Also on the rise are RV rentals. RVs are especially popular vacation options because they are seen as a hassle-free way of seeing the world. They allow greater freedom and flexibility in travel, and people do not have to worry about advanced hotel reservations, although in some instances reservations may be required for stays at RV parks or resorts. RVs are also like a home away from home because they offer comfortable accommodations, TVs, kitchenettes, running water, heat, bathrooms, and air conditioning. RV holidays are typically less expensive than other forms of travel, for people can prepare their own food and sleep in their vehicles.

In the United States and Canada, RVs tend to appeal to various market

Rented RVs are popular lodging options in New Zealand

segments including families with young children seeking to travel to multiple destinations and attractions. The active senior retired market is especially attracted to RV travel and they have become important to the economies of the climatically mild and sunny states of Florida, Texas, Arizona, and California during the winter months from late October to April. The annual migration of retirees trying to escape the long and cold winters in Canada and the US central, mid-western, and eastern states has become known as the snowbird phenomenon. A significant number of these mobile visitors stay at RV resorts and RV parks in major urban areas; however, rural areas in the deserts of Arizona and California, such as Quartzite, have become established RV travel centers. To a lesser extent, regions within the northern Mexican states that share the long border with California, Arizona, New Mexico, and Texas also benefit from RV travel. RV tourists have significant economic impacts at destinations for a numbers of reasons. First, their length of stay ranges from a few weeks to months. Second, because they are very mobile, they have a tendency to impact several communities, sometimes in different states. Some RVers even pull their sedan or SUV vehicles to enable them to travel more economically and conveniently away from the RV park or resort, which serves as a 'base camp'. Third, RV tourists tend to be repeat travelers returning to the same region or destination each year for a number of reasons that include a sense of community with other retirees.

HOUSEBOATS AND YACHTS

Houseboats and yachts have long been a salient part of tourist transportation and accommodation in places where lakes, rivers, and large canals are important tourism resources. Houseboats are particularly popular on the lakes and rivers of the western United States (e.g. Lake Powell and Lake Meade) and the large rivers of the mid-west and east. Riverboats are another favored option on the navigable rivers of the US east and Midwest. Canal barges and motorized boats/yachts are prevalent in Europe, especially in the Netherlands, Belgium, Ireland, the United Kingdom, and France, where intricate networks of canals and rivers allow travelers to navigate their way deep inside the countryside, often seeing sights that would be out of reach for most tourists. River barges are common on Europe's major rivers including the Danube, Rhine, Rhone, Seine, Elbe, and Volga. Comfortable motorized boats are becoming a popular mode of transportation in India and other parts of Asia as well on the major lakes and rivers of the region.

In the United States, houseboats on large water bodies have become a form of second home for some people, even if the boats are rented, for many people spend months at a time on the water. Some houseboats are treated like timeshares, as several people join together to purchase the unit and take turns using it. In Arizona, Lake Havasu and Lake Powell (also in Utah) are popular houseboating destinations for weekend getaways, week-long holidays, or entire seasons. At Lake Havasu, it is not uncommon for retirees from the north to come to the desert to spend the winter months on a boat. Research shows that house-boaters are overall social people, who enjoy encounters with other boaters and travel in groups of family and friends.

Houseboats, while not inexpensive to rent or own, are not as prestigious as charter boats and yachts. These can be found all around the world, but several destinations have become popular for this form of travel, such as Bermuda, the US and British Virgin Islands, the French islands of Guadalupe and Martinique, other Caribbean islands, as well as Hawaii. The Mediterranean region from Spain to Greece is also noted for yachting activity that ranges from construction, sales, rental servicing, and storage. In the Scandinavian region, Norway, Sweden, Denmark, and Finland also have thriving yachting activity, although it is limited mostly to the short summer season. New and emerging yachting destinations include the oil-rich gulf states (UAE, Qatar, and Bahrain). Yachting, according to some observers, involves an entire subculture, including high living standards, fashionable clothing and lifestyles, sexual encounters, and other excesses of life. In most cases, large yachts, or schooners, can be hired with a crew and can house up to 80 passengers, including accommodations. Most yachts, however, are chartered without a crew and carry between four and ten passengers.

All of these issues come to bear on aspects of lodging. Nearly all houseboats, yachts, and canal barges are equipped with beds, toilets, kitchenettes, televisions, and other social amenities. Separate bedrooms for all passengers are difficult to accommodate, since spaces are obviously limited. Many solve this space problem by using bunk-style and foldaway beds. The significance of houseboats and yachts can be seen in some popular tourist destinations where onboard bedrooms outnumber hotel rooms. Like all other forms of accommodation, there are significant environmental concerns associated with houseboats, primarily surrounding issues of water pollution from gas or diesel, exhaust, and human and kitchen waste, as well as direct damage to marine wildlife.

TRAINS

Train travel is still the most popular mode of long distance and intercity travel in Europe, Japan, China, India, and many other parts of the world.

Table 12.1 shows data on passengers in the top ten rail-transporting countries of the world. In Europe, trains provide a relatively cost-effective method of transportation, compared to owning a car, which can be prohibitively expensive and difficult to navigate in centuries-old cities. Trains in Europe and Japan are also highly efficient and punctual compared to those in many other parts of the world and are widely used as a practical means of traveling short and long distances.

In North America the situation is different. A relatively small portion of the population utilizes railways for long-distance travel. In Canada and the United States, trains are used primarily for short-distance trips and daily commutes, and rarely have a pleasure holiday connotation. For some people in North America, however, long-distance rail trips are gaining in popularity—not as a transportation mode but as an entire vacation experience. Traveling by rail from coast to coast exposes people to pristine locations that cannot be seen from most interstate highways. Such trips often take more than a week and require sleeping arrangements on board. Overnight trains in Europe are also very popular, less as a holiday experience, but as an effective method of travel, because considerable distances can be covered while sleeping. In either case, train sleepers are an important itinerant form of tourist accommodation.

Table 12.1	Passengers and Passenger Kilometers in the World's Most Train-Dependent Countries, 2006	
Country	**Total Passengers Carried (Millions)**	**Total Passenger Kilometers Traveled (Millions)**
Japan	8 778	249 029
India	5 378	615 634
Germany	1 850	74 727
Russia	1 320*	173 699
China	1 260	635 327
United Kingdom	1 163	46 764
South Korea	969	31 416
Spain	622	21 520
Italy	592	47 642
Ukraine	522	53 230
Egypt	451	40 837
Netherlands	322	15 414

*2005 data

Source: International Union of Railways (2008).

For short-distant travel (less than a day), most train passengers purchase a ticket for first or second class, depending on the level of comfort they want. This seat then becomes their 'accommodation' while on the train. For many people a seat is enough for short-distance travel. Some customers even elect to stay in a single seat for longer trips of one or more nights. While this is an uncomfortable option, it is seen as a way of reducing travel costs, and some people are willing to endure sitting and sleeping on a chair to be able to travel on a budget. Long-distance trains, however, have other sleeping options. The two primary options are sleepers and couchettes. Couchettes are inexpensive but resemble a youth hostel in that bunk-bed arrangements in cabins (usually in second class) are assigned regardless of gender or familiarity. They typically accommodate several people who share a common berth but have their own bunks with pillow and blanket.

The second overnight alternative is sleeper cars, which are more comfortable and private. In most cases, these contain berths and a private washbasin. First class sleepers usually accommodate one or two passengers, while second class sleepers can accommodate between two and four people. Rates are charged per person, and a family or travel group can share a berth. Some of the more upmarket trains include restrooms in individual sleeper compartments. Nearly always, advanced reservations must be made for sleeper and couchette positions.

Passenger rail transportation played a leading role in the evolution of tourism in the mid to late 1800s with major milestones that include Thomas Cook's organized tours, and George Pullman's individual sleeping compartments. The development of luxury sleeping accommodations combined with restaurants is what elevated rail travel to new heights that found wide public acceptance before the advent of automobile and airline travel. Belgium's George Nagelmackers, who established the more advanced sleeping railcar, also founded the Compagnie Internationale des Wagons Lits, which today is a major rail, catering, and mega-travel agency operation that merged with Carlson Travel. Rail transportation expanded in Europe in the late 1800s and became dominant in the early to mid 1900s, spreading to other parts of the world and contributing to the growth of tourism. The sleeping compartment became a major feature of rail travel with a well-developed luxury segment. Nagelmackers' Orient Express from Paris to Constantinople, which became known as 'the king of trains, the train of kings', established the high standards of today's luxury trains as well as the forerunner to contemporary nostalgic and heritage trains.

Several long-distance rail lines have become popular tourist destinations. The Trans-Siberian Railway, for example, is among the most sought-after experiences for train enthusiasts and people who desire to traverse the width of Siberia and visit Mongolia and China afterward. Several nostalgic railways have also become popular in recent years, including the Orient Express routes in Europe and South America, which are reminiscent of the original Orient Express of the nineteenth century. On these lines, lodging is an essential component of the trip and often adds appeal to the nostalgic flavor of the journey. Australia's trans-continental Indian to Pacific Ocean train provides an alternative way to see some of the remote areas of that vast continent from Sydney to Perth. South Africa's Blue Train from Cape Town to Victoria Falls in Zimbabwe is marketed as the 'World's Leading Luxury Train' that combines the luxury of the world's leading hotels with the charm of train travel.

As noted already, train travel in Europe, Japan, and other parts of the world remains popular. In North America, though, it is less popular, and has in recent decades seen a decline in customers and service routes with the increase in car ownership and less-expensive air tickets following the deregulation of that sector in 1978. This has become a highly controversial and significant point of debate in countries such as the United States and Canada where passenger rail operators such as AMTRAK and Via Rail are heavily subsidized by the national government and continuously operate at a profit loss. There is constant talk of doing away with long-distance passenger service, but it is unlikely this will happen in the near future. Rail company managers are also concerned about safety and security from two perspectives. First, the threat of terrorism is always at the forefront of their plans and management approaches. Second, however, more directly relevant to accommodations, is the notion of the safety of passengers in seats, couchettes, and sleeper cars. Pick-pocketings, thefts, muggings, and violent crimes are not uncommon and are a major concern in the less-private accommodations options aboard trains. European and Japanese passenger rail services have benefitted from improved technology with respect to speed, safety, comfort, convenience, and on-board amenities found in rail systems such as the TGV in France, Inter-City Express (ICE) in Germany and the Bullet Train (Shinkansen) in Japan. Some countries such as China are already building the next generation of the technologically advanced magnetically levitated (MAGLEV) train. Prospects for improved rail passenger service in the United States are pretty high. ACELA, the first high speed train operated by AMTRAK, entered into service in 2000 and currently operates in the Northeast Corridor from Boston to New York and Washington, D.C. As petroleum prices increase, many believe more Americans will travel by train, including long overnight trips that will include expanding overnight accommodation facilities on board.

CRUISES

Like long-distance trains, houseboats, and yachts, accommodation is one of the most important features of cruises. While pleasure cruises began initially in the 1950s and 1960s, they gained most of their current level of popularity in the 1970s, 1980s and 1990s, with 1970s television shows (e.g. *The Love Boat*) depicting the romanticized experience of cruising the oceans of the world. As a result of this growth in popularity, many destinations developed their infrastructure (i.e. ports) to accommodate increasing numbers of cruise ships and passengers. Likewise, this trend of the 1970s–2000s provided a rationale for many less-developed destinations in the Caribbean, Central America, and the Pacific to focus on cruise-based tourism as a tool for economic growth. Many well-defined cruise destinations have thus developed, with the Caribbean being the world's most significant cruise tourism region in terms of ships, passengers, and ports of call. Most cruises to the Caribbean depart from the United States. Approximately 8.3 million cruise passengers traveled from US ports in 2003 and 9.4 million in 2004 to the Caribbean and other destinations (Table 12.2).

A large cruise ship docked at Prince Edward Island, Canada

In most cases, though, the positive economic impact on the port destinations or the entire country is relatively small because passengers disembark, sightsee, and shop for a few hours, and then head back to the ship to eat and sleep. Furthermore, although cruise ships stock huge amounts of provisions, very little is purchased locally at the destinations. That cruise tourists do not spend much money in the destination, because of the all-inclusive nature of cruises, is a major concern among destination planners and business owners. This is even the case in Bermuda, where most cruises stay much longer (in some cases several days) in port than in most other cruise destinations, but they act as floating hotels, where people return to dine and sleep. This, according to local hoteliers and restaurateurs, creates too much competition for Bermuda's other accommodation and dining

Table 12.2   Cruises Departing from the 15 Most Popular US Cruise Ports, 2003–2004

15 Busiest Ports in Order of Rank (2004)	2003 Passengers (thousands)	2003 Cruises	2004 Passengers (thousands)	2004 Cruises
Miami, Florida	1 865	735	1 683	641
Fort Lauderdale, Florida	1 078	544	1 237	637
Port Canaveral, Florida	1 116	451	1 230	466
San Juan, Puerto Rico	571	225	677	322
New York, New York	424	212	547	252
Los Angeles, California	515	225	434	193
Galveston, Texas	377	203	433	208
Long Beach, California	171	70	401	166
Tampa, Florida	418	213	399	198
New Orleans, Louisiana	297	143	396	178
Seattle, Washington	165	78	291	135
San Diego, California	93	65	173	104
Honolulu, Hawaii	172	79	171	90
Jacksonville, Florida	n/a	n/a	114	65
Baltimore, Maryland	57	49	105	55
All other ports	805	471	697	517
Total US cruise ship ports	8 283	3 840	9 417	4 463

Source: Bureau of Transportation Statistics (2005).

options, and an excess of ships in port deteriorates the island's image of a luxury, high-quality destination.

Cruise tourism is considered the fastest growing sector of the leisure tourism market. Figures compiled by Cruise Lines International Association (CLIA) show that since 1970, the number of people taking cruise vacations in the North American region has grown from only 500 000 to 12.6 million in 2007—a 2 100 per cent growth during that period. In 2008, there were nearly 92 million bed days on cruises throughout the world (see Table 12.3). One of the primary reasons for the attractiveness of cruises is that they are a total vacation experience and all-inclusive, with some ships even going so far as to promote themselves as the destination! They are commonly referred to as 'floating resorts'. Cruises provide gourmet food, entertainment, transportation, and comfortable accommodations, in some cases with twice daily cabin service. One purchase price covers all of these service elements that might otherwise have to be found and purchased individually. Interesting routes and ports of call are important factors in deciding on a particular cruise; there are few other options for people to visit multiple destinations without having to pack and re-pack several times. Recent research studies have found that nearly all cruise passengers are satisfied and happy with their

Table 12.3	Geography of Cruise Destinations by Bed Days, 2008 (000's)				
Destination	**2000 Total Bed Days**	**2002 Total Bed Days**	**2004 Total Bed Days**	**2006 Total Bed Days**	**2008 Total Bed Days**
Caribbean	21 510	26 741	31 211	31 956	30 786
Mediterranean	6 277	6 497	9 704	10 504	16 271
Alaska	4 197	5 053	5 914	6 356	6 968
Bahamas	3 200	2 876	3 657	6 073	3 477
Trans Panama Canal	2 573	2 093	2 931	2 804	2 679
Western Mexico	2 681	3 387	4 827	5 214	6 451
Europe	3 745	6 923	7 560	6 800	7 592
Bermuda	988	1 227	1 324	1 388	1 266
Transatlantic	1 016	1 006	1 425	1 467	2 830
Hawaii	857	1 903	2 629	2 885	3 031
South Pacific	1 155	835	683	1 449	1 986
South East Asia	245	346	20	611	527
Africa	503	260	17	43	137
Canada/New England (US)	1 108	1 151	1 489	1 233	1 911
Far East	202	360	404	127	527
Mississippi River	347	0	0	0	137
World	414	582	463	340	1 063
South America	826	1 395	1 089	1 446	2 676
US West Coast	218	216	644	161	225
Indian Ocean	121	94	11	10	229
Trans-Pacific	52	143	12	99	389
US East Coast	1 402	147	60	81	83
Antarctica	49	73	219	197	285
Unclassified	109	234	990	196	449
Total	53 795	63 542	77 283	81 440	91 975

Source: CLIA (2009).

cruising experience and considered their cabins to be comfortable, clean, and a good value.

The accommodations element of cruises is equally as important as food, entertainment, and ports of call. In most large cruise ships, there are several decks devoted to sleeping cabins, or staterooms, as the industry now refers to them. Most cruise lines have four or five levels of luxury available on each sailing. For example, luxury suites are the most expensive and most lavish. These typically contain more than one room, sometimes two bedrooms and a common living room. Most luxury suites include hot tubs, saunas, whirlpool tubs, private concierge service, private balconies, pianos, and bars. Some companies also offer mini-suites, which are a variation of luxury suites.

Balcony rooms are also considered quite elegant and include one or two beds, a living/sitting area, private bath, and a private balcony. A third type of room is 'outside', referring to ocean views from cabin windows. Finally, and least expensive of them all, are interior rooms. These are similar to outside rooms but without the ocean view. Prices between these staterooms vary considerably depending on their location on the ship, the size of room/number of beds needed, and length of the cruise itinerary.

Room management in the cruise sector is very different from that of hotels and resorts in several ways (see Toh et al., 2005). First, most cruise bookings are made several months in advance. Second, the least expensive and most expensive cabins and suites tend to be purchased first, with the mid-range rooms filling up later. Third, most cruise reservations (approximately 90%) are handled by travel agents rather than individuals booking their own passage. Fourth, because no-shows and last-minute cancellations cannot typically be filled on cruises, like they can be in hotels with walk-ins, there are steep cancellation penalties, including

Inside a cruise ship luxury stateroom

a 100% penalty for cancellations within a week of departure. Finally, over-bookings are common on cruises to offset cancellations. These management approaches and others together have created a much higher occupancy rate on cruise ships than the hotel sector sees each year. On average, the occupancy rates on cruises range from 95 to 103%.

One futuristic perspective of on-board accommodations is the idea of apartment ships. This concept is quite unique. A person can purchase an apartment of one to five bedrooms onboard a cruise ship, and prices range in the millions of dollars. These apartments provide an opportunity to live on a ship and spend all of one's time traveling the world. Individuals, couples, or families can live on board and come and go at will from various ports of call or via helicopter at sea. Residents can elect to live full time on board, or rent out their apartments for part of the year. For some residents, the apartments are second homes. One such apartment ship, *The World*, has swimming pools, restaurants, a supermarket, tennis court, dance club, bookstore, mini-golf course, and a helicopter landing pad. Half of the ship's residents are from Europe, 40% from the United States, and 10% from Asia and the Middle East.

Several health concerns have come to the fore in recent years regarding cruises and cabins. There is some concern and talk about the location of rooms increasing or decreasing the likelihood of passengers becoming seasick. However, recent scientific research concludes that cruise cabin location does not affect the probability of seasickness, but the roughness of the seas does. Many medical studies have focused on the spread of diseases and sickness through cruise ships and by utilizing cabins that have housed sick people before. Similarly, there are safety concerns related to the accessibility of cabins during times of emergencies, such as fires.

On the supply side, the growth of accommodation capacity on cruise ships has been quite impressive and underscores the phenomenal rate of growth in the entire cruise line industry. Table 12.4 provides figures for the number of berths (or beds) between 1981 and 2007 that indicates an increase from 41 073 to 268 109 during that period. Almost 40 new ships were built in the 1980s but this doubled in the 1990s when about 80 new ships were built. This pace has further increased and it is estimated that by the end of 2008, over 100 new ships have entered service since 2000. The actual capacity of accommodation facilities and amenities on cruise ships is much higher since cruise ship inventory is measured in lower berths but upper berths that accommodate third and fourth guests are available in most staterooms.

Table 12.4	Growth of North American Cruise Capacity (Lower Berths) 1981–2007	
Year	**Number of Lower Berths**	**Percentage Change**
1981	41 073	–
1991	86 631	3.7
2001	175 855	5.8
2002	197 553	12.3
2003	212 004	7.3
2004	225 714	6.5
2005	230 891	2.3
2006	245 898	6.5
2007	268 103	9.0

Source: CLIA, 2001, 2005a, 2005b, 2007.

SUMMARY AND CONCLUSION

Mobility is at the core of the tourism phenomenon, while overnight stays at destinations are an essential requirement for what functionally constitutes tourism. Various forms of mobile lodging continue to combine these two elements and the future promises even greater utilization of these mobile accommodation units for tourism. Aircrafts currently have seats that recline flat into beds in first and business class, especially on long-haul flights. In addition to beds on the Airbus A380, there are 'personalized suites', hospitality lounges, and other amenities designed to provide a 'resort-like' feel and experience in the air. The A380 aircraft currently being operated by Emirates Airlines has showers for passengers who wake up in first and business class. Emirates Airlines, a trend setter, has ordered about 50 of these mega-aircrafts, and it is very likely that these and other accommodation-related amenities will more than likely be adopted by other major airlines to stay competitive.

The cruise sector is arguably where some of the greatest advances are taking place in mobile lodging. The trend towards the development of mega-equipment and facilities has produced mega-hotels such as the MGM in Las Vegas with 5005 rooms and the Airbus A380 with capacity for 550 to 800 passengers. The new generation of mega-cruise ships have finally arrived. Currently, the two largest ships are Royal Caribbean Cruise Line's *Liberty of the Sea* and *Independence of the Sea* with 160 400 Gross Registered Tonnage (GRT) with accommodation capacity for 3 643 passengers. The new ship, *Oasis of the Sea* that is scheduled to enter service in 2009, will be 220 000 GTR with 2700 staterooms for 5 400 passengers, and will be 16 decks high. Utilizing land-based residential concepts, it will also have seven neighborhoods, a Central Park, boardwalk, and Royal Promenade. The accommodation facilities will include two-level duplexes, suites that range from 2 000 to 3 000 square feet of living space, and balconies that open into a courtyard. With the typical ratio of three guests to one service personnel, this ship will also accommodate an additional 1 800 crew members for a total of 7 200 persons on this mega-floating resort. The increased size of cruise ships has been a trend since the mid-1980s when the *Norway* with capacity for 1 800 passengers was the largest cruise ship. It is therefore likely that the industry will continue to build larger ships.

The growth and widespread use of mobile lodgings have obvious economic and social benefits; however, they also have economic, social, and environmental implications. RVs and caravans may have economic benefits in destinations but they also are among the most fuel inefficient vehicles in both absolute and per capita terms. It has already been noted that cruise ships do not benefit most less-developed destinations in the Caribbean, Central and South America, Africa, Asia, and the Pacific. There is also the issue of low wages and lack of benefits for the large number of crew members recruited from developing countries. Cruise ships and yachts may pollute and dispose of waste material in international waters where their activities are hard to monitor. The adverse environmental impacts are likely to increase as cruise ships become even larger. Many of these ships will not be able to dock in today's ports, forcing some poor countries to invest in port expansion or be excluded as ports of call.

REFERENCES

Bureau of Transportation Statistics, 2005. Top 15 cruise ship ports by port of departure: 2003 and 2004. Online <<http://www.bts.gov/cgi-bin/breadcrumbs/PrintVersion.cgi?date=06172706>> Accessed December 30, 2008.

CLIA, 2001. The cruise industry – an overview. CLIA, New York.

CLIA, 2005a. Cruise industry source book; M. Silver Associates Inc./CLIA, New York.

CLIA, 2005b. Overview of the cruise line industry. CLIA, New York.

CLIA, 2007. Cruise industry source book. CLIA, New York.

CLIA, 2009. 2008 CLIA cruise market overview. Online <<http://www.cruising.org/Press/overview2008/#RecentGrowth>> Accessed January 5.

Curtin, R.T., 2005. The RV consumer: a demographic profile 2005 survey. Recreation Vehicle Industry Association, Reston, VA.

International Union of Railways, 2008. Documentation database. Online <<http://www.uic.asso.fr/uic/spip.php?article1347>> Accessed January 5, 2009.

Toh, R.S., Rivers, M.J., Ling, T.W., 2005. Room occupancies: cruise lines out-do the hotels. International Journal of Hospitality Management 24, 121–135.

FURTHER READING

Becker, R.H., 1979. Travel compatibility on the upper Mississippi River. Journal of Travel Research 18 (1), 33–36.

Berger, A.A., 2004. Ocean travel and cruising: a cultural analysis. Haworth, New York.

Cahill, M., Kisielica, S., 1993. The U.S. riverboat and dockside gaming industry. Hotel Valuation Journal 3, 1–5.

Dickinson, B., Vladimir, A., 1997. Selling the sea: an inside look at the cruise industry. Wiley, New York.

Dowling, R.K. (Ed.), 2006. Cruise ship tourism. CAB International, Wallingford, UK.

Flanagan, B., Garn, A., 2004. The Houseboat Book. Universe Publishing, New York.

Gabor, M., Blaustin, J., 1979. Houseboats: Living on the Water Around the World. Ballantine Books, New York.

Gahlinger, P.M., 2006. Cabin location and the likelihood of motion sickness in cruise ship passengers. Journal of Travel Medicine 7 (3), 120–124.

Klein, R.A., 2002. Cruise ship blues: the underside of the cruise ship industry. New Society Publishers, Gabriola Island, BC.

Kokkranikal, J.J., Morrison, A.J., 2002. Entrepreneurship and sustainable tourism: a case study of the houseboats of Kerala. Tourism and Hospitality Research 4 (1), 7–20.

Kosters, M.J., 1992. Tourism by train: its role in alternative tourism. In: Smith, V.L., Eadington, W.R. (Eds.), Tourism Alternatives: Potentials and Problems in the Development of Tourism. University of Pennsylvania Press, Philadelphia, pp. 180–193.

Lawton, L.J., Butler, R.W., 1987. Cruise Ship Industry-Patterns in the Caribbean 1880–1986. Tourism Management 8, 329–343.

Luck, M. (Ed.), 2007. Nautical Tourism: Concept and Issues. Cognizant Communications, New York.

Lett, J.W., 1983. Ludic and liminoid aspects of charter yacht tourism in the Caribbean. Annals of Tourism Research 10, 35–56.

Miller, L., 1995. Five years in the rise of the modern cruise industry. FIU Hospitality Review 13 (1), 33–40.

Qu, H., Ping, E.W.Y., 1999. A service performance model of Hong Kong cruise travelers' motivation factors and satisfaction. Tourism Management 20, 237–244.

Steinbach, J., 1995. River related tourism in Europe: an overview. GeoJournal 35 (4), 443–458.

Testa, M.R., 2002. Shipboard vs. shoreside cruise operations. FUI Hospitality Review 20 (2), 29–40.

Testa, M.R., Sullivan, K., 2002. Customer satisfaction, quality in cruise industry. FIU Hospitality Review 20 (2), 1–12.

Teye, V.B., Leclerc, D., 1998. Product and service delivery satisfaction among North American cruise passengers. Tourism Management 19 (2), 153–160.

Timothy, D.J., 2004. Recreational second homes in the United States: development issues and contemporary patterns. In: Hall, C.M., Müller, D.K. (Eds.), Tourism, mobility and second homes: between elite landscape and common ground. Channel View, Clevedon, UK, pp. 133–148.

Toh, R.S., Rivers, M.J., Ling, T.W., 2005. Room occupancies: cruise lines out-do the hotels. International Journal of Hospitality Management 24, 121–135.

van Heerden, C.H., 2008. Leisure motorhoming: the case of the motorhome club of South Africa. South African Journal for Research in Sport, Physical Education and Recreation 30 (1), 125–136.

Vladimir, A.N., 1995. Seabourn Cruise Line: a case study in achieving quality. FUI Hospitality Review 13 (1), 7–22.

Widmer, W.M., Underwood, A.J., 2004. Factors affecting traffic and anchoring patterns of recreational boats in Sydney Harbour, Australia. Landscape and Urban Planning 66, 173–183.

Wood, R.E., 2000. Caribbean cruise tourism: globalization at sea. Annals of Tourism Research 27 (2), 345–370.

USEFUL INTERNET RESOURCES

Rail Europe: http://www.raileurope.com/us/rail/about_train_travel/index.htm.

Amtrak: www.amtrak.com.

Via Rail (Canada): www.viarail.ca.

South Africa Blue Train: http://blue-travel.net/bluetrain/.

Houseboat Association of America: www.penrose-press.com/idd/card.php?INDEX= SOC15409&;SUBJECT=SUB10033.

Houseboat Magazine: www.houseboatmagazine.com.

Orient Express: www.orient-express.com/web/luxury/luxury_travel.jsp.

Recreation Vehicle Industry Association: www.rvia.org.

Trans-Siberian Railway: www.trans-siberia.com/.

The World Cruise Ship Apartments: www.theworldsuite.com/index.asp.

Cruise Lines International Association: www.cruising.org.

Royal Caribbean International: http://RoyalCaribbean.com.

Oasis of The Seas: http://oasisoftheseas.com.

Airbus Industries: http://www.airbus.com.

CHAPTER 13

Youth Hostels and Backpacker Accommodation

INTRODUCTION

This chapter examines hostels, their development, and some of the current issues being discussed about them. There are many different types of hostels, including hostels for the homeless, hostels for dying patients, hostels for drug addicts, hostels for religious pilgrims, and hostel accommodation for individual tourists. This chapter is concerned with the last category, or the accommodations most often associated with backpacking youth and a few other types of foreign independent traveler (FIT) tourists who travel on a budget, seek less-expensive accommodations, and who might want to associate with other travelers in their own socio-economic and age category.

Youth hostels have become synonymous with the backpacking and FIT lodging experience. They are a low-budget travel option that appeals to a wide range of travelers, but not just youth. In the past, hostelling was more restrictive and inflexible than it is today. For instance, in some cases guests were required to acquire an International Youth Hostel Federation membership card before being allowed to spend a night at a member establishment. Similarly, both the Young Men's Christian Association (YMCA) and its sister organization, the Young Women's Christian Association (YWCA), originally limited their lodging facilities to members. Many youth hostels also limited their market to people under the age of 26. Today, however, the hostel sector has adapted to changing global demand, and many even cater to families and business travelers who are attempting to travel on a budget.

CONTENTS

Introduction

Backpacker and FIT Tourists

Hostels

Management and Organization

Summary and Conclusion

References

Further Reading

Useful Internet Resources

BACKPACKER AND FIT TOURISTS

FIT tourists, backpackers, and other budget travelers are, according to some observers, leftovers of the hippie era of the 1960s and behave in much the same way the hippies did: seeking freedom and independence, spending little, and wandering from place to place. Some people suggest that they are today's descendants of the Grand Tour youth of the seventeenth and eighteenth centuries, who were affluent drifters who traveled through Europe learning about art and culture, and visiting diverse places to become worldly, refined, and culturally aware. Tourism Australia (2008: 1) defines a backpacker tourist as 'a person who spends at least one night in either a backpacker or hostel accommodation. Visitors do not necessarily spend all nights in backpacker accommodation and may also stay in other types of accommodation'. In most cases, budget travelers/backpackers are young people between the ages of 18 and 30 (although there are significant exceptions to this), who have saved adequate money to get by cheaply on a world journey. Recent trends, however, show that increasingly older people are taking on the persona of backpackers, with 12% of backpackers in Australia being aged 40–49 years old (Tourism Australia, 2008). Some backpackers are known to try to earn a bit of cash along the way working on farms, in restaurants, in hostels, or teaching a language. This is particularly notable in places such as Australia that provide work-holiday visas. They also have time away from school and work to pursue a travel adventure that in most cases lasts longer than package tours. Most backpackers fall within the category of young people on summer breaks from colleges and universities, undertaking gap year (the time between high school and university or between university graduation and work), schoolies/leavers (Australia), spring breakers (US/Canada), railers traveling by train through Europe or Asia, people on work holidays, or young New Zealanders on the Overseas Experience.

Backpackers are essentially independent travelers who desire to see the world on a tight budget, often sacrificing whatever it takes to make the trip possible. Their itineraries are flexible and may change daily, and they tend to take longer trips than other types of tourists. In most cases, ground transportation comprises trains, bicycles, hiking, and hitchhiking, and local transportation is preferred. They try to find the cheapest forms of accommodation, including camping and hostels,

In this Agra, India, backpacker enclave, budget travelers mingle with other backpackers

and many rent rooms in people's homes or stay with friends/relatives. In terms of dining, they are known also to eat cheaply, preferring to purchase their nourishment from markets, stores, and street vendors rather than spending large amounts of money in restaurants and cafes. Budget travelers can be found in nearly every corner of the world, including areas of severe conflict, and their trips number in the hundreds of millions each year.

Many countries have discounted the importance of backpacker and other FIT tourists in the tourism economy, suggesting that because they spend little on accommodations, transportation, and food, they have a relatively small impact on the destination economy while contributing to its socio-cultural and ecological demise, just as other tourists do. In fact, some countries have actively discouraged this form of low-economy travel and established policies to curtail it. For example, Tanzania refused entry to backpackers in the 1970s and early 1980s on social and economic grounds. In most parts of the world, this form of budget travel suffers from a lack of government support and recognition, lack of promotion and marketing, and weak or non-existing industry associations. Backpacking has evolved over time, from drifting nomads, or vagabonds, to the mainstream version of today. The market has expanded so much that it is sometimes hard to differentiate between backpackers and other types of tourists, let alone distinguish between the different types of backpackers.

Certain countries have become well known as backpacker-friendly destinations, and some researchers have argued that small-scale, backpacker-oriented lodging establishments are more sustainable than large hotel corporations. This is because lodging for budget travelers is more likely to be locally owned, employ destination residents, and utilize locally produced goods and services. Among the more open-minded countries as regards accommodating budget travel are Australia and New Zealand, which welcome and encourage backpackers from all over the world, including domestic travelers. Australia was one of the forerunners in accepting back-packer and other budget travel forms as a legitimate and salient contributor to the Australian economy and is one of only a small handful of countries that keep statistics related to backpacker travel (see Table 13.1).

Government leaders and researchers have recognized that many budget travelers, or backpackers as they are generically known in Australia, visit more places and spend more money than non-backpacking tourists owing to their longer average length of stay in the country. Backpackers comprise approximately 10% of international arrivals in Australia. Table 13.2 illustrates figures and characteristics associated with backpackers in Australia.

While backpacker travel has not caught on in North America to the extent that it has in Australia, New Zealand, Asia, and Europe, it is beginning to be

Table 13.1 Backpacker and Hostel Accommodation in Australia, 2005–2007

	2005	2006	2007	Change 2006–2007 (%)
Number of backpacker/hostel properties	456	429	424	−1.1
People employed	3337	3271	3449	5.4
Bed spaces ('000)	48	47	47	0
Guest nights (millions)	8.31	8.54	8.73	2.2
Bed occupancy rates (%)	47.8	49.7	51.2	3.0
Earnings from hostel accommodations (millions AUD $)	192.3	203.4	218.4	7.4

Source: Based on Tourism Australia (2008).

seen as a viable alternative for domestic youth and budget tourists from abroad.

Backpackers have particular relevance for the tourism industry in developing countries, especially during the discovery and early growth stages of the industry. Backpackers tend to be 'explorers' and many prefer destinations in geographic locations that are at the inception or emerging stage of the destination life cycle, including many developing regions in Asia, Africa, and Central and South America. Countries such as Costa Rica, Egypt, Thailand, India, and Fiji view backers as a niche market segment and have strategies to provide amenities beyond lodging facilities. These include Internet cafes, transportation services, extreme recreational activities, restaurants, and

Table 13.2 Characteristics of Backpacker Travel in Australia, 2007

	2000	2001	2002	2003	2004	2005	2006	2007
INTERNATIONAL BACKPACKERS								
Backpacker tourists ('000s)	453	451	479	468	482	499	545	566
Nights in backpacker lodging (millions)	13	11	11	12	13	12	15	15
Average stay in backpacker lodging (nights)	28	25	23	25	26	24	27	26
Nights spent in Australia (millions)	34	33	32	30	33	32	39	40
Average stay in Australia (nights)	75	73	67	64	68	64	72	71
DOMESTIC BACKPACKERS								
Backpacker tourists ('000)	462	283	386	475	439	413	524	500
Nights in backpacker lodging (millions)	2.4	1.2	1.4	1.6	1.4	1.3	1.7	1.7
Average stay in backpacker lodging (nights)	5	4	4	3	3	3	3	3
Nights spent away from home (millions)	3.1	2.1	2.5	2.4	2.2	2.1	2.5	2.9
Average stay away from home (nights	7	7	7	5	5	5	5	6

Source: Based on Tourism Australia (2008).

nightclubs. Researchers have recently become interested in backpackers. For example, they have found that backpackers spend a large portion of their total expenditure at the destination and provide direct economic benefits to the host populations. Economic, environmental, and cultural sustainability, especially in rural destinations in developing countries, can benefit from backpacker travel development, because a lot of backpackers are more likely to travel to less developed regions, spend more time, and be more willing to endure hardships in comparison to most mass tourists. Backpackers often spend more money in a country than other types of tourists, and they can have a greater impact on local economies because their spending could result in less leakage. Furthermore, a large number of backpackers have above-average lengths of stay and therefore spend significant amounts of money in developed enclaves, and consume many of the same types of products as more traditional tourists.

HOSTELS

Hostels are a form of budget accommodation where short-term, individual travelers can rent a bed in a dormitory-style room and which offer shared facilities and common areas. While some newer hostels also offer single or double rooms with private baths, the primary defining characteristic of a hostel is shared rooms of a dormitory nature that cater to individual travelers. Beds are usually bunk beds, although some hostels have free-standing units too. In most cases, tenants share a bathroom,

This backpacker facility is located in Rotorua, New Zealand

kitchen, reading lounge, Internet desks, and television area. The rooms often house men and women together, but some have single-gender rooms and toilet and bath facilities. Hostel staff members are often vagabond travelers, who stay in one place for longer periods of time than most other tourists. In exchange for their work, they are allowed to stay at the hostel for free or at much lower rates. Hostels have been built from old farmhouses, schools, homes, and other structures, while others have been purpose built. They vary in their service levels, with some providing breakfast with other meals available, and others providing little by way of food and other services. In Great Britain, certain hostels have been designated bunkhouses or camping barns, although few other countries make this distinction.

There are many advantages associated with youth hostels. Probably the most salient of these is cost. As already noted, hostels are frequently the accommodation of choice for backpackers and other budget tourists, and are nearly always less expensive than hotels and other more formal lodging operations. Prices may range from a few dollars per night with no bed sheets or pillows to a few hundred dollars, depending on location, level of privacy, and services offered. Another advantage often identified by hostel guests is the opportunity to meet like-minded people. Associating with a wide array of global travelers is part of the product and experience of hostelling. Stories are shared, photographs exchanged, recommendations made for other voyage destinations, and in some cases romances are kindled. Some studies show that hostellers believe this kind of social interaction can help facilitate cross-cultural understanding and promote a degree of peace building. Although many budget travelers have an avid interest in meeting local people, this is sometimes secondary in importance to meeting other travelers and learning about their experiences and their homelands.

Youth hostels provide dormitory-style lodging for budget travelers

Another advantage is that many hostels also have Internet access free of charge or for minimal cost, and book exchanges are common. Accessibility is another important factor. In most instances, hostels are located in areas of high amenity, near or relatively near important natural and cultural tourist attractions.

Although there are many advantages associated with staying at hostels, there are also several notable disadvantages, which are a constant concern to owners and managers. Lack of privacy is the most common issue, although most guests are aware of this situation and agree to accept this condition when they register for their stay. Shared sleeping quarters are uncomfortable options for many tourists, so for some people other options are selected. A related problem is theft, which can be a chronic matter in common living spaces. Secure rooms, lockers, or safes are becoming more prevalent in youth hostels around the world. Even though most backpackers and independent tourists do not travel with large reserves of money or expensive jewelry, it is common for cameras, bags, watches, credit cards, wallets, purses, and even shoes to be stolen in communal settings. One of the least controllable aspects of hostel accommodations is noise. People entering a room during the night, leaving early in the morning, having sexual encounters, or snoring can be significant deterrents to getting adequate sleep. Finally, there is a tendency for sickness and various forms of infections to be easily passed along in dormitory-like settings. Colds, flus, and other contagious sicknesses are easily transferred to other guests in closed quarters and in bunk-bed settings.

The concept of hostels began in 1909 and 1912 in Germany, when Richard Schirrmann established the first youth hostel (*Jugendherberge*). The idea originated with the broader youth improvement movement that encouraged young people to enjoy the outdoors and experience places beyond their home environments. Originally, guests were expected to help manage and care for the hostels by cleaning, cooking, and doing yard work. Today, in some locations, this original model where guest do chores to help pay for their stay is still followed, but it is quickly becoming a thing of the past. In nearly all cases, guests are not expected to care for the hostel but instead pay for its upkeep through their fees. Although the original intent was to provide inexpensive lodging for young people, including in some cases school-age children, few hostels in the world today restrict their use only to youth. In fact, more older people, including pensioners, are using hostels than in the past, although hostels research indicates that the older a traveler is, the more willing he/she is to pay more for more privacy and comfort. Because of this demographic change, the term 'youth hostel' is becoming obsolete in most places, being superseded simply by the 'hostel'. In Australia and New Zealand, the more common term is backpackers' hostel, which in most everyday speech is shortened to backpackers.

Another budget option besides official hostels is student housing (dorms) located at or near university and college campuses. During summer or winter breaks, it is not uncommon for institutes of higher learning to rent out rooms in student residence halls to travelers. This provides low-cost accommodation for FIT and backpacking tourists and helps the institution supplement its income during a time when it would not otherwise be generating revenue from student residents.

Dormitories near James Cook University in Cairns, Australia, double as a cheap lodging option

MANAGEMENT AND ORGANIZATION

Hostels have grown in importance and number in the past quarter century, although they have been popular since the early 1900s. The idea is so catching that many accommodation providers are beginning to call themselves hostels even if they do not fit the established and globally accepted criteria of shared dormitory space, common areas, low cost, and short-term stays. Some hotels have reportedly even converted one of their private rooms into a five- or six-bed dormitory so they will qualify and be able to join a hostel association and get listed on the association's reservations systems. There is a considerable debate going on among lodging specialists about what exactly a hostel is and what hotels or bed and breakfasts would need to qualify as a hostel. Many proponents argue that the meaning of hostel should be definitively set to preclude non-hostels from claiming to be hostels. Some suggest that for a lodging facility to call itself a hostel, it should have at least 50% of its beds in dorm rooms, provide traveler facilities (e.g. kitchenettes, Internet, common areas, laundry facilities), be low-budget oriented, provide a personal atmosphere conducive to meeting other travelers, and accept individual walk-ins. Since the term 'hostel' is not copyrighted or owned by any one individual or company, as noted above, its use has become more widespread by establishments that do not traditionally meet the basic hostel defining criteria. This is a significant source of consternation in the hostel management circuits and among the formalized hostel associations.

In general hostels can be viewed from two network perspectives. The first group comprises hostels that are members of Hostelling International, a non-profit hostel membership organization that promotes youth exchanges, experiential learning and travel, and outdoors-oriented activities. The other form comprises independently operated hostels that are not necessarily members of national or international bodies. This independent hostel movement has grown considerably in recent years and is now reflected in the development of hostel chains in many countries and regions (see Table 13.3).

There are nearly 100 youth hostel organizations throughout the world, and many individual countries have their own associations. A few examples include the Italian Youth Hostel Association, the German Youth Hostel Association, the Youth Hostels Association of India, China Youth Hostel Association, and the Kenya Youth Hostels Association. Hostelling International (HI) (formerly the International Youth Hostel Federation) is the largest network of hostels in the world. More than 4500 hostels in over 80 countries and 90 national and regional hostel associations have joined Hostelling International because of its brand image and the valuable and widespread

Table 13.3	A Selection of International Hostel Chains	
Chain	**Country/Region**	**Number of Hostels**
MacBackpackers	UK	8 hostels
Nomads Hostels	Australia/New Zealand/Fiji	14 hostels
Jazz Hostels	USA/Canada	7 hostels
Loftstel	USA	4 hostels
Meininger Hostels	Germany/Austria/UK	9 hostels
Xanascat	Spain	47 hostels
BASE Backpacker Hostels	Australia/New Zealand	13 hostels
Pirwa Hostels	Peru	4 hostels

Sources: www.hostelmanagement.com; http://nomadshostels.com; www.meininger-hostels.com; www.jazzhostels.com; www.loftstel.com; www.macbackpackers.com; www.xanascat.cat; www.pirwahostelscusco.com.

network it provides. Some budget travelers have become accustomed to the HI brand and seek out HI hostels because they know what to expect.

The International Youth Hostel Federation was founded in 1932 in Amsterdam with representation from hostelling associations in Germany, the Netherlands, Norway, Denmark, Great Britain, Switzerland, Ireland, Czechoslovakia, France, and Belgium. Hostelling International coordinates collaborative efforts between national organizations, assists in policy making, and provides services for travelers. In addition to its accommodations function, it also promotes international student exchanges and youth work experiences. In 2003, Hostelling International signed an agreement with the United Nations Educational, Scientific, and Cultural Organization (UNESCO) to campaign for international peace and understanding by promoting cultural understanding, educational travel, and youth exchanges. It also aims to build awareness of AIDS and celebrate International Youth Day.

There are several Internet-based organizations, industry clearinghouses, and help sources for the hostel sector. HostelManagement.com was formed in 2004 as a resource for hostel managers and owners. It provides information for people who have an interest in opening a hostel and provides planning and marketing information to improve the product and the guest experience. There are also several online reservation systems and travel agencies that deal specifically with budget accommodations, including hostels. Hostelworld.com is one such reservation and travel planning site that specializes in hostels and backpacker travel and allows customers to search more than 17 000 hostels in some 168 countries.

The most salient form of promotion for hostel owners and managers is word of mouth. Part of the socialization processes for which backpacker tourism is known is travelers making recommendations on where to stay and what to see and do. Likewise, recommendations are made regarding which hostels to avoid. Thus, not only can word of mouth be a powerful tool to draw budget travelers to a hostel, but it can also become a tool to dissuade potential guests from staying. This word of mouth feedback takes place in person-to-person interactions at hostels and on trains, via letters in newspapers and magazines, and more recently in online discussion venues, where travelers can vent their frustrations or pleasures associated with any given hostel.

Several research studies have illustrated the most important characteristics that create satisfied hostel guests or that are most influential in a person's decision process in selecting a hostel. One of these is staff friendliness. This plays an important role in online and in-person word of mouth recommendations. According to a study by Murphy (2001), hostels with the most 'working backpackers' (those who stay for longer periods to work for their accommodations) are less friendly and less customer oriented, because the staff members already have made friends, become cliquish, and make little effort to interact with the short-term guests. Cleanliness and comfort are critical characteristics as well. This is particularly important from the perspective of the bathrooms, dorms, and kitchen, but is also a salient issue in terms of overall cleanliness and building maintenance. Social atmosphere is also important, and as already noted is an essential part of hostels and hostelling. Facilities including bars, reading rooms, TV rooms, and a common kitchen are important venues in the sociability of the establishment. Location is also a critical factor, relative to attractions, transportation, and dining options. Guests also need to feel a sense of security, so a location in a safe area is also important. Likewise, security inside the hostel is important in terms of offering lockers, locked doors and windows, and having 24-hour on-duty staff. Low price is a requirement to be considered as a hostel, but it is also an important point in decision making among travelers; however, low price alone is not as important as value for price, as many hostels are seen to be cheap but not of good quality. Amenities (e.g. table tennis, pool tables, and Internet) and home-style extras (e.g. free coffee and tea) are weighty variables, too. One of the earlier, but out-of-date characteristics of hostels was daytime lock-out periods (so that guests were essentially forced to sightsee and spend time outdoors) and early curfews. A lack of these curfews and lockouts is also of consequence in deciding which hostel to use. Size and level of intimacy are also important, with smaller hostels typically being more conducive to social interactions and friendly atmosphere than larger ones. The number of beds in each room and the gender mix are also important elements in satisfaction and guest decision making.

Recent research suggests that youth budget travelers, many of whom tend to be more environmentally conscious than other tourists, also place a higher value on hostels that abide by green practices such as recycling, energy efficiency, water conservation, and eco-friendly waste management.

SUMMARY AND CONCLUSION

This chapter examined backpacker tourists, youth hostels, and some of the issues related to this market segment and lodging category respectively. A number of important concluding observations can be made in relation to the travel industry. First, technology, including the Internet and digital cameras, have also led many backpackers to check their email regularly, logon to online community websites (e.g. Facebook and Myspace), update blogs, and post their digital pictures to be shared with friends and family back home as well as to communicate with fellow travelers on the road. When combined with the mainstreaming of backpacker travel, a new more affluent and technologically savvy sub-segment has emerged, often referred to on internet forums as *flashpackers*, who are less likely to worry as much about traveling on a tight budget, and will often splurge on more expensive restaurants, accommodations, and activities. This is a major shift from the traditional backpacker traveler which also has economic implications for destinations.

Secondly, most backpackers tend to participate in diverse activities unique to a destination. Many backpackers who may have concerns about keeping on a tight budget will often save up money by living with even more hardships, in order to participate in an expensive activity, such as bungee jumping or scuba diving, because they see it as a once-in-a-lifetime experience.

Third, backpacker tourism infrastructure has experienced extensive development to include hostels, trains and train passes, backpacker enclaves, backpacker specific tours, and hop-on hop-off bus routes. Much of the infrastructure follows specific backpacker trails, on which FITs are guided by one of the 'backpackers' bibles'—*Lonely Planet*, *Let's Go*, or *Rough Guide*. There have been recent tourist infrastructure developments that cross the boundaries between backpacker tourism and mass tourism. Budget airlines specifically are used in great numbers by all segments of tourists, but some, such as Ryanair, have started to create partnerships with leading suppliers to backpacker tourism. Ryanair has a successful partnership with the largest online hostel booking website, HostelWorld.com. To meet the demands of this expanding market segment, specialized service providers have evolved including travel agencies such as STA Travel and tour operators like Contiki Tours. Finally, the educational component of backpacking and youth hosteling is very important. Many students studying abroad for a few weeks, a semester or a whole year, usually extend their educational experience by backpacking at the end of their programs or on weekends and breaks during their programs.

REFERENCES

Murphy, L., 2001. Exploring social interactions of backpackers. Annals of Tourism Research 28 (1), 50–67.

Tourism Australia, 2008. Backpackers in Australia, 2007. Tourism Research Australia, Belconnen.

FURTHER READING

Chadee, D.D., Cutler, J., 1996. Insights into international travel by students. Journal of Travel Research 35 (2), 75–80.

Cohen, E., 1973. Nomads from affluence: Notes on the phenomenon of drifter-tourism. International Journal of Comparative Sociology 14 (0), 89.

Firth, T., Hing, N., 1999. Backpacker hostels and their guests: attitudes and behaviours relating to sustainable tourism. Tourism Management 20 (2), 251–254.

Grassl, A., Heath, G., 1982. The magic triangle: a short history of the world youth hostel movement. International Youth Hostel Federation, Welwyn Garden City, UK.

Hannam, K., Ateljevic, I. (Eds.), 2008. Backpacker tourism: concepts and profiles. Channel View, Clevedon, UK.

Hampton, M., 1998. Backpacker tourism and economic development. Annals of Tourism Research 25, 639–660.

Heath, G., 1962. Richard Schirrmann, the first youth hosteller. International Youth Hostel Federation, Copenhagen.

Hecht, J., Martin, D., 2006. Backpacking and hostel-picking: an analysis from Canada. International Journal of Contemporary Hospitality Management 18 (1), 69–77.

Horak, S., Weber, S., 2000. Youth tourism in Europe: problems and prospects. Tourism Recreation Research 25 (3), 37–44.

Loker-Murphy, L., Pearce, P.L., 1995. Young budget travelers: backpackers in Australia. Annals of Tourism Research 22 (4), 819–843.

McCulloch, J., 1992. The Youth hostels association: precursors and contemporary achievements. Journal of Tourism Studies 3 (1), 22–27.

Moscardo, G., 2006. Backpackers and other young travelers to the Great Barrier Reef: An exploration of changes in characteristics and behaviors over time. Tourism Recreation Research 31 (3), 29–37.

Murphy, L., 2001. Exploring social interactions of backpackers. Annals of Tourism Research 28 (1), 50–67.

Nash, R., Thyne, M., Davies, S., 2006. An investigation into customer satisfaction levels in the budget accommodation sector in Scotland: a case study of backpacker tourists and the Scottish Youth Hostels Association. Tourism Management 27 (3), 525–532.

Obenour, W., Patterson, M., Pederson, P., Pearson, L., 2006. Conceptualization of a meaning-based research approach for tourism service experiences. Tourism Management 27 (1), 34–41.

O'Regan, M., 2008. Hypermobility in backpacker lifestyles: the emergence of the Internet café. In: Burns, P.M., Novelli, M. (Eds.), Tourism and Mobilities: Local-Global Connections. CAB International, Wallingford, UK, pp. 109–132.

O'Reilly, C.C., 2006. From drifter to gap year tourist: Mainstreaming backpacker travel. Annals of Tourism Research 33, 998–1017.

Papis, J., 2006. Understanding the workforce: the key to success in a youth hostel in Scotland. International Journal of Contemporary Hospitality Management 18 (7), 593–600.

Peach, H.G., Bath, N.E., 2000. Health and safety problems and lack of information among international visitors backpacking through north Queensland. Journal of Travel Medicine 7 (5), 234–238.

Prideaux, B., Shiga, H., 2007. Japanese backpacking: the emergence of a new Market sector–a Queensland case study. Tourism Review International 11 (1), 45–56.

Richards, G., Wilson, J., 2004. The global nomad: backpacker travel in theory and practice. Channel View, Clevedon, UK.

Rogerson, C., 2007. The challenges of developing backpacker tourism in South Africa: an enterprise perspective. Development Southern Africa 24 (3), 425–443.

Scheyvens, R., 2002. Backpacker tourism and third world development. Annals of Tourism Research 29, 144–164.

Scheyvens, R., 2006. Sun, sand, and beaches: Benefiting from backpackers – the Samoa way. Tourism Recreation Research 31, 75–86.

Sørensen, A., 1999. Travelers in the periphery: backpackers and other independent multiple destination tourists in peripheral areas. Bornholm Tourism Research Center, Bornholm, Denmark.

Sørensen, A., 2003. Backpacker ethnography. Annals of Tourism Research 30, 847–867.

Thyne, M., Davies, S., Nash, R., 2004. A lifestyle segmentation analysis of the backpacker market in Scotland: a case study of the Scottish youth hostel association. Journal of Quality Assurance in Hospitality and Tourism 5 (2), 95–119.

Visser, G., 2004. The developmental impacts of backpacker tourism in South Africa. GeoJournal 60 (3), 283–299.

Westerhausen, K., Macbeth, J., 2003. Backpackers and empowered local communities: Natural allies in the struggle for sustainability and local control? Tourism Geographies 5 (1), 71–86.

USEFUL INTERNET RESOURCES

German Youth Hostel Association: www.jugendherberge.de/en.

Hostelling International: www.hihostels.com.

Hostelling International Canada: www.hihostels.ca.

Hostelling International USA: www.hiusa.org.

Hostel Management: www.hostelmanagement.com.

Hostelworld.com: www.hostelworld.com.

Irish Youth Hostel Association: www.anoige.ie.

Italian Youth Hostel Association: www.ostellionline.org.

Japan Youth Hostels: www.jyh.or.jp.

UK Youth Hostel Association: www.yha.org.uk.

Youth Hostels.com: www.youthhostels.com.

Youth Hostels Association of India: www.yhaindia.org.

YHA Australia: www.yha.com.au/.

YHA New Zealand: www.hihostels.com/dba/country-NZ.en.htm.

European Hostels: www.europeanhostels.com/.

CHAPTER 14

Camping

INTRODUCTION

Camping is one of the most popular recreational activities in the western world today and a favored type of accommodation. Camping is perhaps the oldest form of accommodation in the world. Hunters and gatherers, early pilgrims, conquerors, and explorers all participated in camping in one form or another. In modern times, people around the world are becoming more convinced of the value and enjoyment associated with camping. Even for people who can afford the comforts, convenience, and amenities of hotels and resorts, camping provides an out-of-the-ordinary lodging option, regardless of socio-economic status.

Europeans, especially French and Germans, are particularly known for their interest in commercial camping, while Americans and Canadians are known for both commercial and wilderness camping activities. The natural and human environments of North America and Europe are particularly conducive to all forms of camping. In these regions, nature preserves have historically been part of the social and economic development strategies at the national, state, and local levels. These developments also apply to countries like Australia and New Zealand that have fine national and regional parks systems, which provide accommodation and other amenities for domestic and international visitors. In most of the less-developed world, with the exception of hunting camps, camping is a less preferred form of accommodation owing to inhospitable climates or a fear of disease-carrying insects and water bodies. Likewise, most people in the developing world rarely think of leisure activities like camping, and their travel opportunities otherwise are few and far between. The limitations to greater participation in outdoor recreational activities that involve use of camping facilities in developing regions range from perceptions and attitudes to lack of protected natural areas with even minimum facilities. In areas where these exist, such

CONTENTS

Introduction

Categories of Camping

Motives and Demand for Camping

Management Concerns

Summary and Conclusion

References

Further Reading

Useful Internet Resources

as Costa Rica, economic considerations, including entrance fees, tend to discourage greater participation.

This chapter describes this pervasive form of tourist accommodation and highlights experiential issues among campers themselves and management issues that planners, developers, and managers face.

CATEGORIES OF CAMPING

There are several ways of categorizing camping areas, none of them being mutually exclusive, however. From a venue or locational features perspective, camping and campgrounds as a tourist lodging option can be divided into wilderness and non-wilderness camping. Within this simplistic categorization, there are many degrees of development or remoteness. On one end of the spectrum is complete wilderness (backcountry or primitive) camping, where no planned or organized facilities exist for overnighters. In this instance, camping locations are typically accessed by foot, horseback, or mountain bike and are usually associated with hiking, fishing, hunting, and trekking. Often this setting is non-fee-based but might be subject to land regulations and property ownership, although some popular hiking countries in Europe have freedom of access laws that allow trekkers to camp anywhere, even on private property. Some primitive camping, though, requires a fee and permit if it takes place on public lands. On the other end of the spectrum are luxury RV and camping resorts, complete with amenities and facilities such as tennis courts, saunas, spa tubs, mini golf, swimming pools, cafeterias, and even gift shops. While these resemble nothing like backcountry camping, they are nonetheless an important part of the outdoor lodging experience. Between these two extremes are wilderness camps where toilets (outhouses), picnic tables, and fire pits are provided but no running water or electricity. Closer to villages, towns, and cities, campgrounds tend to have more services, such as sewer and water hookups, electric plugs, and hot showers.

Another way of looking at campgrounds is ownership and management. Many campgrounds are owned by individuals or companies, and some are even franchised (e.g. Kampgrounds of America (KOA)). These for-profit camping areas are often referred to as commercial campgrounds and can range from simple sites beside a road or on a farm to major camping resorts. The most successful private campgrounds, including KOA, are located near water bodies, major highways, and population centers. Commercial camping tends to be more expensive than wilderness camping, sometimes costing as much as USD $100–150 per night, but it offers more modern amenities, such as electricity, water, showers, flushing toilets, swimming pools, and other entertainment features. In the United States, there are approximately 16 000 campgrounds, of which some 8 500 are privately owned and operated. Private campgrounds provide some three quarters of the US demand for camping with more than one millions campsites (Jensen and Guthrie, 2006).

Public agency-owned campgrounds are typically not as commercialized and do not usually attempt to capture additional tourist spending by offering golf, bowling, and arcades. Instead they are subsidized by governments and seen as non-profit or self-sustaining enterprises; they usually offer either no amenities (except nature and scenery)

This family is camping at a partially serviced National Forest Service campground in the USA

or very rudimentary services (e.g. toilets, fire pits, car parks, and occasional electric hookups). In most countries, forest services, national parks services, and other land management agencies provide campgrounds and campsites for outdoor enthusiasts. The US National Park Service operates 776 campgrounds with 26 830 campsites. Several other US agencies, such as the Bureau of Land Management and the National Forest Service, also operate camping areas.

Campgrounds might also be classified by the type of shelters or lodging accoutrements offered or allowed. Some areas allow only tents, owing to ecological sensitivities. Some commercial camping resorts allow only RVs, mobile homes, or motorhomes, precluding tent-based camping, and some even require memberships. Both public and private sites, however, offer combined RV and tent camping capabilities. Other campgrounds provide cabins or immobile tents and trailers on site for rent. In campgrounds that allow both tent and RV camping, the two unit types are often separated because the clientele is different in their tastes and interests, which can result in conflicts.

MOTIVES AND DEMAND FOR CAMPING

People camp for a variety of reasons. The first reason is economic, since camping is almost always less expensive than other lodging options, even at some RV resorts. Camping near amusement parks, cultural sites, and other attractions can save money that might be used for other holiday experiences.

Comfortable cabins can be rented by campers in areas of high amenity

It is not uncommon for individuals and families to camp as a way of making a vacation more affordable. The second reason is social. It allows families and friends to spend quality time together in sometimes rugged natural settings. Some parents camp with their families as a way of getting their children to learn about and appreciate non-urban environments. The third reason is environmental. Camping in wilderness areas tends to bring people closer to nature and may help create an appreciation and awareness for the environment. Another reason could be spiritual. Studies of campers and other outdoor enthusiasts have found that being close to nature is a spiritually moving experience for many people, and spending time in nature, including camping, enlarges a spiritual sense of co-existing with nature or connecting with deity. Finally, people do not have to travel far to feel they are away from home. With widespread car ownership, city dwellers in most parts of the world can be in a natural setting within a few minutes or a few hours.

There has been a notable growth in outdoor adventure travel and outdoor recreation, as the traveling public has become more health conscious and weary of urban living. Sales of camping equipment, such as tents, sleeping bags, backpacks, and cooking utensils, have grown a great deal in recent years, and with the global economic crisis of 2007–2008, sales of some items have increased because of public interest in saving money on travel accommodations. As a result, there has also been an increase in camping activities, particularly in wilderness settings, and other less-expensive camping holiday packages. By the same token, as noted in an earlier chapter, RV sales and rentals have increased dramatically during the past two decades, resulting in more travelers opting for partial- or full-service campgrounds. Many countries of the world and most states and provinces in North America have developed campground associations to help handle this increase in interest and to act as marketing networks. Campers tend to be quite active, compared to some other tourists and participate in a wide range of activities, such as walking, cycling, fishing, swimming, and reading. Table 14.1 illustrates the

Table 14.1	Top Ten Activities Undertaken by KOA Campers in 2007
Activity	**Percentage of KOA Users**
Walking	71%
Reading	67%
Exploring nature	59%
Shopping	58%
Swimming	57%
Visiting heritage sites	53%
Participating in campground activities	53%
Hiking	49%
Fishing	37%
Visiting theme parks	35%

Source: KOA 2008.

main activities undertaken by campers at commercial KOA campgrounds in the US and Canada.

The Travel Industry Association of America suggests that almost 5% of all domestic travelers in the United States utilized RV and tent camping as their accommodation of choice in 2006, although tents are utilized by twice as many campers as RVs are, likely because of the lower expenses involved. The primary users of organized campgrounds are family groups and youth groups traveling together on holiday breaks. Small hiking groups, couples, and individuals tend to be the most predominant users of primitive camping areas and do so in an effort to seek solitude. Most campers at non-managed primitive sites are more predisposed to wilderness experiences, possess more survival skills than other campers, and see camping as a more central part of their lives.

MANAGEMENT CONCERNS

Probably the most significant management concern in the public domain, and in natural areas in the private domain, is the environmental impact of camping. Compacted soils, damaged natural vegetation, forest fires, and vandalism are among the biggest problems in both primitive and organized settings. Fires are often started by campers who smoke or do not fully extinguish their campfires. These often destroy hundreds or thousands of acres of forests, which can take hundreds of years to regenerate. Compacted soils result in increased erosion, water runoff and flooding, and a lack of vegetation growth. Campers often cut trees or gather wood for fires, which damages the ecosystem balance and makes the wilderness area unsightly. Carved names in rocks and trees, litter, spray painted trees and picnic tables, and broken fire pits and interpretive signs are all forms of vandalism that are common in camping areas.

Besides the cost of repairing these damages, and while the direct ecological outcomes of careless recreationists and masses of campers are a salient matter, many scientific studies show that there are also social consequences related to environmental degradation and vandalism. Potential campers are often turned off by the presence of litter, vandalism, erosion, compacted soils and resource damage, and may choose to camp elsewhere.

Overcrowding is another source of dissatisfaction among wilderness campers. The presence of too many campers can dissuade people from staying at certain campgrounds. In fact, according to White et al. (2001), the decision of where to camp is influenced more by social conditions than by natural conditions for approximately three out of four wilderness campers. Similar results have been found in studies of commercial campgrounds, although the tolerance threshold for large crowds in the commercial context is much higher. Nonetheless, issues that cause less than satisfactory camping experiences at more developed sites are long waits at the restrooms, noise, litter, closeness between tents and trailers, and large numbers of tents and campers. Factors that result in satisfactory camping experiences in both developed and wilderness settings include cleanliness, a feeling of safety and security, interesting environment, and a well-maintained campground.

Contact with wild animals is a primary concern among backcountry campsite managers. Too often, campers and other users get too friendly with animals, which can alter habitats, migration and mating patterns, and diets. It causes wild animals to become overly dependent on handouts from tourists and makes tourists more prone to being attacked. Stories abound of bears, wolves, and other creatures sneaking into campsites and campgrounds to rummage for food. Such occurrences are not restricted only to wilderness camping but sometimes occur even in urban or suburban settings.

Often campsite managers have to take drastic steps to intervene before the negative impacts of use overwhelm a site. These include relocating campsites to new areas, restricting or banning fire use, setting carrying capacities, replanting areas severely affected by compaction and erosion, hardening sites with gravel or wood planks, and imposing heavy fines for mistreating property. Such actions are seen to improve the conditions that are most important to visitors, and in most cases, strict camping policies result in more satisfied campsite users because of the protection that such policies ensure.

Fees are another management issue that are highly controversial. Some users believe they should not be required to pay fees in publicly owned campgrounds, because they are the public. However, most users are willing to pay fees and will still continue to camp if fees are levied. While some public lands managers do not wish to charge the public to utilize camping areas, they realize the need to acquire funds for maintenance, even though most fees today do not cover the costs of operating public campgrounds.

Research shows that there is a common willingness among wilderness campers to pay more for the use of public campgrounds, but this depends largely on the characteristics of the campground and the campground user. For the most part, there is a direct link between scenic beauty and willingness to pay for camping.

Another interesting but critical management issue is the spread of sickness and disease. Medical science has shown many times that crowded campgrounds, particularly developed sites in urban areas are prone to the spread of diseases such as viral meningitis and influenza. Crowded RVs and common areas (e.g. swimming pools) have been blamed in the past for outbreaks and spread of certain sicknesses.

There are other impacts of camping accommodations besides those associated with the environment in a negative light. Camping contributes to local economies in many parts of the world, and some smaller communities might be almost entirely dependent on camping as the sole lodging sector income earner, especially if they are located in areas of high amenity. In the southwestern United States, for example, several desert communities depend almost exclusively on 'camping tourists' for their economic well being, particularly each winter, spurring large crowds of northerners who come to escape the cold winters. While seasonal migrants, many of whom reside temporarily in RVs and campgrounds, have a notable economic impact on their destinations of choice, overnight and short-term campers have been shown to contribute more to local economies than seasonal campers.

SUMMARY AND CONCLUSION

This chapter has examined camping accommodation facilities and some of the management issues surrounding them. The relationship between the establishment of protected areas, camping facilities, and the travel industry is significant. The first national protected area in the world is Yellowstone National Park, established in 1872. It was followed by several national parks throughout the United States and Canada that are administered by the

US National Parks Service and Parks Canada. A major factor in this development was the transportation system that provided capital, access, and management capacity; in the United States, it was originally the rail companies followed by the automobile. Similar developments occurred in Canada where the Canadian Pacific (CP) and Canadian National (CN) rail companies not only teamed up with the national government to establish national parks, but also actually built some of the classic park accommodation facilities such as the Chateau Lake Louis in Banff National Park in Alberta. Today, national and state/provincial parks in most industrialized countries are major tourism destinations, and a significant proportion of their visitors utilize camping facilities. Unfortunately, most developing countries lack camping facilities for both domestic and international visitors.

From a purely demand and marketing perspective, studies indicate that camping in the United States and other developed countries has very low participation rates by ethnic and racial minorities. For example, both Washburne (1978) and Philipp (1999) found that African Americans were significantly underrepresented in undeveloped outdoor recreation areas. More recently, data compiled by the Washington State Parks and Recreation Commission show that many African Americans 'for a variety of reasons are not frequent users of the state's 250 000 acres of parkland, particularly for activities like camping' (The Seattle Times 2005).

Developing countries are facing dual exponential forces of high population growth rate and depletion of their ecological resources such as the rainforest. One solution is environmental preservation, including the establishment of protected areas with camping facilities for both domestic and international visitors. This is already taking place in countries such as Costa Rica, Belize, and Botswana but there is much more work to be done.

REFERENCES

Jensen, C.R., Guthrie, S.P., 2006. Outdoor recreation in America, sixth ed. Human Kinetics, Champaign, IL.

KOA 2008. Kamping trends, 2007. Online <<http://koapressroom.com/storystarters/2007KampingTrendsPage4.pdf>> Accessed December 23.

Philipp, S.F., 1999. Are we welcome? African American racial acceptance in leisure activities and the importance given to children's leisure. Journal of Leisure Research 31 (4), 385–403.

Wanted: African–American campers. The Seattle Times July 6, 2005.

Washburne, R.F., 1978. Black under-participation in wildland recreation: alternative explanations. Leisure Sciences 11, 11–28.

White, D.D., Hall, T.E., Farrell, T.A., 2001. Influence of ecological impacts and other campsite characteristics on wilderness visitors' campsite choices. Journal of Park and Recreation Administration 19 (2), 83–97.

FURTHER READING

Abdullah, M., Yaman, A.R., Choonkeat, T., Wai, Y.H., 2005. Campers' characteristic, recreation activities and related forest camping attributes in Shah Alam Agriculture Park, Selangor. Journal of Applied Sciences 5 (9), 1546–1552.

Arimond, G., Lethlean, S., 1996. Profit center analysis within private campgrounds. Journal of Travel Research 34 (4), 52–58.

Baud-Bovy, M., Lawson, F., 1998. Tourism and Recreation Handbook of Planning and Design. Architectural Press, Oxford.

Beaman, J., Hegmann, S., DuWors, R., 1991. Price elasticity of demand: a campground example. Journal of Travel Research 30 (1), 22–29.

Becken, S., Gnoth, J., 2004. Tourist consumption systems among overseas visitors: reporting on American, German, and Australian visitors to New Zealand. Tourism Management 25, 375–385.

Bell, S., 2008. Design for Outdoor Recreation. Taylor and Francis, Abingdon, UK.

Brown, R.N.K., Rosenberger, R.S., Kline, J.D., Hall, T.E., Needham, M.D., 2008. Visitor preferences for managing wilderness recreation after wildfire. Journal of Forestry 106 (1), 9–16.

Buckley, R. (Ed.), 2004. Environmental Impacts of Ecotourism. CAB International, Wallingford, UK.

Christensen, N.A., Stewart, W.P., King, D.A., 1993. National forest campgrounds: users willing to pay more. Journal of Forestry 91 (7), 43–47.

Cole, D.N., Monz, C.A., 2003. Impacts of camping on vegetation: response and recovery following acute chronic disturbance. Environmental Management 32 (6), 693–705.

Cole, D.N., Spildie, D.R., 2006. Restoration of plant cover in subalpine forests disturbed by camping: success of transplanting. Natural Areas Journal 26 (2), 168–178.

Cooper, R.B., 1999. Campground Management: How to Establish and Operate Your Campground. NetLibrary, Dublin, OH.

Cottrell, S., Cottrell, R., 2003. Happy campers: fun-filled programs as management intervention in family camping. Parks and Recreation 38 (10), 36–40.

Daniel, T.C., Brown, T.C., King, D.A., Richards, M.T., Stewart, W.P., 1989. Perceived scenic beauty and contingent valuation of forest campgrounds. Forest Science 35 (1), 76–90.

Daniels, M.L., Marion, J.L., 2006. Visitor evaluations of management actions at a highly impacted Appalachian Trail camping area. Environmental Management 38 (6), 1006–1019.

Erdoğan, N., 2005. Environmental problems and visitor behavior at the Olimpos National Park, Turkey. Journal of Applied Sciences 5 (5), 868–872.

Farooquee, N.A., Budal, T.K., Maikhuri, R.K., 2008. Environmental and socio-cultural impacts of river rafting and camping on Ganga in Uttarakhand Himalaya. Current Science 94 (5), 587–594.

Fesenmaier, D.R., Roehl, W.S., 1985. Locational analysis in campground development decisions. Journal of Travel Research 24 (3), 18–22.

Gibbs, K.C., 1980. Public campgrounds: are they profitable? Journal of Forestry 78 (8), 466–468.

Gibbs, K.C., van Hees, W.W.S., 1981. Cost of operating public campgrounds. Journal of Leisure Research 13 (3), 243–253.

Henderson, K.A., Cooper, R., 1983. Characteristics of campers in private and state-owned campgrounds in Wisconsin. Journal of Travel Research 22 (1), 10–14.

Hoffman, W.L., Romsa, G.H., 1972. Some factors influencing attendance at commercial campgrounds: a case study. Land Economics 48 (2), 188–190.

Hultsman, J.T., Cottrell, R.L., Hultsman, W.Z., 1987. Planning Parks for People. Venture, State College, PA.

Ibrahim, H., Cordes, K., 2003. Parks, Recreation and Leisure Service Management. Eddie Bowers Publishing, Peosta, Iowa.

Jensen, C.R., Guthrie, S.P., 2006. Outdoor recreation in America, sixth ed. Human Kinetics, Champaign, IL.

Lindberg, K., Aylward, B., 1999. Price responsiveness in developing country nature tourism context: review and Costa Rica case study. Journal of Leisure Research 31 (3), 281–299.

Lucas, R.C., 1990. How wilderness visitors choose entry points and campsites. USDA Forest Service, Intermountain Research Station, Ogden, UT.

Marion, J.L., Cole, D.N., 1996. Spatial and temporal variation in soil and vegetation impacts on campsites. Ecological Applications 6 (2), 520–530.

Marion, J.L., Farrell, T.A., 2002. Management practices that concentrate visitor activities: camping impact management at Isle Royale National Park, USA. Journal of Environmental Management 66 (2), 201–212.

McFarlane, B.L., 2004. Recreation specialization and site choice among vehicle-based campers. Leisure Sciences 26 (3), 309–322.

Moore, R.L., Driver, B.L., 2005. Introduction to Outdoor Recreation: Providing and Managing Natural Resource Based Opportunities. Venture, State College, PA.

More, T.A., Dustin, D.L., Knopf, R.C., 1996. Behavioral consequences of campground user fees. Journal of Park and Recreation Administration 14 (1), 81–93.

Nelson, H., Wearing, S., 1999. A campground strategy for ACT parks and forests. Australian Parks and Leisure 1 (4), 6–8.

Oh, K.S., Shelbey, B., 1998. Norms for behavior and conditions in two national park campgrounds in Korea. Environmental Management 22 (2), 277–285.

Reid, S.E., Marion, J.L., 2005. A comparison of campfire impacts and policies in seven protected areas. Environmental Management 36 (1), 48–58.

Reiling, S.D., Criner, G.K., Oltmanns, S.E., 1988. The influence of information on users' attitudes toward campground user fees. Journal of Leisure Research 20 (3), 208–217.

Tourism Industry Association of America, 2007. Domestic Travel Market Report. Travel Industry Association, Washington, DC.

Turton, S.M., 2005. Managing environmental impacts of recreation and tourism in rainforests of the Wet Tropics of Queensland World Heritage Area. Geographical Research 43 (2), 140–151.

van Heerden, C.H., 2008. Leisure motorhoming: the case of the motorhome club of South Africa. South African Journal for Research in Sport, Physical Education and Recreation 30 (1), 125–136.

White, D.D., Hall, T.E., Farrell, T.A., 2001. Influence of ecological impacts and other campsite characteristics on wilderness visitors' campsite choices. Journal of Park and Recreation Administration 19 (2), 83–97.

USEFUL INTERNET RESOURCES

Kampgrounds of America (KOA): www.koa.com.

The Camping and Caravanning Club (UK): www.campingandcaravanningclub. co.uk.

The Caravan Club (UK): www.caravanclub.co.uk.

Camping and Budget Travel in Europe: www.karmabum.com/camping.htm.

Accessible Camping in Europe: www.geocities.com/Paris/1502/accessiblecamping ineurope.htm.

Camping Card International: www.campingcardinternational.com/published/cci/ content/pagina/homepage/homepage.nl.html.

The Camping Club: www.thecampingclub.com/.

Camping Club Europe: www.campingclubeurope.com/.

International Camping Club: www.internationalcampingclub.com/.

CHAPTER 15

Novelty and Alternative Lodging

INTRODUCTION

As already noted throughout the previous chapters, there have been many socio-cultural, political, and economic changes throughout the world during the past quarter century. These changes have manifested in various ways on both the supply and the demand sides of tourism. One of these, the sophistication of tourist demand, is evident in many people's desire to forego the lackluster destinations of the past in favor of exploring new places where few tourists go and where new and unusual experiences can be sought.

From a lodging perspective, this translates into people wanting to stay in innovative and novel forms of accommodations that can offer something beyond the ordinariness of resorts, hotels, motels, hostels, or inns. Not only do novel, post-modern genres of accommodation offer exclusive opportunities but also, many of them, especially the most extreme and bizarre, come with bragging rights. To be able to claim that one has spent a night or two in a hotel made of ice, for instance, is well worth a high price for many people who have an interest in doing things 'off the beaten path' and which most of their acquaintances might never even have dreamed of doing.

This pattern can now be seen on nearly every continent and appears in many different forms. This chapter describes a variety of new, or novel, types of accommodations that convey an attractiveness unlike any of the others so far discussed in this book. They are products of creative minds and entrepreneurial spirits that have identified a market niche or distinctive type of curious traveler that desires to be a pioneer in the lodging experience.

ICE HOTELS

The first ice hotel was established in northern Sweden in 1989, with other developments following suit during subsequent years. While this type of accommodation facility is obviously limited to regions that get cold enough to

CONTENTS

Introduction

Ice Hotels

Ecolodges

Tree House Lodging

Indigenous Dwellings

Caves and Underground Lodges

Historic Buildings

Capsule Hotels

Mega Multi Malls

Pilgrim Rest Houses and Spiritual Retreats

Plastic Surgery Resorts

Outer-Space Experiences

Sand Hotel

Summary and Conclusion

References

Further Reading

Useful Internet Resources

maintain icy conditions for several months each winter, the idea is spreading, and ice and snow hotels have been established in Greenland, Canada, Sweden, Norway, Finland, Switzerland, the United States (Alaska), and in the mountains of Romania. These 'hotels' are constructed when snow can be well compacted and when ice begins to form in thick layers on lakes and rivers, typically between December and March. Blocks are cut or formed, and igloo-like structures are built, with check-in counters and reception areas, bedrooms, dining rooms, movie theaters, art galleries, skating rinks, and other activity spaces. It is extremely labor intensive, and the window of opportunity is fairly narrow and the season relatively short. Nonetheless, the structural investment is much less than that for a traditional building, so that if such an establishment does not meet its financial goals, it melts away in the spring with no permanent investment or upkeep.

Demand for ice hotel accommodation usually comprises adventurous and outdoors-oriented travelers who aspire to sleep cold but wrapped in warm furs, blankets, and sleeping bags that can withstand temperatures of 40 or 50°C below zero on beds made of ice and snow. Although the rooms are cold, often below zero, they are significantly warmer than the outdoors. Most of these unique establishments also boast amenities such as ice bars, where guests drink from glasses made of ice and dine on tables made of ice. The Ice Hotel Quebec, in Canada, has in the past even offered weddings in its wedding chapel. Staying in an ice hotel is expensive. Most prices range between $300 and $400 per night, although some reach nearly $1000 per night for a double room.

Cold weather activities are important attractions to guests who elect to stay at ice hotels and provide revenue sources for these properties. Some of these hotels supplement the sub-zero experience with snow golf, which is usually played on firm pack-ice with brightly-colored balls that can be seen against a white background. Ice fishing, snow-mobile excursions, ice swimming, wildlife watching trips, snow hikes, and dog sledding tours are among the many other activities organized by some of these establishments and which fit in line with their purpose of offering a highly immersed winter experience. Among the most prominent examples today are the Hotel Igloo Village in Greenland, the Jukkasjärvi Ice Hotel in Sweden, Ice Hotel Quebec in Canada, Lainio Snow and Ice Hotel in Finland, the Aurora Ice Museum in the United States, and the Alta Igloo Hotel in Norway.

ECOLODGES

Another interesting trend that is growing with the popularity of eco-tourism and other forms of nature-based travel is ecolodges and ecoresorts.

One of the underlying philosophies of the ecolodge phenomenon is that humans are a part of nature and that they belong to nature, not nature to people. As part of the broader green movement discussed in an earlier chapter, ecolodges and ecoresorts have developed in response to traditional hotels and resorts that have been associated with mass tourism and largely blamed for the deterioration of ecological and cultural environments.

Today there are thousands of so-called ecolodges throughout the world that cater primarily to hard-core ecotourists, or tourists who desire to

These units are part of a certified ecolodge in Costa Rica

reduce their carbon footprint. Ecolodges are typically small in size in terms of total area and/or number of rooms available. They are also usually located in relatively remote locations and most often associated with rainforest environments, although this is not a necessity. Ecolodges cater to environmentally sensitive tourists, are often education-oriented, and operate according to strict ecologically friendly guidelines that set them apart from other inns and bed and breakfast establishments.

While some small-scale quarters might label themselves 'ecolodges', the industry has become more self-regulating in recent years and has begun to require adherence to principles and codes of conduct in order for a lodge to be an officially authorized 'ecolodge'. In Costa Rica, for example, the Certification for Sustainable Tourism (CST) was developed by the Sustainability Programs Department of the Costa Rica Tourist Board and the Costa Rica National Accreditation Commission to distinguish tourism businesses that adhere to principles of ecological sustainability and those that do not. Accommodation firms that comply with CST principles of sustainable development can be officially certified ecolodges. Similarly, Ecotourism Australia is a non-profit organization that regulates tourism and environmental regulations in Australia. As part of its mandate, the organization certifies guides, operators, and lodging businesses as eco-friendly firms that are committed to sustainable practices. As of November 2008, there were 81 eco-certified accommodations establishments in Australia, many of which market themselves as ecolodges or eco-cottages. This Australian eco-certification program was one of the first of its kind and is now being used in other parts of the world where nature-based tourism has become an important part of the tourism landscape.

The Australian and Costa Rican certification programs, and others, require ecolodges to adhere to strict regulations related to water use, waste management, energy use, and recycling, all in an attempt to reduce the carbon footprint of tourism and to build awareness among tourists of the need to be environmentally sensitive. To receive and maintain official 'eco-lodge' or 'ecoresort' designation, the establishments should abide by several common policies and practices.

- Construction should be done in such a way that minimizes disturbance to nature, is ecologically less-intrusive, and environmentally friendly construction materials should be used. Some ecolodges have utilized scrap wood, surplus timber, and recycled materials, including lumber from other demolished buildings. The design of the lodge should also be harmonious with the natural landscape in which it is located.

- Facilities should be designed in a manner that minimizes energy use. For instance, a northern, southern, or western building orientation can maximize natural sun light for illumination and heat. Skylights can reduce the need for artificial lighting, and low energy bulbs help reduce the consumption of electricity. Breezeways can be designed in place of fans or air conditioners.

- The use of natural water sources is preferred. Ground water can be pumped and filtered, while gutters and roofs can be used to collect rainwater for bathing and watering plants. Gray water can also be treated and re-used for watering plants and landscaping.

- Only food and cleaning products that come in recyclable containers should be used. Composting toilets and composting bins convert human and kitchen waste into valuable organic fertilizer for gardens and landscaping.

- Ecolodges and ecoresorts must have functioning recycling programs in place. Glass, paper products, and cans should be collected and recycled. Likewise, stationary, toilet paper, and promotional materials ought to be made from recycled materials.

- Chemical usage should be reduced where possible. Biodegradable cleaning liquids and powders should be used. Chemical pesticides should not be used; instead, manual weeding and pest control should be undertaken.

- Products purchased and used on site should be locally produced inasmuch as possible. Vegetables, fruits, bread, meat, eggs, and milk can often be purchased from clean and reliable sources in the local area. This reduces cost and waste, provides fresh produce daily, and brings economic benefits to the local community, who will in turn become more supportive of tourism.

- While not a requirement of all certification programs, many ecolodges and ecoresorts include an educative element in their product. Trail walks, rainforest treks, and educational centers feature strongly in most ecolodges and helps fulfill the mandate to minimize ecological disturbances by working to modify visitor behavior.

Many ecolodges charge higher rates than hotels and other mainstream forms of accommodation. However, some research studies suggest that hard-core ecotourists are willing to pay substantially more money for their stay if they are certain that the money will be spent on conservation or that the firm is abiding by sustainable tourism practices.

TREE HOUSE LODGING

Several important nature destinations have begun to develop 'tree house hotels' and lodges. Many of these are also certified and operated as ecolodges, but they are unique in this category because of their locations in treetops or on stilts at treetop canopy level. These types of lodging provide opportunities to become immersed in the rainforest canopy to observe bird and animal life, or a good overview of happenings on the ground. They range from individual 'cabins' in a single tree to a series of rooms connected by suspended walkways several meters above the ground.

Dozens of these tree house hotels have been built in Asia, Africa, the Pacific, North America, Latin America, and Europe (Table 15.1). The Woodpecker Hotel in Sweden is typical of a one-room establishment located some 13 m above the ground. Access is by ladder, and food is delivered via a pulley and basket system. One night at the Woodpecker ranges from $250 to 350, depending on season. The Sanyan Nanshan Tree house Resort and Beach Club in China comprises four tree houses, connected by catwalks. From the rooms, visitors can observe rain forests, botanical gardens, white sand beaches, and the famed Nanshan Mountains. Rooms at this resort also range between $250 and 350 per night.

Units at the Fur 'n' Feathers Rainforest Tree Houses near Cairns, Australia, are set on tall poles in the rainforest canopy of the Wet Tropics area of northern

Table 15.1	Examples of Tree House Accommodations and their Characteristics	
Tree House Hotel	**Location**	**Average Cost Per Night**
Alaska's Tree House	Seward, USA	<$100
Ariau Amazon Towers Hotel	Manaus, Brazil	$250–350
Baumhaus Hotel	Gorlitz, Germany	$150–250
Cedar Creek Treehouse	Ashford, USA	$250–350
Hana Lani	Hana, USA	$150–250
Kadirs Tree House Hotel	Antalya, Turkey	<$100
Out'n'about Treesort	Takilma, USA	$150–250
Parrot Nest Lodge	Cayo, Belize	<$100
Safariland Treehouse Resort	Nilgiris, India	$150–250
Tree Houses Hotel	Santa Clara, Costa Rica	<$100
Wild Canopy Reserve	Masinagudi, India	$150–250
Winvian	Litchfield, USA	$350
Woodpecker Hotel	Vasteras, Sweden	$250–350

Source: www.unusualhotelsoftheworld.com; www.treehouseshotelcostarica.com.

Queensland. The self-catering units are situated in the rainforest canopy and feature lounges, fireplaces, telephones, TVs, and laundry facilities. The units include kitchens where visitors can prepare their own meals. Activities include trail walks, river tubing, and wildlife viewing. While this particular establishment features a dishwasher, kitchen, laundry machines, and covered parking, it utilizes eco-friendly sewage treatment and natural rainwater supplies. This represents an up-market establishment, but many others are more basic in the experiences they offer.

While the novelty of these establishments includes their location in treetops or on stilts and the views that such a location commands, there are several management challenges. The most important of these is accessibility. Clearly this type of establishment is not well suited to consumers with physical disabilities, and if located too high, supplying construction and maintenance materials can be a significant constraint. Safety and security are also problems that must be addressed by managers, including legal issues related to liability.

INDIGENOUS DWELLINGS

As part of people's desires to explore the world and be immersed in different cultures, there is a long trend related to indigenous housing being utilized as tourist accommodations. This type of lodging underscores the true meaning of hospitality in the travel industry because it combines indigenous accommodation with the traditional warmth and friendliness of the local host. From the very beginning of global travel, explorers and early adventurer tourists stayed in the homes of indigenous peoples before formal and dedicated traveler accommodations were established. This trend still continues in more remote parts of the world, but today most of this phenomenon is geared toward purpose-built native lodging. Some of these have been constructed according to traditional design explicitly for tourist use, while others are extant homes that have been refurbished to accommodate tourists. Also, in some cases they provide affordable alternatives for less-affluent backpacker tourists, while at the same time they provide foundations of some of the world's most luxurious and exclusive resorts.

Traditional Fijian grass homes, *bures*, are used throughout the Fiji islands as small-scale tourist accommodations. In most cases, they are purpose built for tourism, some retaining traditional characteristics while others don more modern design elements, including glass windows, air conditioners, and en-suite showers. Even the most luxurious resorts in the islands have adopted many traditional design elements for several reasons, including the esthetic appeal that they provide, the cost effectiveness of building units that are not made entirely of wood and metal, and to satisfy the desires of guests who might want to stay in a 'traditional' abode but have access to all the modern amenities of a mega resort.

Similar use has been made of traditional Samoan dwellings, *fales*, in both resort and other contexts. Many of the *fales* of Samoa, however, are linked more directly to budget travelers—backpackers—who do not mind sleeping in a traditional home with no walls, as long as it is inexpensive and accessible. Most of the dozens of tourist *fales* that have been built on the islands cost approximately USD $25 per night and include one or two meals and bedding.

Many families or villages have built *fales* in an effort to earn additional income from small-scale tourism. The primary advantages of families offering small-scale *fale* accommodations are that nearly all the money earned from backpackers or other guests stays in the local

This resort unit in Fiji is designed to resemble a traditional Fijian 'bure'

economy, they employ local people and local skills, they utilize locally grown products, do not require large start-up costs, and diversify the range of accommodations available to tourists. Another positive characteristic of *fale*-based accommodations is that visitors are submerged in Samoan culture and have opportunities to learn about Samoan traditions and family life. Compared to other island destinations worldwide, Samoa has been successful in retaining domestic control over its hotel and lodging establishments. The *fale* idea contributes to the longevity of that pattern and is well suited for a tropical island country in the pacific.

Many other examples can be found in all parts of the world, from the longhouses of Sarawak (Indonesia), *marae* of New Zealand's Maoris, to Bedouin tents in the deserts of the Middle East and North Africa. These Bedouin tents have become important tourist accommodations, particularly in Jordan and Egypt, where guests can spend one or more nights in the desert, learning about Bedouin lifestyles and traditions, assisting in the care of horses and camels, and eating the traditional foods of the desert nomads. A similar situation can be found in Mongolia, where tourists can arrange stays in traditional felt *gers* (yurts) in the countryside. *Ger* camps have been built in some of Mongolia's national parks because they are seen to be more ecologically sustainable than wood or concrete structures and offer visitors a glimpse of what life might be like for traditional Mongolian nomads. Several camps in North America (e.g. Colorado) have also modeled their own lodging establishments after Mongolian *gers* and Bedouin tents. More upscale indigenous facilities are emerging in the oil rich states of the Middle East, including the United Arab Emirates, Qatar and Bahrain. A good example of this kind of luxurious establishment is Bab Al Shams Desert Resort and Spa in Dubai.

Tourists can stay at a traditional Maori family compound, a marae, in New Zealand

Finally, many lodging providers in North America have capitalized on traditional Native American dwellings by opening facilities in the form of teepees, wigwams, and hogans. Some entrepreneurs have even built them in Europe and Australia. These range from tacky replicas built of concrete, steel, and bricks, where tourists can stay cheaply beside a highway, to higher-end edifices made in more authentic style of skins, wood poles, and canvas. These high-end accommodations are especially popular in US and Canadian natural areas and often try to target nature-based tourists and spiritual retreaters, who desire to be close to nature and discover themselves within it. Some higher-end teepees have earthen floors, while others are made of wood. They are furnished with beds, pillows, buffalo furs, chairs, and fireplaces, and meals are prepared and served in central eating quarters.

Although many of the teepee lodging establishments attempt to be ecologically and culturally sensitive in their portrayals of native history and culture, conflicts have occurred in the past regarding cultural property rights infringements and a sense of exploitation among Native Americans and Canadian First Nations. This is common in places where tourism relies heavily upon native cultures, including dwellings, for its appeal. Often, indigenous people consider the unauthorized utilization of their traditional homes as lodging as offensive and disrespectful. In New Zealand, where tourists sometimes stay at a traditional marae, or meeting place where traditions are celebrated and tribes united, the Maori people are heavily involved in tourism. The use of Maori cultural symbols and spaces is heavily regulated by the Maoris themselves. In other countries, this relationship is not as well developed, and in the case of the United States, it has led to conflict and unresolved discontent between Native Americans and tourism developers.

CAVES AND UNDERGROUND LODGES

Several caves have been developed into tourist lodging, and others have been built far underground. In most cases, developers blend history and nature to create a unique product that is isolated and sheltered from the outside elements. Extant caves have been converted into hotels and inns. Others have been built completely underground in deserted mine shafts or in purpose-built holes. Messerli and Sterling (2005) outline several advantages of this type of location, not least of which are that these dwellings stay cool in the summer and warm in the winter. Typically, these enterprises are located in areas of high natural or cultural amenity and are especially popular in the United States, Turkey, Australia, France, and Spain (Table 15.2).

HISTORIC BUILDINGS

One of the most demanded genres of tourist accommodation is renovated or remodeled historic buildings that once served a different function. Much of this is part of a broader movement toward preserving historical buildings and utilizing them for alternative purposes rather than tearing them down to make way for new developments. There are countless examples throughout the world of barns, factories, jails, stores, castles, mansions, convents, post offices, and even churches being refurbished and turned into tourist housing.

Table 15.2	Examples of Cave and Underground Tourist Accommodations	
Property	**Location**	**Features**
Beckham Creek Cave Haven	Eureka Springs, USA	Multi-room house built in Ozarks cave.
Cuevas Pedro Antonio De Alarcón	Guadix, Spain	Prehistoric cave converted into tourist chalets
Elkep Evi	Urgup, Turkey	Ancient cave dwelling converted to 23-room hotel
Gamirasu Cave Hotel	Urgup, Turkey	18-room cave house built into the mountains
Kokopelli's Cave	Farmington, USA	23-m deep blasted cave with Native-American theme
Le Prince Noir	Les Baux de Provence, France	Bed & Breakfast carved out of a mountainside
PJ's Underground Bed & Breakfast	White Cliffs, Australia	Underground guesthouse built in converted old mine

Source: Messerli and Sterling 2005; www.unusualhotelsoftheworld.com.

Such establishments appeal to heritage aficionados and have added appeal because of their previous functions. Their degree of appeal and the audience they appeal to depend largely on what their former function was. For example, old churches or convents might be most appealing to religious tourists. Jails and prisons no doubt have an appeal for people interested in outlaws and criminal history.

Several prisons associated with the communist past in Eastern Europe have been converted into pensions and inns. Napier Prison Backpackers Lodge in New Zealand was created from an old inmate quarry and prison, and the 1989 Langholmen Hotel in Sweden was the state prison until the mid 1970s.

Similarly, old railway cars and stations have been transformed into upper-class accommodations in a number of countries, including the United Kingdom, the United States, India, New Zealand, and the Netherlands. Typically, several train cars are linked together but stationary and are often located at former railway stations. Several of these offer bed and breakfast packages, and others are considered luxury suites and offer fine food in the dining car. These train suites cater especially to railway enthusiasts and history buffs. The B&B trains are relatively inexpensive (under US $100 per night), but the luxury suites can cost upwards of $500 per night.

Lighthouses are another element of built heritage that have recently developed as lodging options for tourists (Table 15.3). Many lighthouses throughout the world have been preserved as an important part of maritime heritage. In many countries, lighthouses are owned and preserved by national parks agencies, non-profit societies, land trusts, or private investors. One way of funding their preservation is to allow people to sleep in the lighthouses themselves or in the caretaker's cottage, which is often attached to the lighthouse or located nearby. This form of accommodation is becoming more popular in the United States, United Kingdom, Ireland, Netherlands, Canada, and Australia.

Converted castles, convents, and monasteries abound in Europe and have become a preferred form of accommodation for luxury tourists and even business travelers. In Spain and other countries that were historically influenced or colonized by Spain, this unique form of lodging is known as a *parador*, or a luxury hotel that has been transformed from previous aristocratic edifices such as castles, monasteries, or convents. Paradors are similar to the castle-type accommodations found throughout Europe, especially in the British Isles and in Italy. Entire castles or paradors can be rented for weddings, receptions and other major events, or family reunions. More often, however, they are hired out room by room and are typically quite expensive.

Table 15.3	Examples of Lighthouse Accommodations	
Lighthouse	**Location**	**Features**
Cape Otway Light Station	Cape Otway, Australia	Guests stay in the keeper's quarters
Great Orme Lighthouse	Conwy, UK	Guests stay in the keeper's suite and lighthouse
Lighthouse Harlingen	Harlingen, Netherlands	Guests stay in the converted lighthouse
Sand Hills Lighthouse Inn	Ahmeek, USA	Guests stay in converted lighthouse and keeper's quarters
Saugerties Lighthouse	Albany, USA	Guests stay in converted lighthouse and keeper's quarters
Smoky Cape Lighthouse	Smoky Cape, Australia	Guests stay in converted lighthouse
Wicklow Head Lighthouse	Wicklow, Ireland	Guests stay in converted lighthouse

Source: www.travel-quest.co.uk/blue/bd_special_light.htm; www.unusualhotelsoftheworld.com.

CAPSULE HOTELS

Capsule hotels, or pod hotels, began in 1979 and have become fashionable in Japan with limited acceptance outside the country, although a few, and similar models, are being considered in Europe and North America. These establishments comprise small-space fiberglass pods with little more room than a coffin (2 m × 1 m × 1.25 m). The pods are stacked side by side, and usually two units high, resembling the body storage compartments at a morgue or in a mausoleum. Many of them include wireless Internet connections, televisions, and radios. Bathrooms and toilets are shared, and most of the hotels have restaurants and entertainment facilities.

Several of the Japanese pod hotels are used exclusively by men, while others cater to men and women. In the past they were associated with sex and prostitution, with some of the earlier hotels being located in or near urban red light districts and sometimes being dubbed 'love hotels'. Today, however, they have become a more legitimate form of accommodation, particularly for male business travelers who can ill afford commute time between home and office, although all budget-conscious travelers are welcome to stay. The primary advantages of pod hotels are their convenience and price, ranging from $15 to $45 per night. Such accommodation is probably not suitable for people who require larger spaces or who want more privacy, but they are becoming more popular among foreign travelers in general in Japan.

MEGA MULTI MALLS

Several mega malls have developed during the past 25 years, including the world's largest, West Edmonton Mall (WEM), in Alberta, Canada, and the Mall of America (MOA), the second largest in the world, located in Minnesota, USA. Other malls have been or are currently being developed according to the WEM and MOA model, although at a smaller scale. Besides their sheer size, the most unique feature of this new genre of shopping center is the ancillary entertainment provided alongside shopping. Bowling alleys, skating rinks, water parks, petting zoos, mini golf, and a variety of other added amenities accompany the traditional shops and eating establishments to comprise what many observers are calling a 'total vacation experience'. Thus, instead of being simply a shopping mall with a variety of stores and restaurants, these new mega multi malls, as they are often called, have begun positioning themselves in the global market as complete holiday destinations, with travel agencies, hotels, and amusement parks built into the property.

Of particular interest to this book is the idea of malls being home to hotels or other lodging establishments. With the inclusion of hotels, mega malls have become self-contained holiday destinations, where in the cases of WEM and MOA, tour groups arrive from Japan or Europe, spend a week or long weekend shopping and playing at the mall, and returning to their home countries, often without ever leaving the mall property. At WEM, for example, Fantasyland Hotel offers 120 themed rooms (e.g. Hollywood, Polynesian, Arabian, Igloo, African) inside the mall, and the MOA is planning to build a world-class hotel as part of its second development phase. With the changing role of large shopping centers and mega malls into capitals of 'shoppertainment', it is likely that embedded accommodation facilities will become more commonplace in the future and will spread to other parts of the world. Dubai's Mall of the Emirates (MOE) is a mixed land-use mega mall that includes the 5-Star Kempinski Hotel. Suites in this hotel average over $8,000 a night. Similar mega malls have been planned for the UAE, Russia, India, and China.

PILGRIM REST HOUSES AND SPIRITUAL RETREATS

Pilgrimage is often cited as one of the earliest forerunners to the modern-day notion of long-distance travel and has existed for thousands of years, including early records of Buddhist and Hindu devotees traveling to places known to be sacred to their religious affiliations. An important component of the original notion of pilgrimage was hardship, or strenuous efforts to arrive at a destination by following a prescribed trail or pilgrim route from the pilgrim's home to the holy sites. By following these prescribed trails, typically by foot or on horseback, a pilgrim can humble himself/herself and thereby become closer to God and more sensitive to spiritual matters, as well as demonstrate remorse for committing sin.

Along these pilgrimage routes, accommodations developed through the centuries to cater to the needs of traveling pilgrims. In most cases they were, and continue to be, fairly spartan in appearance (except those inside important monasteries) and substance, and usually could be utilized by religious travelers free of charge. These rest houses, guesthouses, pilgrims' rests, or hospices, as they are variously known, still exist along major pilgrimage routes (e.g. the route to Santiago de Compostela, Spain) and at significant religious pilgrimage destinations throughout the world (e.g. Varanasi (India) and Jerusalem). Today, most of these pilgrim hospices are operated by volunteer religious organizations and welcome people of their own religious persuasions to stay for free or for a minimal surcharge. In many cases, non-pilgrims (i.e. tourists who do not belong to the specific religion being represented) may also stay in these establishments for a nominal fee. Jerusalem, one of the most significant pilgrimage destinations in the world, is home to many pilgrimage lodging establishments that are used by various Christian groups and non-pilgrimage tourists. Likewise, various forms of pilgrim accommodations have been developed in Mecca, Saudi Arabia, for travelers undertaking the annual Hajj.

The idea of pilgrim guesthouses has grown to encompass spiritual retreats, or getaways for people seeking to enhance their spiritual channels. These tend to be less spartan and can in fact resemble higher class hotels or resorts. What makes them unique is their concentration on enhancing people's spirituality by connecting to nature, yoga and meditation, indigenous knowledge, and religious exercises.

This historic pilgrim rest house in Jerusalem is still used by pilgrims today

Spiritual retreat houses are especially popular in the United Kingdom and United States and typically offer short-term accommodations for travelers seeking a getaway for spiritual rejuvenation. Many of these overlap with health spas and resorts, but others are more clearly defined as spiritually oriented sanctuaries that cater specifically to guests seeking spiritual growth, peace, and quiet conditions. They tend to focus on nature adulation, reflexology, aromatherapy, naturopathic treatments, yoga, meditation, 'holistic holidays', and other new age-associated practices. The spiritual retreats are typically located in places of extraordinary natural beauty and may in some cases be located in renovated historic buildings. In the UK, these retreat houses are fairly basic, reflecting their 'back-to-nature' theme, and often lack basic amenities such as televisions and minibars. In the United States, however, they tend to be more luxurious and more recently constructed for the purpose of providing a more lavish atmosphere.

Not all spiritual retreats are of a new age order. Several mainstream religions, such as the Roman Catholic Church and some of the Orthodox churches, also maintain retreats for religious adherents who wish to get away on short-haul and short-term breaks to revitalize their spiritual and mental self, to pray in humble environments away from the hustle and bustle of the city, and to reflect on their spiritual lives. In Europe, these can be found in old monastic houses, medieval cloisters, or old churches.

PLASTIC SURGERY RESORTS

Part of the now recognized realm of health or medical tourism, another new phenomenon of the modern day is plastic surgery resorts. With skyrocketing costs of surgery in the developed world, thousands of people have opted to travel to less-affluent countries to engage in 'plastic surgery tourism' or other types of operations. These 'medical tourists' travel to a selected destination, undergo surgical procedures, and then recuperate in on-site health resorts or nearby spas and resorts that have been booked in conjunction with their operations. For a fraction of the cost of plastic surgery alone in the North, medical tourists can travel to the South, undergo surgery, and recover in relaxing and lavish surroundings, engaging in golf, swimming, pedicures, spa treatments, and other holiday-related diversions. The most popular destinations for these surgery and recovery stays are India, China, Thailand, Mexico, Costa Rica, and Brazil. Many more developing world destinations, however, have seen the potential for this type of health tourism and have begun development efforts.

OUTER-SPACE EXPERIENCES

Every couple of years, news headlines around the world spotlight a 'space tourist' who spent millions of dollars to travel to a space station or to experience life in the outer reaches of the earth's atmosphere and beyond. Many observers predict that this activity, space travel, will become more common and less expensive in the future, and many hotel and resort companies are banking on it. Since the beginning of the new millennium, some of the world's largest hotel chains (e.g. Hilton and Budget Suites) have invested millions of dollars into researching the feasibility of developing space resorts, either floating or grounded on the moon. Civil and aerospace engineering research has been funded by large hotel companies to conduct feasibility studies, including how empty rocket and shuttle fuel tanks floating as space rubbish can be collected, assembled, and turned into floating resorts. These futuristic complexes are expected even to boast mini golf and tennis, space walks, and space gardening activities. According to Thompson's (2007) report, the first space hotel, Galactic Suites, is set to open in 2012, with a three-night package starting at $4 million. Tourists can, according to the website, 'see the sunrise 15 times a day', travel around the world in 80 min, and bathe in a bubble filled with water.

Until that time, several hotels are already beginning to develop space-themed accommodations on earth that send visitors on virtual voyages and present 'fantasy' suites that make guests feel they are staying beyond the atmosphere. Three-dimensional projections, sounds, and space-related paraphernalia en suite create the illusion of being in outer space. Some observers believe this is just the next step before actual space travel and accommodations are developed.

SAND HOTEL

In July 2008, the so-called 'world's first hotel made of sand' opened for business on the beach in Dorset, England. Entrepreneurs took eight days to construct the small 15-m square castle, which included open-air rooms with bed and sofas made of sand. The initial cost per night was 10 pounds ($18) and was booked full for the season. The lack of privacy was said to be compensated by good sea views and the novelty factor. While this was the first attempt of its kind, it is likely that, given the preponderance of innovation and entrepreneurialism in the world today, other unusual and strange ideas for accommodation forms will develop in the future.

SUMMARY AND CONCLUSION

The lodging sector of the tourism industry has expanded beyond the traditional accommodation facility. With the rapid growth of the tourism industry in the last quarter century, the expansion of travel market segments have led to the need for diverse lodging facilities. Several factors that have influenced or facilitated these novel or non-traditional lodging facilities include improved technology as in the case of Ice Hotels and Galactic Suites. The environmental movement, global warming, the need for conservation, and ecological issues facing the planet are some of the principal driving force behind the tremendous development of Ecolodges particularly in developing regions of the world where sustainable tourism development is being embraced. For example, Eco Hotels of the World, an independent guide to lodging establishments that are considered the greenest hotels in the world, listed about 110 ecolodges in 2008. Most of these are located in ecological hotspots in developing countries. Another important factor influencing the development of these novel lodging properties is the imperative need to conserve, preserve, and restore the built environment, which includes cultural heritage. Heritage hotels fulfill this need while indigenous properties incorporate the preservation component while adding both educational and hospitality dimension at the communal level. Future development of these types of unique lodging facilities is likely to include underwater hotels, more elaborate space hotels, and submarine cruises with staterooms.

REFERENCES

Messerli, H., Sterling, D.S., 2005. Alternative accommodation. Travel and Tourism Analyst 6, 1–37.

Thompson, A., 2007. Space hotel slated to open in 2012. Online at http://www.space.com/news/070811_space_hotel.html

FURTHER READING

Adcock, J., 1999. Lighthouse Accommodation: Britain and Worldwide. Joy Adcock, London.

Al-Oun, S., Al-Homoud, M., 2008. The potential for developing community-based tourism among the Bedouins in the Badia of Jordan. Journal of Heritage Tourism 3 (1), 36–54.

Ayala, H., 1995. Ecoresort: a 'green' masterplan for the international resort industry. International Journal of Hospitality Management 14 (3/4), 351–374.

Ayala, H., 1996. Resort ecotourism: a master plan for experience management. Cornell Hotel and Restaurant Administration Quarterly 37 (5), 54–61.

Ayala, H., 1996. Resort ecotourism: a paradigm for the 21st century. Cornell Hotel and Restaurant Administration Quarterly 37 (5), 46–53.

Ayala, H., 1997. Resort ecotourism: a catalyst for national and regional partnerships. Cornell Hotel and Restaurant Administration Quarterly 38 (4), 34–45.

Beck, A., 2005. The Treehouse Village Ecoresort: a model for successful sustainable tourism. Development Bulletin 67, 71–72.

Brown, F., 2004. The final frontier? Tourism in space. Tourism Recreation Research 29 (1), 37–43.

Buselle, M., 1989. Castles in Spain: A Traveller's Guide Featuring the National Parador Inns. Salem House Publishers, Topsfield, MA.

Collins, P., 2002. Space hotels: civil engineering's new frontier. Journal of Aerospace Engineering 15 (1), 10–19.

Connell, J., 2006. Medical tourism: sea, sun, sand and … surgery. Tourism Management 27 (6), 1093–1100.

Coy, W.G., Høgh, L., 2002. Endangered visitors: a phenomenological study of eco-resort development. Current Issues in Tourism 5 (3/4), 254–271.

Crouch, G.I., 2001. The market for space tourism: early indications. Journal of Travel Research 40 (2), 213–219.

de Arrellano, A.B.R., 2007. Patients without borders: the emergence of medical tourism. International Journal of Health Services 37 (1), 193–198.

Fennell, D., 2008. Ecotourism, third ed. Routledge, London.

Grant, J., 2005. Staying at a Lighthouse: American's Romantic and Historic Lighthouse Inns, Second Edn. Globe Pequot, Guildford, CT.

Harris, R., Leiper, N. (Eds.), 1995. Sustainable Tourism: An Australian Perspective. Butterworth Heinemann, Sydney.

Hawkins, D. (Ed.), 1995. The Ecolodge Sourcebook: for Planners and Managers. International Ecotourism Society, Burlington, VT.

Holjevac, I.A., 2003. A vision of tourism and the hotel industry in the 21st century. International Journal of Hospitality Management 22 (2), 129–134.

Magenheim, H., 2001. Quebec proves ice is nice as hotel reopens. Travel Weekly 60 (98), 37.

Messerli, H., Sterling, D.S., 2005. Alternative accommodation. Travel and Tourism Analyst 6, 1–37.

Osland, G.E., Mackoy, R., 2004. Ecolodge performance goals and evaluations. Journal of Ecotourism 3 (2), 109–128.

Pearce, A.B., Ocampo-Raeder, C., 2008. A Montana lodge and the case for a broadly defined ecotourism. In: Stronza, A., Durham, W.H. (Eds.), Ecotourism and conservation in the Americas. CAB International, Wallingford, UK, pp. 114–124.

Pizam, A., 1999. Life and tourism in the year 2050. International Journal of Hospitality Management 18 (4), 331–343.

Pizam, A., 2008. Space tourism: new market opportunities for hotels and cruise lines. International Journal of Hospitality Management 27 (4), 489–490.

Sanders, E.G., Halpenny, E., 2001. The Business of Ecolodges: A Survey of Ecolodge Economics and Finance. International Ecotourism Society, Burlington, VT.

Shackley, M., 2004. Accommodating the spiritual tourist: the case of religious retreat houses. In: Thomas, R. (Ed.), Small Firms in Tourism: International Perspectives. Elsevier, Amsterdam, pp. 225–237.

Scheyvens, R., 2002. Backpacker tourism and third world development. Annals of Tourism Research 29, 144–164.

Scheyvens, R., 2005. Growth of beach fale tourism in Samoa: the high value of low-cost tourism. In: Hall, C.M., Boyd, S.W. (Eds.), Nature-based Tourism in Peripheral Areas: Development or Disaster? Channel View, Clevedon, UK, pp. 188–202.

Smith, V.L., 2000. Space tourism: the 21st century 'frontier'. Tourism Recreation Research 25 (3), 5–15.

Timothy, D.J., White, K., 1999. Community-based ecotourism development on the periphery of Belize. Current Issues in Tourism 2 (2/3), 226–242.

Warnken, J., Bradley, M., Guilding, C., 2005. Eco-resort vs. mainstream accommodation providers: an investigation of the viability of benchmarking environmental performance. Tourism Management 26, 367–379.

Weaver, D.B., 2002. Hard-core ecotourists in Lamington National Park, Australia. Journal of Ecotourism 1 (1), 19–35.

Wheat, S., 2004. Back to nature. Leisure Management 24 (2), 76–79.

Whitehead, A., 2001. Snapshot: Ice Hotel Quebec. Architectural Record 189 (2), 59–65.

Wight, P.A., 1997. Ecotourism accommodation spectrum: does supply match the demand? Tourism Management 18, 209–220.

Wilson, J., 2000. Postcards from the moon: a lunar vacation isn't as far-out an adventure as you think. Popular Mechanics June, 97–99.

World Tourism Organization, 2003. Sustainable Development of Ecotourism: A Compilation of Good Practices in SMEs. UNWTO, Madrid.

USEFUL INTERNET RESOURCES

West Edmonton Mall: www.fantasylandhotel.com/home/wemindex.asp.

Mall of America: www.mallofamerica.com.

Mall of the Emirates: www.malloftheemirates.com.

Hotel Igloo Village, Kangerlussuaq, Greenland: www.greenland-guide.gl/igloo/default.htm.

Jukkasjärvi Ice Hotel, Sweden: http://www.icehotel.com/Winter/Home/.

Paradors in Spain: http://www.parador.es/es/portal.do;jsessionid=17B8E86133D-93C1D441DB7D45F3364DE.

Bab Al Shams Desert Resort & Spa: http://www.jumeirahbabalshams.com.

Ecolodge certification in Costa Rica: http://www.turismo-sostenible.co.cr/EN/home.shtml.

Ecotourism Australia certifies accommodations: http://www.ecotourism.org.au/neap.asp.

Green hotels and ecolodges: www.planeta.com/ecotravel/tour/hotels.html

Eco Hotels of the World: http://www.ecohotelsoftheworld.com.

Rancho Margot Ecolodge, Costa Rica: http://www.ranchomargot.org.

Laguna del Lagarto Eco Lodge, Costa Rica: www.lagarto-lodge-costa-rica.com.

Chan Chich Jungle Lodge and nature Reserve, Belize: http://www.chanchich.com.

Cotton Tree Lodge, Belize: www.cottontreelodge.com.

Unusual Hotels of the World: http://www.unusualhotelsoftheworld.com/.

Lighthouse hotel directory: http://www.travel-quest.co.uk/blue/bd_special_light.htm.

Japanese Capsule Hotels: http://gojapan.about.com/cs/accommodation/a/tokyocapsule1.htm.

CHAPTER 16

Critical Issues and the Future of Lodging

The purpose of this book was to provide an overview of the accommodation sector within the context of tourism, not separated from tourism as is often done in the hospitality literature. Various types of tourist lodging have been examined within the framework of social, environmental, managerial, and political thought. While the book has not presented a hospitality management approach, the issues discussed clearly have management implications. This last chapter draws ideas together from the text and considers possible future directions for tourist accommodations.

Tourism is clearly one of the most pervasive and largest industries in the world. Some commentators suggest that tourism itself is not a single industry but a system of industries that work together to produce a complete product. Regardless of the terminology used, tourism and its various sectors (e.g. transportation, lodging, food, shopping, etc.) are extremely political, ecological, economic, geographical, and anthropological phenomena that affect all areas of the world through economic and social multipliers, even places where full-fledged tourism does not exist. Tourism is also very large, comprising nearly 10% of the world's total economy (GDP) and resulting in billions of international and domestic trips away from home each year.

Given the magnitude of tourism and the number of people involved, it is not surprising that lodging is one of the most important service sectors in tourism, and usually when people think about 'tourism' the image that most often comes to mind is hotels and resorts. Given that the industry has grown continuously every year, with only a few exceptions (e.g. 2001), it will likely continue to grow as new destinations choose to become more involved in tourism because of its economic promise and as political climates change, opening more doors to the outside world. Destinations that have heretofore resisted the urge to target tourism have caved to the economic stresses of the new millennium. Likewise, tourists are becoming more sophisticated in their demands for destinations and experiences. We will certainly see the blossoming of new and unusual destinations, such as Rwanda, Angola, Sao Tome et Principe, Nicaragua, Mozambique, Malawi, Congo, Mauritania, Mali,

CONTENT

References

Swaziland, Gabon, Suriname, Uruguay, Djibouti and various other countries that have a great deal to offer visitors but which the world has yet to target for mass tourism. Antarctica, which has also seen phenomenal growth in arrivals (on cruises, overflights, and visits to scientific stations) during the past 15 years, is expected to host even more tourists in the future—more than the 45 000–50 000 who already visit each year. Some commentators predict that outer space will become the next frontier in tourism, with demand for floating hotels and resorts a realistic possibility in the next generation or two.

Manifestations of globalization, such as supranational alliances and improved international relations, will likely continue into the future, improving the tourism product and facilitating a freer flow of international travelers, industry workers, and information, as has already occurred in the European Union. Likewise, the future will certainly bring about additional international legislation to deal with security, standardized service and hygiene ratings, and accessibility in the lodging sector. Although most of the world is set to bring down the traditional barrier effects of political boundaries through cross-border cooperation, the United States is erecting new ones—literally and figuratively—to help monitor terrorist threats and assure the security of its citizens.

More than any other country in the world, perhaps with the exception of Israel, the United States is concerned about safety and security, owing to its position as a prime target for terrorists who are bent on thwarting its influence around the world. This has a considerable bearing on safety and security issues related to hotels and other lodging facilities. Only a few decades ago, security departments in hotels and resorts were almost unheard of. Today, however, these comprise some of the biggest departments and are staffed by trained security personnel. Biosecurity and food security have come to the fore in recent years with increases in terrorist activity and liability litigation. Given the most evident possibility of security breaches and threats to customer safety, lodging companies have begun to require employee training courses and develop emergency plans to cope with potential security contingencies.

Tourism has a long history of causing environmental problems. The authors are cognizant of the fact that tourism is only one of many forces that have brought about environmental degradation in tourism destinations. Nonetheless, without careful planning and monitoring, tourism has been allowed to grow unmitigated for far too long in too many parts of the world. While urban and regional planners have realized the importance of community-based planning and development and environmental conservation in regional planning exercises, this has become a central part of tourism development only since the late 1980s. Thus, there is a lot to catch up on in this regard. As established destinations continue to develop and as new destinations are 'discovered', careful environmental planning is an absolute necessity for places to remain viable into the future.

As the environmental ethics movement continues to grow in tourism, hotels, resorts, guesthouses, inns, hostels, campgrounds, cruise lines, and other accommodation providers will continue to realize that reducing their carbon footprint on the environment translates into good business. Some are already implementing high-quality recycling and waste water management programs at a significant cost, more than they save, as a way of demon- strating their commitment to sustainable tourism for generations to come. This is great news, but there is more to be done, especially among the tourists themselves, who seem to have yet to catch the same vision that so many lodging providers have adopted. Best practices and codes of ethics research continues in tourism studies in the realm of lodging. It will likely continue into the future, involving a tourist education component that so many observers have already recommended.

One of the problems for researchers interested in the supply of tourism services is the classification of various accommodation types, for researchers and marketers favor definitions and typologies. The lines between classifi- cations of lodging facilities are blurry, and there is no universal standard definition of what hotels, resorts, bed and breakfasts, inns, paradors, or hostels are. In fact, even though some states, provinces, or countries have worked out 'official' definitions of lodging types, in most destinations owners are free to call their establishments whatever they wish. It is common for basic hotels to be labeled 'resorts' or bed and breakfasts to operate under the name of 'hotel'. These definitions will continue to be refined, which will be instrumental in product development and scientific research.

In spite of these blurred boundaries, it is likely that new forms of accommodation will continue to appear on the tourism scene. Creative people have already begun to capitalize on tourists' propensity toward odd- ness, curiosity fulfillment, unusualness, otherness, being 'the first', and seeking titillating experiences. The establishment of ice hotels, sand hotels, lighthouse lodges, cave and underground hotels, and tree house lodges attests to this. The future will no doubt reveal additional novelty forms of lodging that will be irresistible to travelers seeking unusual destinations and sleeping experiences. As modern life continues to become more rushed and frenetic in urban areas, albeit constrained by economic pressures, we will continue to see adaptations to traditional lodging, such as the capsule hotels described in Chapter 15, which have become popular and inexpensive options for busi- ness people in many Japanese and European cities.

Just as new lodging types will continue to appear and with an ever more diverse demand for tourism products and services, as illustrated by adaptations being made for people with disabilities, new definitions of tourists will emerge. People who have traditionally been overlooked in tourism statistics will eventually be counted as part of the global tourism phenomenon. This includes informal traders who cross national boundaries, spend a night on the opposite side, purchase goods abroad, and sell them at home, or sell goods from home while they are abroad. Timothy and Teye (2005) examined this phenomenon along the border of Ghana and Togo in West Africa, where traders cross the international boundary to buy and sell their wares. These, they argue, are the third world's version of business travelers and their volume is much higher than the more commonly accepted view of business tourists who wear suits and fly in airplanes. This part of the population will become more mobile in the future and their demands for accommodations will increase as well. Cross-border trade exists throughout the world and the expansion of the definition of tourists and tourism will no doubt provide a more complete picture of the worldwide phenomenon of global mobility.

All of the trends and issues identified so far in this concluding chapter will either necessitate the construction of additional accommodation facilities or change the face of existing hospitality services. Multinational corporations will no doubt penetrate these new markets to become involved as franchisers and management contractors, as developers and investors realize the latent and existing new demand for lodging facilities. There has even been talk by Argentina about building a Holiday Inn in Antarctica to facilitate tourists' interest in staying there and to assert Argentina's claim of sovereignty over a portion of the southernmost continent. Whether or not this ever comes to fruition is a point of debate and will not likely happen for many years to come, but it is an interesting argument that would be worth following in the future. The lodging sector is among the most pervasive, dynamic, and economically and socially important elements of the tourism industries. The earliest pilgrims, traders, and Grand Tour participants would hardly recognize the accommodation landscape of today. Its future is certain in that growth will continue, but the growth to come will be determined by social, environmental, and economic forces, many of which are still unknown in the twenty-first century.

REFERENCES

Glassner, M.I., Fahrer, C., 2004. Political geography, third ed. Wiley, Hoboken, NJ.

Timothy, D.J., Teye, V.B., 2005. Informal sector business travelers in the developing world: a borderlands perspective. Journal of Tourism Studies 16 (1), 82–92.

Index

accessibility, 72–73, 84, 244, 260
accidents, 102
Accor, 38, 68, 92, 94, 139
accounting, 30, 64
adventure tourism, 21
Africa, 15, 22, 64, 76, 82, 83, 106,
    134, 142, 143, 168, 177,
    184, 187, 216, 243, 262
agriculture, 20, 88, 120, 183,
    189
agritourism, 183–184, 189
aid agencies, 146
air quality, 81
air travel, 4, 18, 89, 169, 202
airlines, 14, 38–39, 54, 81
airplanes, 2, 14, 89, 187
airport taxes see taxes
airports, 20, 22, 49, 106, 136
Albania, 21, 66
alternative tourism, 57, 83
altruism, 19
amenities, 138, 200, 208, 222,
    228–229, 240, 250
amenity migration, 155, 159,
    161–162, 199
American Bed and Breakfast
    Association, 181
American Resort Development
    Association (ARDA), 164,
    166–167
Americans with Disabilities Act
    (ADA), 34, 72–73
Amerisuites, 137
amusement parks, 143, 229,
    250
Angola, 16, 259
Antarctica, 15, 67, 94, 260, 262
Antigua, 25
apartments, 155, 161, 164
architecture, 145, 187
Argentina, 120, 262
Aruba, 140, 144, 166

Asia, 2, 15, 16, 22, 37, 53, 64,
    65, 83, 90, 124, 133, 134,
    135, 140, 145, 156, 168,
    177, 184, 199, 208, 214,
    215–216, 243
attachment to place, 159
attractions, 6, 13, 24, 48, 54, 63, 89,
    122, 137, 199, 218, 222, 229
Australia, 2, 35, 51, 52, 66, 82,
    86, 90, 93, 119, 120, 121,
    136, 138, 144, 156, 168,
    178, 184–185, 198, 203,
    214–215, 219, 227, 243,
    246, 247, 249
Austria, 156, 181, 189
authenticity, 55–56, 179
automobiles, 2, 3, 15, 81, 89, 133,
    139, 161, 178, 185, 187,
    202, 230
Azerbaijan, 16

baby boomers, 21, 167
backpacker tourists, 51, 182,
    213–223, 245
backpacking see backpacker
    tourists
Bahamas, 25
Bahrain, 163, 200, 246
balance of payments, 47
banks, 48, 50
bars, 90, 118–119, 133, 178, 181,
    206, 222, 240
Bed and Breakfast Association
    (UK), 181
bed and breakfasts (B&Bs), 7,
    29, 40, 49, 54, 55, 75, 81,
    85, 104, 108, 121, 135,
    177–183, 189, 220, 248
bed taxes see taxes
Belgium, 144, 181, 199, 202
Belize, 57, 163, 234
Bermuda, 22, 144, 163, 200, 204
Bhutan, 135

biometric security measures, 109
bioterrorism 103
    see also terrorism
boosterism, 47, 55, 83
Bosnia and Herzegovina, 65
Botswana, 143, 187, 234
boutique accommodation, 7,
    177–189
brands, 51, 52, 69, 122
brand loyalty, 24, 37, 39
branding, 118
Brazil, 253
British Virgin Islands, 200
Brunei, 16
Buddhism, 1, 251
budget accommodation, 25, 51,
    137, 138, 155, 213–223,
    229, 245, 250
budgets, 5, 7
building codes, 109
Bulgaria, 21, 65, 66
Burger King, 119, 121
business travel, 13, 15, 16, 20, 21,
    92–94, 95, 125, 133, 136,
    137, 213, 262

cabins, 243, 19, 155, 229–230
    see also second homes
cafés, 14, 90, 118–119, 181, 215,
    228
Cambodia, 15, 16, 22, 122
campers see recreational vehicles
campgrounds, 7, 20, 25, 49, 55,
    89, 105, 110, 122, 261
camping, 19, 142, 186, 187, 197,
    214, 227–234
    categories of, 228–229
Canada, 3, 22, 23, 34, 37, 49, 50,
    51, 52, 53, 55, 120, 122,
    133, 143, 146, 156, 169,
    178–179, 182, 184, 186,
    187–188, 198–199, 201,
    203, 214, 231, 240, 249

Canada (*continued*)
  Alberta, 3, 123, 188, 250
  British Columbia, 3, 140, 146
  Manitoba, 123, 156
  New Brunswick, 3, 123
  Nova Scotia, 3
  Ontario, 3, 121, 123, 146
  Quebec, 3, 161, 240
  Saskatchewan, 3, 123
canal barges, 197, 199
Candlewood Suites, 137
Cape Verde, 16
capitalism, 22, 66, 167
capsule hotels, 250, 261
caravan parks, 162
  see also campgrounds; RV parks
caravans *see* recreational vehicles
Caribbean, 22, 33, 53, 64, 65, 67,
  75, 83, 88, 106, 111, 124,
  134, 135, 145, 156, 159,
  163, 180, 200, 204
carrying capacity, 76, 159–160,
  208, 209–210, 232
cars *see* automobiles
casinos, 121–124, 20, 30, 65
  see also gambling
castles, 247, 249, 254
Cayman Islands, 106, 163
Central America, 216, 16, 163,
  204
  see also Latin America
certification, 181, 29
  see also eco-friendly
    certification
chambermaids *see* housekeeping
chambres d'hotes, 180
Chile, 16, 121, 143, 189
China, 16, 22, 24, 35, 38, 64, 66,
  119, 163, 167, 200, 203,
  243, 251, 253
China's Approved Destination
  Status (ADS), 16, 35, 66, 71
'choose to reuse' *see* towel reuse
  program
Christianity, 1, 252
churches, 48, 161, 247, 252
cities, 48, 158, 181, 182–183, 185,
  186, 228, 230, 232, 261
cleanliness, 24, 101, 102, 181,
  222, 232
climate, 22–23, 145, 162, 184,
  227
climate change, 89, 259

Club Med, 25, 141
codes of conduct, 94, 241, 261
colonialism, 2, 3, 55, 134, 187
'comforts of home', 137, 147–148,
  150
commissions, 39
communism, 16, 21, 22, 38,
  65–66, 144, 167
community-based tourism, 5,
  56–57, 83, 90
complaints, 71
composting, 85–86, 242
condominiums, 137, 155, 164
conferences, 5, 117, 124–126
consolidation, 38, 67–68, 146
consumer-generated media
  (CGM), 40–41
convention centers, 125, 135
conventions *see* conferences
corruption, 70
Costa Rica, 16, 90, 163, 189, 216,
  228, 234, 241, 253
credit cards, 109, 169, 218
crime, 56, 101, 105–106, 124,
  159, 218
crises, 107–111
  responses to, 107–110
Croatia, 65
cross-border trade/cooperation,
  260, 64, 160
  see also supranationalism
cross-cultural knowledge, 35,
  70–71, 218
Cruise Lines International
  Association (CLIA), 205
cruises, 19, 39, 55, 66, 75, 102,
  110, 111, 118, 204–208,
  260
  apartment cruises, 4, 207
cruise ships, 4, 40, 65, 81, 88,
  102–103, 106–107, 109,
  121, 124, 197, 204, 261
cuisine, 14, 30, 117–118, 119,
  120, 148
culinary arts *see* cuisine
culinary heritage *see* heritage
cultural arrogance, 148
cultural tourism *see* heritage
customs controls, 48
Cyprus, 122, 140
Czech Republic, 21, 160
Czechoslovakia, 144

demand, 3, 4, 5, 7, 13–25, 40, 52,
  53, 66, 69, 84, 119, 120,
  121, 125, 133, 134, 137,
  141, 144, 149, 158, 160,
  165, 187, 213, 223, 234,
  229–231, 239, 247, 262
demand shifters, 20–23, 69
demographics, 20, 21, 24–25, 34
Denmark, 156, 200
developing countries, 15, 51, 55,
  57, 101, 147, 182, 216, 217,
  227, 261
dharamshalas, 2
dining establishments *see*
  restaurants
  see also cafés
disabilities, people with, 34,
  71–74, 244
disciplinary actions, 108
discrimination, 33–34, 72
diseases, 101, 102–104, 107, 111,
  144, 219, 221, 227, 233
Disney, 143, 164, 165–166, 169
diversification, 69
Djibouti, 260
domestic tourism, 4, 15, 17,
  75, 134, 156, 160, 185,
  215–216, 227, 259
Dominica, 51, 88
dormitories, 20, 217, 219–220,
  222
dude ranches, 20, 185–186
Dubai *see* United Arab Emirates

earthquakes, 53, 106
eco-friendly certification, 89–91,
  241–243
ecohotels, 19, 90
ecolodges, 19, 85, 90, 177, 186,
  240–243
e-commerce, 24, 29, 38–41, 69, 182
economic development, 122, 227
economic impacts, 47–54, 124,
  148, 162–163, 189, 215, 217
economic leakage, 51–52, 55, 57,
  147, 148, 189, 217
ecoresorts *see* ecolodges
eco-taxes, 87–89
ecotourism, 19, 21, 57, 83, 89,
  240, 242–243
educating tourists, 92–94, 189, 242
education, 24, 34–35, 41, 54, 147,
  189

educational travel, 19, 20, 21, 57
Egypt, 16, 102, 105, 144, 216, 246
El Salvador, 65
emergency plans, 107
employment, 5, 47, 48, 49, 65,
    124, 182, 189, 246
energy use/conservation, 19, 65,
    81, 82, 86–87, 89–90, 93,
    223, 242
England, 254, 140, 180
    see also United Kingdom
entertainment, 148, 205–206,
    229, 250
entrepreneurialism, 5, 47, 50, 182,
    184, 239, 246, 254
environmental ethics, 94, 261
environmental impacts, 5, 47, 55,
    57, 81–84, 88, 159–160,
    231, 241, 260
environmental protection, 160, 260
ethnic minorities, 55, 161, 234
ethnicity, 21, 24
Europe, 1–2, 21, 22, 33, 35, 37, 52,
    64, 65, 68, 69, 83, 88, 110,
    118, 120, 124, 133, 136,
    141, 143, 144, 156, 157,
    159, 160, 164, 177, 180,
    184–185, 186, 198, 199,
    200–201, 203, 208, 214,
    227, 243, 250, 251
European Monetary Union, 64, 69
European Union, 64, 160, 168, 260
event management, 29
events, 5, 20, 22
exchange rates, 21, 160
Expedia.com, 40, 150

Faeroe Islands, 120
Fairmont Hotels and Resorts, 3,
    188
families, 21, 24, 25, 54, 74,
    141, 143, 155, 158–159,
    164, 180, 182, 185, 189,
    199–200, 207, 213, 230,
    231
family-owned operations, 177–188
family reunions, 54, 126, 249
family vacations see families
farm stays, 20, 88, 183–186
fast food, 119–120
festivals, 20, 177
Fiji, 33, 118, 140, 142, 143, 169,
    216, 245

Finland, 53, 156, 160, 163, 200,
    240
fire safety, 108
fires, 106–107, 208, 231
floods, 53
folklore, 156
    see also heritage
food and beverage (F&B), 5, 7, 30,
    33, 40, 41, 48, 49, 50, 82,
    84, 90, 92, 117–122, 124,
    126, 148, 206
food poisoning, 103
food safety, 260, 103
    see also cleanliness
food services see food and beverage
food trails 121
    see also wine routes
foreign independent travelers
    (FIT), 213–223, 51
    see also budget
        accommodations;
        backpacker tourists
foreign tourists, 185, 18, 22, 93,
    105, 106, 134
    see also international tourism
formal economy 50
    see also informal economy
Four Seasons, 169
France, 51, 121, 140, 146, 156,
    180, 184, 189, 199, 203, 247
franchises, 36–38, 70
frequent stay programs, 39
    see also brand loyalty

Gabon, 260
gambling, 148, 5, 20, 56, 117,
    122–124, 143
    see also casinos
garbage disposal, 82
gas stations, 6, 162
GDP (Gross Domestic Product),
    16, 259
geographic information systems
    (GIS), 40
geotourism, 57, 83
Germany, 35, 134, 144, 156,
    180–181, 184, 203, 219
Ghana, 189, 262
globalization, 5, 7, 29, 30, 35, 37,
    40, 63–70, 141, 146, 155,
    160, 260
golf, 54, 87, 141, 142, 143, 207,
    228, 229, 240, 250, 253

Google Earth, 40–41, 42
Grand Tour, 2, 214, 262
Great Britain see United Kingdom
Greece, 156
green movement, 5, 19, 81–95, 223
Green Seal, 90–91
Greenland, 53, 120, 240
groundskeeping, 7, 30
Guadalupe, 200
Guatemala, 65
guesthouses, 261, 19, 40, 51, 85,
    102, 106, 134, 148, 178,
    252
    see also homestays
guest ranches see dude ranches

hajj, 252, 19
    see also pilgrimage; religious
        tourism
handicrafts, 84, 48, 55–56
    see also souvenirs
Harrah's, 143
health consciousness, 120, 144,
    155, 183, 208, 230
health spas see resorts, spa; spas
health tourism, 253
heritage, 8, 20, 21, 57, 82, 88–89,
    118, 120, 137, 148, 179,
    183, 185, 188, 202, 218,
    246, 248–249, 252
heritage tourism see heritage
highways, 133, 138–139, 178, 228
hiking, 142, 156, 184, 186, 187,
    214, 228, 240
Hilton, 36, 38, 68, 122, 169, 253
Hinduism, 1, 35, 251
historic hotels, 137–138, 247–249
holiday homes see second homes
Holiday Inn, 36, 135, 137, 262
holidays, 20, 22
Holy Land, 1
homestays, 180, 51, 178
    see also guesthouses
homosexuals, 24, 25, 34, 75, 141
Honduras, 16
honeymoons, 25, 179
hospitality, 8, 33, 34, 41, 42, 49,
    64–65, 71, 94, 108, 110,
    136, 146, 147, 150, 164,
    177, 181, 183, 245, 254,
    259, 262
hostages, 104, 105
Hostelling International, 220–221

hostels, 7, 20, 49, 54, 55, 104, 202, 213–223, 239, 261
hotel chains, 38, 69, 125, 146, 189
hotel management, 5, 7, 8, 29, 91, 105, 147
hotels, 2, 3, 5, 7, 14, 19, 20, 29, 36, 38–39, 40, 41, 49, 50, 51, 54–55, 64, 65, 68, 70, 72, 73, 81, 83, 86, 87, 90, 101–103, 104, 106, 108–109, 110, 120, 122, 124, 133, 134–138, 140, 146, 147, 148, 149, 169, 177–178, 181, 182, 197, 207, 218, 227, 239, 241, 251, 261
    airport, 136
    commercial, 136
    conference, 136
    extended stay, 137
    gaming, 136
    luxury, 3, 179, 245
    residential, 136–137
    see also historic hotels
Howard Johnson, 36
houseboats, 197, 199–200, 204
housekeeping, 7, 29, 30
human resources, 5, 7, 29–36, 65
Hungary, 144, 156
hunting camps/lodges, 186–187, 227
hurricanes, 53, 106, 145
Hyatt Corporation, 38, 164, 166, 169
hygiene see cleanliness

ice hotels, 7, 239–240, 261
Iceland, 64, 156
image, 102, 107, 205
immigration, 65, 21, 48, 54
    see also migration
impacts of tourism see environmental impacts; social impacts; economic impacts
inclusiveness, 30, 33, 70–75
India, 1–2, 3, 19, 24, 70, 102, 105, 140, 163, 199, 200, 214, 216, 251, 253
    n gaming 122
    also gambling; Native
        mericans
        ming Regulatory Act, 122
        lodging, 57, 244–247

indigenous people, 245, 48, 56
    see also Native Americans
Indonesia, 3, 51, 102, 106, 119, 122, 140, 147, 246
Industrial Revolution, 2
inflation, 54, 160
informal economy 50–51
    see also formal economy
information search, 41
information technology see technology
inns, 261, 2, 7, 49, 55, 65, 73, 85, 90, 118, 119, 133, 177–183, 239, 241
    see also bed and breakfasts
insurance, 108, 111
InterContinental Hotels Group, 19, 67, 135, 137
International Ecotourism Society, 92, 94
international tourism, 4, 14, 16–17, 21, 63, 75, 134, 215–216, 227, 245, 259, 262
international corporations see multinational lodging companies
Internet, 4, 24, 29, 38–41, 84, 105, 108, 135, 136, 179, 182, 216, 217, 221, 223, 250
interpersonal skills, 36
Interval International (II), 164
intervals see timeshares
investments
    international investments, 146
    private, 146, 163
Ireland, 179, 180, 181, 199, 249
Islam, 35, 149
Israel, 2, 119–120, 177, 184, 185–186, 260
Italy, 35, 120, 121, 133, 156, 180, 184, 249

Jamaica, 25, 106, 144, 148
Japan, 7, 16, 35, 120, 163, 184, 185, 200–201, 203, 250, 251
Jerusalem, 1, 251–252
job satisfaction, 33, 36
jobs see employment
Jordan, 246

Kampgrounds of America (KOA), 228, 231
Kentucky Fried Chicken (KFC), 119

Kenya, 90, 187, 189
kibbutz, 185–186
Korea, North, 6
Korea, South, 35, 66

labor force, 49
languages, need for, 35
Laos, 122
Latin America, 15, 16, 21, 22, 64, 65, 90, 111, 140, 141, 145, 156, 243
law enforcement, 108
laws 34
    see also legal issues
leakage see economic leakage
legal issues, 108
leisure travel, 13, 15, 16, 18, 21, 95, 104, 133
length of stay, 18, 88, 126, 134, 199, 215, 217
Lesotho, 143
Libya, 16
Liechtenstein, 181
lighthouse accommodations, 7, 177, 249, 261
'local tourists', 149
lodges, 186–188, 5, 81, 121
    see also ski lodges; national park lodges
Lonely Planet Thorn Tree Travel Forum, 40
'love motels' see sex and tourism
    see also motels, negative connotations
loyalty see brand loyalty

Macau, 16, 122
Madagascar, 146
maintenance, 29, 30, 38, 39, 89, 167, 169, 222, 233
Malawi, 259
Malaysia, 16, 122
Maldives, 148–149
Mali, 259
malls, 48, 50, 250–251
management contract, 37–38, 67, 70, 262
management information systems, 5
market catchment area, 40, 141, 165
market segmentation, 24–25, 66, 197

marketing, 7, 13, 30, 37, 38, 65,
    91, 107, 118, 135, 141, 182,
    215, 221
markets (niches), 13, 21, 34, 36,
    37, 40, 52, 63, 66, 67, 69,
    71, 73–75, 84, 183, 187,
    216, 239
Marriott International, 38, 92,
    164, 166
Martinique, 200
mass tourism, 55–56, 57, 83, 89,
    217, 241
Mauritania, 259
Mauritius, 146
McDonalds, 119–120, 121
meal plans, 118, 135
media, 20, 107, 167
meetings, incentives, conferences
    and exhibitions (MICE)
    tourism, 117, 124, 126
mergers, 38, 67–69
Mexico, 16, 22, 35, 65, 83,
    103–104, 120, 157, 159,
    161, 169, 199, 253
Middle East, 1, 16, 37, 70, 135,
    177, 208, 246
migration, 232, 65
    see also immigration; amenity
    migration
mobile homes, 162, 229
mobile lodging, 7, 162, 197–210
Monaco, 122
monasteries, 133, 249–250,
    251
Mongolia, 22, 203, 246
Montenegro, 16
Morocco, 140, 144
Motel 6, 139–140
motels, 4, 5, 7, 20, 25, 40, 49, 65,
    73, 81, 102, 104, 108, 122,
    138–140, 177–178, 239
    negative connotations, 139–140
motives, 13, 18, 19–20, 24, 92,
    110, 158, 185, 229–231
motor coaches, 6, 14, 89
motor homes see recreational
    vehicles
motor hotels see motels
Mozambique, 259
multinational lodging companies,
    262, 50, 51, 67–69, 82, 109,
    125, 147
    see also globalization

multiplier, economic, 48, 259
museums, 163
Myanmar, 122

Namibia, 16, 143, 187
national monuments, 137
national park lodges, 121, 186
national parks, 82, 89, 121, 187,
    227, 229, 233, 246
National Register of Historic
    Places, 188
nationality 35
    see also ethnicity
Native Americans, 246–247
natural disasters, 106–107, 52, 69,
    101
    see also floods; hurricanes;
    earthquakes; tsunamis
nature, 148, 158, 186–187, 218,
    227, 230, 240
neocolonialism, 55
Nepal, 1
Netherlands, 35, 199, 249
New Zealand, 35, 118, 138, 144,
    156, 168, 178–179, 180,
    184–185, 198, 214–215,
    219, 227, 246, 247, 248
Nicaragua, 259
non-profit organizations, 84, 229
North America, 2, 37, 64, 67, 68,
    71, 82, 110, 120, 124, 140,
    143, 144, 156, 163, 164,
    179, 180, 182, 184, 187,
    198, 201, 203, 205, 215,
    227, 230, 243, 250
Norway, 23, 53, 64, 156, 163, 200,
    240
novelty accommodations, 102,
    239–255

Orbitz.com, 40, 150
organic food, 120, 144, 183
Orient Express, 202–203
outer space accommodations,
    253–254, 260
outsourcing, food, 121
overcrowding, 56, 160, 232
overdependence on tourism, 52–
    53, 106

Pacific Islands, 22, 33, 66, 83, 124,
    134, 142, 204, 243
Palestine, 2, 177

Panama, 16, 163
paradors, 247–249, 261
partnerships, 38
passports, 22, 66
pensions, 55, 178, 180–181
pick-pocketing, 203, 105
    see also crime
pilgrim rest houses, 2, 19,
    251–252
pilgrims, 1–2, 19, 133, 177, 213,
    227, 262
pilgrimages, 251, 1, 19, 133, 177
    see also religious tourism
Pizza Hut, 119
placelessness, 148
planning, 13, 55, 83, 101, 260–261
'plastic surgery resorts', 145, 253
Poland, 21, 66
political unrest, 101, 7, 21, 52,
    69–70
    see also war; terrorism
pollution, 65, 81, 82, 90, 200, 210
ports, 106, 205
Portugal, 121, 180
post offices, 48
poverty, 48, 55, 103, 147
private ownership, 64
Professional Association of
    Innkeepers International,
    181
promotions see marketing
promotion, blind see boosterism
Promus Hotel Corporation, 122
pro-poor tourism, 83, 5
    see also poverty
prostitution, 50, 56, 105, 250
public relations, 107
pubs see bars

Qatar, 16, 163, 200, 246
quality of life, 54, 64, 90

race see ethnicity
rail travel see railways
railway hotels, 188
railways, 248, 2, 133, 178, 185,
    187, 201–203
    see also trains
Ramada Worldwide, 19, 36, 169
real estate, 36–37, 64, 157, 160,
    161, 165, 167–168
recreational properties see second
    homes

recreational vehicles (RVs), 197–199, 209, 228–229, 230, 231
recruitment and retention, 30–34
recycling, 65, 81, 84–85, 223, 242, 261
regional income, 5, 47–48, 53, 147
regions of high amenity, 7, 52, 157, 161, 164, 177, 178, 186, 218, 252
Register of Historic Places, 3
religion, 24, 33, 35, 70
religious tourism, 248, 19
  see also pilgrimage
renewable energy *see* energy use/ conservation
rental cars, 18, 38–39, 54, 87
reservations systems, 7, 37, 39, 42, 68, 182, 207, 220
residential tourism *see* second homes
resort communities, 140, 178
Resort Condominiums International (RCI), 164
resorts, 2, 5, 7, 29, 36, 40, 41, 49, 51, 54, 65, 70, 75, 81, 83, 86, 87, 90–91, 101–102, 104, 106, 110, 120, 121, 124–125, 140–145, 149, 161, 177, 182, 187, 207, 227, 239, 241
  all-inclusive, 118, 141, 147, 148
  beach/island, 19, 55, 106, 142
  casino, 20, 121–122, 124, 143
  coastal, 3
  diving, 25
  golf, 25, 143–144, 149
  mega-resorts, 55, 141, 148, 245
  RV, 198–199
  ki, 24, 25, 54, 85, 102, 142–143, 145, 149, 164, 187
  25, 144–145
  e park, 143
  o ski lodges
  s, 6, 14, 24, 38, 50, 65, 0, 102, 103, 104, 105, 09, 110, 117–120, 2, 181, 202, 207, 5–216, 250
  s *see* casinos
  200
  –2, 133
  5, 66, 144, 240

room service, 118
rural areas, 20, 48, 160, 182, 184, 217
Russia, 71, 251
Rwanda, 16, 259
ryokan, 7–8

safety and security, 5, 70, 87, 101–111, 159, 181, 182, 203, 222, 232, 244, 260
  responses to, 107–110
  see also security department
Samoa, 245
sand hotel, 254, 261
Sandals, 25
Sao Tome and Principe, 16, 259
satisfaction, 6, 7, 32–33, 39, 41, 63, 71, 118, 185, 205, 222, 232
Saudi Arabia, 16, 19, 252
saunas, 135, 156, 206, 228
scale, 58, 83–84, 85–86, 120, 121, 184, 188, 241, 245
Scandic Hotels, 68
Schengen Agreement, 64
schools, 41, 48, 56, 92, 94, 161
Scotland 121
  see also United Kingdom
seasonal homes *see* second homes
seasonality, 22–23, 39, 53–54, 142, 145, 149, 169, 183, 240
second homes, 7, 155–170, 199, 207
security cameras, 110
security department, 260, 30, 108, 182
  see also safety and security
self-catering, 137, 155, 198, 244
sense of place, 159, 199
Serbia, 21, 65
service quality, 24, 30, 34–36, 68, 71, 181
sewage disposal, 82, 244
sex and tourism, 250, 140, 219
  see also prostitution
Sheraton Hotels and Resorts, 36, 38, 122
shopping, 48, 54, 71, 250, 259
shopping centers *see* malls
shops, 6, 40, 48, 50, 71, 119, 141, 148, 215
shuttles, 6, 136
sickness *see* diseases

Sierra Leone, 120
Singapore, 66, 122, 137
ski lodges, 19, 85, 186
skills *see* staff training
Slovakia, 65
slow food movement 120–121
  see also food and beverage
small and medium enterprises (SMEs), 48
'snowbirds', 162, 199
social capital, 54
social impacts, 54–57, 83, 124, 148, 159, 215
South Africa, 120, 121, 122, 143, 156, 157, 168, 187, 189, 203
South America, 216, 67, 111, 184, 203
  see also Latin America
South Asia, 1, 106, 148
Southeast Asia, 16, 106, 134, 142, 156, 180, 187
souvenirs, 6, 14, 40, 50, 51, 71, 84, 148, 162, 170
Soviet Union, 21, 66
space travel 253–254
  see also outer space accommodation
Spain, 88, 121, 140, 141, 156, 161, 180, 247, 249, 251
spas, 252, 54, 135, 141, 142, 143, 164, 179
  see also resorts, spas
spiritual retreats, 252
spirituality, 19
sports, 20, 23, 48, 141, 142, 186, 187
Sri Lanka, 23, 106
St Lucia, 25
staff training, 29, 34–36, 90, 91–92, 107
star rating system, 135
Starwood Resorts, 166
staterooms 207–208
  see also cruises
Staybridge Suites, 137
stock market, 70
street vendors, 50, 119
student housing *see* dormitories
Subway, 119
summer cottages *see* second homes
Sun International, 143

sun, sea and sand (SSS), 83, 52
  see also resorts, beach; resorts,
    coastal
supermarkets, 48, 50, 103, 110,
  162, 207
Super 8, 139
supply chain management, 19, 20
supranationalism, 260, 5, 64, 72,
  76, 89
  see also globalization
Suriname, 260
sustainable development *see*
  sustainability
sustainability, 261, 5, 7, 56–57,
  65, 81–95, 103, 120, 147,
  188, 217, 241–243, 246
  see also green movement
Swaziland, 120, 143, 260
Sweden, 53, 89, 156, 158, 160,
  161, 163, 200, 239–240,
  243, 248
swimming pools, 87, 102, 135,
  140, 141, 164, 207, 228,
  233
Switzerland, 64, 156, 181, 240

Taiwan, 120, 184
Tanzania, 215
taverns *see* bars
tax incentives, 157, 163, 165
taxes, 5, 47, 49–50, 53, 64, 69,
  87–89, 147, 157, 159–160,
  162, 165, 167, 177, 184
taxis, 18, 50, 148
tea houses, 119
technology, 4, 5, 14, 29, 38, 40, 63,
  108, 145, 150, 184, 197,
  223
tents, 19, 187, 229, 230, 246
terrorism, 260, 20, 21, 22, 102,
  104–105, 203
  see also bioterrorism
Thailand, 66, 106, 122, 140, 216,
  253
theme parks *see* resorts, theme
  park
  see also amusement parks
timeshares, 39, 140, 155, 163–170
tour guides, 6, 48
tour operators, 14, 38, 48, 50, 88,
  89–90, 91–92, 118
tourism satellite account (TSA), 47

tourist enclaves, 147–148, 214,
  217, 223
tours
  familiarization, 107
  package, 107, 149, 214
towel reuse program, 87, 92, 94
trailers *see* recreational vehicles
training *see* staff training
trains, 222, 2, 14, 197, 200–203,
  204, 214
  see also railways
transit, 6, 22, 48, 118, 136, 197
transportation, 4, 8, 13, 14, 30, 48,
  49, 50, 63, 82, 83, 84, 89,
  90, 92, 147, 157, 169, 197,
  199, 201, 202, 205, 214,
  215–216, 222, 259
Trans-Siberian Railway, 202–203
travel agents, 6, 14, 38, 39, 40, 91,
  94, 250
Travelocity.com, 40, 150
tree house lodging, 7, 102,
  243–244, 261
Tripadvisor.com, 40
tsunamis, 106, 109
'turnkey', 164
Turkey, 136, 247
Turks and Caicos, 144

Ukraine, 65
underground lodging, 247, 261
unemployment, 20, 21, 52, 101,
  147, 169
UNESCO, 221
United Arab Emirates (UAE), 16,
  146–147, 149, 163, 200,
  246, 251
United Kingdom, 2, 37, 51, 52, 83,
  133, 137, 140, 178, 179,
  181–182, 184, 199, 217,
  249, 252
United States of America, 4, 15,
  18, 21, 30, 34, 35, 37, 49,
  51, 52, 53, 55, 65, 69, 72,
  83, 86, 90, 103, 118, 119,
  120, 122–123, 124, 133,
  134–135, 137, 143, 146,
  155, 157, 160, 162,
  164–165, 169, 178–179,
  182, 184–185, 186, 187,
  198–199, 201, 203, 204,
  208, 229, 231, 233, 240,
  247, 249, 252, 260

Alaska, 50, 53, 240
Arizona, 54, 123, 139, 143, 149,
  161–162, 185, 187, 199, 200
Baltimore, 2
Boston, 2
California, 50, 53, 121, 123,
  143, 146, 161–162, 187, 199
Colorado, 185, 246
Connecticut, 143
Florida, 4, 50, 53, 123, 135, 140,
  146, 161–162, 164, 199
Georgia, 123
Hawaii, 134, 135, 144, 146,
  159, 163–164, 200
Illinois, 122
Indiana, 122
Iowa, 123
Las Vegas, 53, 87, 122, 123, 149
Louisiana, 122
Massachusetts, 123
Michigan, 123
Minnesota, 123, 251
Mississippi, 123
Missouri, 123
Montana, 185
Nevada, 146, 162, 185
New Mexico, 162, 185, 199
New York, 2, 50, 137, 203
Oklahoma, 123
Philadelphia, 2
San Francisco, 50
South Carolina, 123
Texas, 161, 199
Utah, 185, 187, 200
Washington, DC, 203
Wisconsin, 123
Wyoming, 185, 187
universities, 35, 92, 214, 219
urbanization, 158
Uruguay, 260
US Virgin Islands, 147, 200

vacation properties *see* second
  homes
vandalism, 82, 231–232
Vanuatu, 16
Vietnam, 15, 16, 22, 122
violence, 104, 159
visas, 22, 64, 66, 214
visiting friends and relatives (VFR)
  tourism, 20, 215
volunteer tourism, 57
volunteerism, 49, 163

war, 21, 103
waste management, 19, 81, 85–86,
    88, 89–90, 121, 223, 242,
    261
water conservation, 86–87, 90, 92,
    223, 242
water quality, 81–82, 103
wear and tear, 82
weddings, 42, 54, 126, 240
weekend trips, 158, 200, 251
Westin Hotels and Resorts, 36
willingness to pay, 84, 92–93, 110,
    233

Wimpy Burgers, 119
wine, 121, 189
wine routes, 121
women, 48, 55, 71
World Bank, 146
World Tourism Organization
    (UNWTO), 17, 21, 66, 163
World Trade Organization (WTO),
    64
World Travel and Tourism Council
    (WTTC), 16, 48
World War Two, 2, 14, 22, 36, 55,
    63, 64, 81, 134, 137, 178

Wyndham Hotels and Resorts, 67,
    139, 169

yachts, 197, 199–200, 204
yield management, 39
youth exchanges, 220–221
youth hostels see hostels
Yugoslavia, 144

Zimbabwe, 187, 203
zimmer, 180–181